Bildung-Psychology

The concept of Bildung-Psychology, as developed by Christiane Spiel and her colleagues, combines ideas from developmental and educational psychology to describe educational processes with a strong focus on lifelong learning. Bildung-Psychology is concerned with all educational processes contributing to the development of individuals, as well as all conditions and measures potentially influencing these processes, and it aims to stimulate integrative use inspired basic research in the field of education. The structural model of Bildung-Psychology contains three dimensions: (1) the Bildung-career, (2) several functional areas, and (3) different levels of activities. The theoretical framework systematically classifies psychological actions in the field of education.

This book combines theoretical pieces discussing important conceptual topics within Bildung-Psychology, with empirical contributions focused on different phases of the Bildung-career. The studies were conducted in countries across Europe, and across the various age-specific educational phases in the Bildung-career.

This book was originally published as a special issue of the *European Journal of Developmental Psychology*.

Dagmar Strohmeier is Professor at the University of Applied Sciences Upper Austria, Linz. She studies peer relations among (immigrant) adolescents with a cross-cultural and cross-national perspective. She developed and cross-nationally implemented the ViSC Program in schools and is the principal investigator of the EU funded "Europe 2038" project.

Petra Wagner is Professor at the University of Applied Sciences Upper Austria, Linz. She has a broad experience in psychological research as well as teaching. Her research focuses on self-regulation, scholastic stress factors, time management, social work in schools, and evaluation and is published in various international journal articles.

Barbara Schober is Professor of Psychological Research on Education and Transfer at the University of Vienna, Austria. Her main research activities focus on lifelong learning, learning motivation and its development, gender differences in educational contexts, self-regulation, teacher training, development and evaluation of intervention programs in educational context and implementation research.

Bildung-Psychology

Theory and Practice of Use Inspired Basic Research

Edited by
Dagmar Strohmeier, Petra Wagner and Barbara Schober

LONDON AND NEW YORK

First published 2018
by Routledge
2 Park Square, Milton Park, Abingdon, Oxon, OX14 4RN, UK

and by Routledge
711 Third Avenue, New York, NY 10017, USA

Routledge is an imprint of the Taylor & Francis Group, an informa business

Introduction, Chapters 1-7 © 2018 Taylor & Francis
Chapter 8 © 2016 Willem Koops, Michael van den Kerkhof, Carlien Ostermeier
and Rens van de Schoot. Originally published as Open Access.

With the exception of Chapter 8, no part of this book may be reprinted
or reproduced or utilised in any form or by any electronic, mechanical,
or other means, now known or hereafter invented, including photocopying
and recording, or in any information storage or retrieval system, without
permission in writing from the publishers. For details on the rights for
Chapter 8, please see the chapter's Open Access footnote.

Trademark notice: Product or corporate names may be trademarks or
registered trademarks, and are used only for identification and
explanation without intent to infringe.

British Library Cataloguing in Publication Data
A catalogue record for this book is available from the British Library

ISBN 13: 978-1-138-57428-1

Typeset in Myriad Pro
by RefineCatch Limited, Bungay, Suffolk

Publisher's Note
The publisher accepts responsibility for any inconsistencies that may have
arisen during the conversion of this book from journal articles to book chapters,
namely the possible inclusion of journal terminology.

Disclaimer
Every effort has been made to contact copyright holders for their permission to
reprint material in this book. The publishers would be grateful to hear from any
copyright holder who is not here acknowledged and will undertake to rectify
any errors or omissions in future editions of this book.

Contents

Citation Information	vii
Notes on Contributors	ix

Introduction: Bildung-Psychology: Theory and practice of use
inspired basic research   1
Petra Wagner, Dagmar Strohmeier and Barbara Schober

1. Overcoming the ivory tower: Transfer and societal responsibility
as crucial aspects of the Bildung-Psychology approach   11
*Barbara Schober, Laura Brandt, Marlene Kollmayer and
Christiane Spiel*

2. Social-emotional development: From theory to practice   27
Tina Malti and Gil G. Noam

3. Bildung-Psychology and implementation science   41
Dean L. Fixsen, Marie-Therese Schultes and Karen A. Blase

4. Gender role self-concept at school start and its impact on academic
self-concept and performance in mathematics and reading   56
Ilka Wolter and Bettina Hannover

5. School burnout and engagement profiles among digital natives
in Finland: a person-oriented approach   79
*Katariina Salmela-Aro, Joona Muotka, Kimmo Alho, Kai Hakkarainen
and Kirsti Lonka*

6. Fostering pupils' lifelong learning competencies in the classroom:
evaluation of a training programme using a multivariate multilevel
growth curve approach   94
*Marko Lüftenegger, Monika Finsterwald, Julia Klug, Evelyn Bergsmann,
Rens van de Schoot, Barbara Schober and Petra Wagner*

7. The implementation and evaluation of the ViSC program in Cyprus:
challenges of cross-national dissemination and evaluation results   112
*Olga Solomontos-Kountouri, Petra Gradinger, Takuya Yanagida and
Dagmar Strohmeier*

CONTENTS

8. A Bildung-psychological investigation into student motives: McKinsey- or von Humboldt-oriented? 131
Willem Koops, Michael van den Kerkhof, Carlien Ostermeier and Rens van de Schoot

Index 151

Citation Information

The chapters in this book were originally published in the *European Journal of Developmental Psychology*, volume 13, issue 6 (November 2016). When citing this material, please use the original page numbering for each article, as follows:

Editorial
Special Issue: Bildung-Psychology: Theory and practice of use inspired basic research
Petra Wagner, Dagmar Strohmeier and Barbara Schober
European Journal of Development Psychology, volume 13, issue 6 (November 2016), pp. 625–635

Chapter 1
Overcoming the ivory tower: Transfer and societal responsibility as crucial aspects of the Bildung-Psychology approach
Barbara Schober, Laura Brandt, Marlene Kollmayer and Christiane Spiel
European Journal of Development Psychology, volume 13, issue 6 (November 2016), pp. 636–651

Chapter 2
Social-emotional development: From theory to practice
Tina Malti and Gil G. Noam
European Journal of Development Psychology, volume 13, issue 6 (November 2016), pp. 652–665

Chapter 3
Bildung-Psychology and implementation science
Dean L. Fixsen, Marie-Therese Schultes and Karen A. Blase
European Journal of Development Psychology, volume 13, issue 6 (November 2016), pp. 666–680

CITATION INFORMATION

Chapter 4
Gender role self-concept at school start and its impact on academic self-concept and performance in mathematics and reading
Ilka Wolter and Bettina Hannover
European Journal of Development Psychology, volume 13, issue 6 (November 2016), pp. 681–703

Chapter 5
School burnout and engagement profiles among digital natives in Finland: a person-oriented approach
Katariina Salmela-Aro, Joona Muotka, Kimmo Alho, Kai Hakkarainen and Kirsti Lonka
European Journal of Development Psychology, volume 13, issue 6 (November 2016), pp. 704–718

Chapter 6
Fostering pupils' lifelong learning competencies in the classroom: evaluation of a training programme using a multivariate multilevel growth curve approach
Marko Lüftenegger, Monika Finsterwald, Julia Klug, Evelyn Bergsmann, Rens van de Schoot, Barbara Schober and Petra Wagner
European Journal of Development Psychology, volume 13, issue 6 (November 2016), pp. 719–736

Chapter 7
The implementation and evaluation of the ViSC program in Cyprus: challenges of cross-national dissemination and evaluation results
Olga Solomontos-Kountouri, Petra Gradinger, Takuya Yanagida and Dagmar Strohmeier
European Journal of Development Psychology, volume 13, issue 6 (November 2016), pp. 737–755

Chapter 8
A Bildung-psychological investigation into student motives: McKinsey- or von Humboldt-oriented?
Willem Koops, Michael van den Kerkhof, Carlien Ostermeier and Rens van de Schoot
European Journal of Development Psychology, volume 13, issue 6 (November 2016), pp. 756–774

For any permission-related enquiries please visit:
http://www.tandfonline.com/page/help/permissions

Notes on Contributors

Kimmo Alho is Professor of Psychology at the University of Helsinki, Finland.

Evelyn Bergsmann is based at the Vetmed Vienna, Internal Quality Management at the Vice Rectorate for Teaching, Austria.

Karen A. Blase is Senior Scientist Emerita at the Frank Porter Graham Child Development Institute, University of North Carolina at Chapel Hill, USA.

Laura Brandt is a university assistant (postdoctoral) at the Faculty of Psychology, Department of Applied Psychology: Work, Education, University of Vienna, Austria.

Monika Finsterwald is based at the Institute for Systemic Organisational Research (I.S.O.), Vienna, Austria.

Dean L. Fixsen is an Implementation Scientist, WHO Collaborating Center for Research Evidence for Sexual and Reproductive Health, University of North Carolina at Chapel Hill, USA.

Petra Gradinger is based at the School of Applied Health and Social Sciences, University of Applied Sciences Upper Austria, Linz.

Kai Hakkarainen is Professor of Education at the Institute of Behavioural Sciences, University of Helsinki, Finland.

Bettina Hannover is Professor at the Department of Education and Psychology, Freie Universität Berlin, Germany.

Julia Klug is Professor of Educational Psychology at the Department of Educational Sciences and Research, PH Salzburg, Austria.

Marlene Kollmayer is based at the Faculty of Psychology, Department of Applied Psychology: Work, Education, University of Vienna, Austria.

Willem Koops is Professor at the Department of Developmental Psychology, Utrecht University, The Netherlands.

Kirsti Lonka is Professor of Educational Psychology and Director of the Research Group of Educational Psychology, University of Helsinki, Finland.

NOTES ON CONTRIBUTORS

Marko Lüftenegger is Assistant Professor of Developmental and Bildung-Psychology at the University of Vienna, Austria.

Tina Malti is Professor at the Department of Psychology, University of Toronto, Canada.

Joona Muotka is University Teacher at the Department of Psychology, University of Jyväskylä, Finland.

Gil G. Noam is the Founder and Director of The PEAR Institute, Harvard Medical School and McLean Hospital, USA.

Carlien Ostermeier is based at the Department of Education and Pedagogics, Utrecht University, The Netherlands.

Katariina Salmela-Aro is Professor of Educational Psychology and Educational Sciences, University of Helsinki, Finland.

Barbara Schober is Professor of Psychological Research on Education and Transfer at the University of Vienna, Austria.

Marie-Therese Schultes is a Research Associate at the Gillings School of Global Public Health, University of North Carolina at Chapel Hill, USA.

Olga Solomontos-Kountouri is based at the Theology School of the Church of Cyprus, Cyprus.

Christiane Spiel is Professor at the Faculty of Psychology, Department of Applied Psychology: Work, Education, Economy, University of Vienna, Austria.

Dagmar Strohmeier is Professor at the University of Applied Sciences Upper Austria, Linz.

Michael van den Kerkhof is based at the Department of Developmental Psychology, Utrecht University, The Netherlands.

Rens van de Schoot is Associate Professor at the Department of Methodology and Statistics, Utrecht University, The Netherlands.

Petra Wagner is Professor at the University of Applied Sciences Upper Austria, Linz.

Ilka Wolter is a Junior Research Group Leader at the Leibniz Institute for Educational Trajectories, Bamberg, Germany.

Takuya Yanagida is based at the Faculty of Psychology, Department of Applied Psychology: Work, Education, Economy, University of Vienna, Austria.

INTRODUCTION

Bildung-Psychology: Theory and practice of use inspired basic research

1. Introduction

This special issue consists of eight papers addressing specific aspects of Bildung-Psychology. The concept of Bildung-Psychology was developed by Christiane Spiel and her colleagues to offer a theoretical perspective and a structural model to stimulate use inspired basic research in the field of education and learning. Bildung-Psychology combines ideas from developmental and educational psychology to describe educational processes over the whole educational career among individuals and has a strong focus on lifelong learning. The concept systematically classifies psychological actions in the field of education and learning and deals with questions like, e.g.,: What is lifelong learning? How can competencies for lifelong learning be fostered throughout the life span? Which measures are needed to sustainably implement evidence-based innovations in educational systems?

In the following, we will present the most important principles of Bildung-Psychology, and describe the emergence of this new concept in a chronological order.

Initially, Spiel and Reimann (2005a) published the concept of Bildung-Psychology in the journal *Psychologische Rundschau*, the official journal of the German association of psychology. In this discussion paper, Spiel and Reimann (2005a) presented four arguments why they decided to develop the new concept of Bildung-Psychology: (1) The term 'Bildung' which has no precise equivalent in English, was chosen because the term was well accepted in science as well as in society in the German speaking countries, encompassed the broad area of education and learning, but had implications beyond educational psychology. (2) The internally perceived achievements and potentials of psychology in the educational field were not visible enough in society. (3) The profile of educational psychology was considered as 'vague'. (4) Previous structural approaches within educational psychology were perceived as failed. Based on these arguments, Spiel and Reimann (2005a) outlined the importance and additional benefit of the new concept of Bildung-Psychology and introduced the structural model of Bildung-Psychology for the first time (see Figure 1).

Bildung defines education and learning on both a formative and a substantive level. On the formative level, Bildung is understood as a product as well as a process. Bildung as a product refers to the characteristics of a person which are desirable from a normative perspective. Bildung as a process focuses on the development of these desirable traits. The substantive level of Bildung deals with the question which

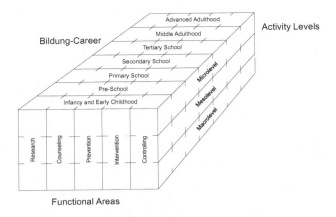

Figure 1. Structural model of Bildung-Psychology.

characteristics of a person who has acquired some Bildung are really desirable (cp. Spiel, Reimann, Wagner, & Schober, 2008). Spiel and Reimann (2005a) argue that over its history, the meaning of Bildung has often changed. The most prominent person associated with the term 'Bildung' is Wilhelm von Humboldt, who advanced Bildung as the basis for a program of education. Current debates on the meaning of Bildung are strongly influenced by the context in which the concept is used. Therefore, the meaning of Bildung as product is dynamic and always embedded in a specific historical context.

According to Spiel and Reimann (2005a), Bildung-Psychology is concerned with all educational processes contributing to the development of individuals, as well as all conditions and measures potentially influencing these processes, i.e., to initiate, maintain, support, and/or optimize them. Hence, Bildung-Psychology is systematically structured and has a strong focus on lifelong learning. Furthermore, Bildung-Psychology understands itself neither as a pure basic research discipline nor as a pure applied research discipline, but covers research activities from basic research to evidence-based practice. Thus, Bildung-Psychology is comparable to the use-inspired research approach by Stokes (1997; cp. Spiel, Schober, Wagner, Reimann, & Strohmeier, 2011), and classifies the most important topics and activities in the broad field of education and learning within a structural model (see Figure 1).

The structural model of Bildung-Psychology introduced by Spiel and Reimann (2005a) contains three dimensions: (1) the Bildung-career, (2) several functional areas, and (3) different levels of activities. The innovation of this model is that all conditions and measures which can influence educational processes are systematically linked.

Bildung-Career. The main assumption of Bildung-Psychology is that every individual passes through a chronological Bildung-career, which neither begins nor ends with traditional schooling. Consequently, the entire life-span is the explicitly declared object of Bildung-Psychology. Accordingly, Spiel and Reimann (2005a) see an analogy to the life-span perspective of developmental psychology (e.g., Baltes, Lindenberger, & Staudinger, 2006). In addition, the dimension Bildung-career is linked to the concept of lifelong learning. Continuous learning in terms of lifelong learning has been accorded a central significance in international educational policy for several years (e.g., European Commission, 2001; cp. Schober et al., 2007), and is defined as 'all purposeful learning activity, undertaken on an ongoing basis with the aim of improving knowledge, skills and competence' (Commission of the European Communities, 2000, p. 3). Lifelong learning operates as link between theories and practice, and therefore makes a contribution to achieve evidence-based practice.

Functional Areas. For the promotion of evidence-based practice the functional areas of Bildung-Psychology are highly relevant. Spiel and Reimann (2005a) defined five functional areas, namely, research, counselling, prevention, intervention, and controlling (evaluation) as equitable fields of Bildung-Psychology.

Activity Levels. The above described functions of Bildung-Psychology are accomplished on various activity levels, which are oriented in accordance with the ecological model of developmental environments presented by Bronfenbrenner (1979) and Bronfenbrenner and Morris (2006). Spiel and Reimann (2005a) take into account the micro-level, meso-level, and macro-level of the Bronfenbrenner model. The micro-level is the immediate environment in which the individual is living; particularly relevant here are individual learning conditions e.g., those associated with scholastic instruction. The meso-level is the institutional level; e.g., the institutions an individual attends over the course of his/her educational career. The macro-level refers to the entire system which is at work during education; political guidelines and conditions which are legally binding are significant here. In sum, Spiel and Reimann (2005a) emphasize that a common feature to all three structural dimensions is that their subject matter is not isolated from that of the other two.

The presented concept of Bildung-Psychology resulted in an intensive discussion with heterogeneous comments and reactions within the German psychological community (e.g., Greve, 2006; Lang, 2005; Leutner, 2005; Renkl, 2005; Silbereisen, 2005; Spiel & Reimann, 2005b). The representative of the professional association of psychology commented the new concept very positively (Lang, 2005). He found that the concept of Bildung-Psychology was very suitable to support the contribution of psychology to the challenging societal processes and the increasing needs in the educational field. Also, he liked that the message of the concept was very plausibly communicable to politicians and citizens. He also prognosticated a high political and societal acceptance of the concept. In contrast, representatives of the discipline within educational psychology criticized the concept very much. Renkl (2005) argued that the term 'Bildung' was not primarily linked with psychology, but rather with educational science, sociology or economy. He especially criticized that the meso- and marco-level of the model were concerned with the education system or educational politics, and not with the core competencies of educational psychologists.

In 2008, a paper with the title 'Bildung-Psychology: The substance and structure of an emerging discipline' was published by Spiel and her colleagues. Aim of this paper was to introduce the concept of Bildung-Psychology to the international scientific community.

In 2010, the first textbook of Bildung-Psychology was published by Spiel, Schober, Wagner, and Reimann in german. The innovation of this book is the systematic structure. The book, which addresses researchers, teachers, students of psychology and related disciplines, as well as practitioners in the field of Bildung-Psychology, is designed along the three dimensions of Bildung-Psychology (see Figure 1). Section 1 includes seven chapters giving an overview about all segments of the Bildung-career each with two examples of use-inspired research approaches; Section 2 gives an overview about the five functional areas, and Section 3 summarizes the three different levels of activities each with two typical research examples. Today, the book is used as teaching and learning material in many Bachelor's and Master's degree programmes in the German speaking countries.

In the meantime, further contributions to Bildung-Psychology were published in various journals and edited books, each of these contributions discusses special aspects of Bildung-Psychology (e.g., Spiel, 2012; Spiel et al., 2011; Spiel, Schober, Wagner, & Reimann, 2014), and at the university of Mannheim the first professorship of Bildung-Psychology was established.

Now, the focus of this special issue is on both theories and practice of use inspired basic research in the field of Bildung-Psychology. Each of the following eight papers addresses specific cells respectively dimensions of the structural model of Bildung-Psychology.

2. Overview of contributions to the special issue

The aim of this special issue is to illustrate the potential of the structural model of Bildung-Psychology for developmental and educational research as well as significant research activities in this field. The eight contributions were selected because each of them demonstrates important features of the structural model of Bildung-Psychology. Hence, in the following the findings of each paper will be summarized, and the papers will be classified according to the dimensions of the structural model (see Figure 1). The special issue contains three theoretical and five empirical papers. While the theoretical papers discuss important topics of Bildung-Psychology, the five empirical papers cover a broad spectrum of the Bildung-career. The studies were conducted in different European countries – Germany, Finland, Austria, Cyprus, and The Netherlands –, and refer to various age-specific educational phases in the Bildung-career, from primary school to tertiary school (see Figure 1).

In the first paper, *Schober, Brandt, Kollmayer, and Spiel* discuss the specific potential of the concept of Bildung-Psychology to succeed in overcoming the theory-practice problem of universities in the field of education. The relevance of this problem is explained by elaborating the important role of universities in transferring evidence-based knowledge from educational research to decision-makers and practitioners. There is an emerging expectation for universities to explicitly take responsibility for demands of the society and to address social, economic and societal challenges – the so called 'Third Mission'. The Third Mission has two key priorities: (1) targeted use and transfer of scientific knowledge to help resolve diverse societal challenges, and (2) transfer of technologies and innovations in the form of cooperations with public and private enterprises. The authors argue that Bildung-Psychology is of high relevance for this mission, also beyond its specific research topics. Bildung-Psychology delivers a helpful integrative perspective that can be considered as one desideratum for the development of a systematic 'Third Mission Strategy'. Therefore, Bildung-Psychology can be considered also as model for other disciplines.

To illustrate this argumentation, two examples from the field of Bildung-Psychology are presented, which combine the domain specific approach and the general mission. One example contains an innovative and evidence-based teaching concept in higher education – Vienna E-Lecturing, and the training program REFLECT – Gender Competence through Reflective Coeducation – is an example of a responsible research activity in the field of Bildung-Psychology.

The core areas of this theoretical paper are related to the cell 'Tertiary school' (Dimension: Bildung-career) of the structural model of Bildung-Psychology (see Figure 1).

In the second paper, *Noam and Malti* introduce a new conceptual framework to understand and enhance child and adolescent social-emotional development (SED). SED was defined as an umbrella term that describes individuals' various interpersonal and intrapersonal skills in the domain of social and emotional competencies, and entails (1) an individual's understanding of emotional experiences in the self and others, (2) the ability to express emotions in an age-appropriate way, and (3) emotion regulation capacities. The authors argue that while much research on SED has been conducted and various evidence-based programs on social-emotional learning have been widely implemented, there are still significant gaps in the research-practice connection. Based on this conceptualization, core dimensions of SED (action orientation, emotion control, assertiveness, sympathy, trust, self-reflection, optimism) were defined and a tool through which children, teachers, and caregivers are able to report on dimensions of SED was developed. This tool is called the Holistic Student Assessment and it generates individual, classroom, and whole school profiles of SED. Furthermore, it is illustrated how these profiles can be used to inform intervention planning and to implement developmentally sensitive strategies to promote SED and to intervene in the case of psychopathology among children and youth. Finally, the authors discuss how their developmental and holistic approach to better understand and assess SED relates to Bildung-Psychology. They argue that cultivating human minds involves not only thoughts and abstract reflection but that an equal emphasis on educating emotions, natural instincts, and regulatory capacities in everyday social interactions is needed. Therefore, SED describes processes that contribute to the development of Bildung of an individual over the lifespan, leading to an educated individual and ultimately to a mature self.

The core areas of this theoretical paper are related to the cell 'Research' (Dimension: Functional areas) of the structural model of Bildung-Psychology (see Figure 1).

In the third paper, *Fixsen, Schultes, and Blase* focus on implementation science. The authors point out similarities between implementation frameworks and the Bildung-Psychology model. The integrated view offered by Bildung-Psychology regarding lifelong learning as influenced by factors on the micro-, meso-, and macro-level (Spiel et al., 2008) corresponds well to the findings from the developing field of implementation science. In line with lifelong learning, implementation is a growing science built on research and evaluation of practices that unfold over years and decades. This theoretical paper illustrates the relationship between implementation science and Bildung-Psychology by presenting a cascading logic model that guides implementation activities on the micro-, meso- and macro-level. The authors provide a historical overview of the emergence of implementation science based on experiences with the implementation of a concrete intervention (Teaching-Family Model), which was developed over time into a systematic implementation approach covering different system levels (Teaching-Family Sites). The Teaching-Family Model was developed as a family-style, group home (residential) treatment program for teenagers referred from the delinquency system. Although the treatment was already effective in the pilot phase, the implementation to produce sustainable success took years to evolve. Based on this example, the authors summarize the importance of implementation science for putting effective interventions into practice with the following formula: effective innovations x effective implementation x enabling contexts = socially significant outcomes. The authors also present the cascading logic model which includes activities on the micro-, meso-, and macro-level. The paper demonstrates that the cascading logic model makes an important contribution to a sustainable use of implementation research in the field of Bildung-Psychology.

The core areas of this theoretical paper are related to the cell 'Intervention' (Dimension: Functional areas) of the structural model of Bildung-Psychology (see Figure 1).

In the fourth paper, *Wolter and Hannover* focuses on the role of gender stereotypes to better understand gender differences in academic self-concept and performance outcomes in mathematics and reading among primary school students. In line with basic assumptions of the structural model of Bildung-Psychology, this study incorporates gender stereotypes as a relevant factor in explaining educational trajectories with respect to gender differences in subject domains in the early Bildung-career. The authors assume that to the extent that girls and boys ascribe gendered attributes to themselves (gender role self-concept), their academic self-concepts and performances are consistent with gender stereotypes half a year later, at the end of the first grade in primary school. The authors measured gender role self-concept, and analysed its impact on children's academic self-concepts, performance in mathematics, and reading half a year later. As expected, girls ascribed more feminine and boys more masculine-stereotyped behaviours to themselves. Furthermore, the more feminine children described themselves the better was their reading performance half a year later, while no indirect effects, mediated via the academic self-concept, appeared. Also, the more masculine children described themselves, the higher were their mathematics related ability self-concepts half a year later. However, maths achievements were unrelated to any of the other variables. The authors conclude that gender stereotypes need to be targeted already in pre-school as they predict ability self-concepts already in the first year of primary school. Thus, in line with basic assumptions of the structural model of Bildung-Psychology and its focus on lifelong learning, preschool years are an important developmental period to prevent 'gendered' Bildung-careers. More studies are needed to better understand how gender role self-concepts of young children impact the development of gendered academic self-concepts and skills in adolescence and adulthood.

This empirical paper can be placed in the cell 'Primary school/Research/Microlevel' of the structural model of Bildung-Psychology (see Figure 1).

BILDUNG-PSYCHOLOGY

In the fifth paper, *Salmela-Aro, Muotka, Alho, Hakkarainen, and Lonka* examine school burnout and engagement profiles and investigate whether these profiles differ depending on the socio-digital participation among pre-adolescents. Following a person-oriented approach, latent profile analysis revealed five groups: Engaged students, who formed the majority (50%); stressed students, who reported high exhaustion and high inadequacy as a student (4%); students with high scores on all the components of school burnout, particularly cynicism, but also on exhaustion and inadequacy as a student (burnout group; 5%); students, whose cynicism was directed in particular towards studying and school (moderate in cynicism; 15%); bored students, whose feelings of cynicism were nevertheless elevated (emerging cynicism; 26%). Overall, the results revealed that almost half of the pre-adolescents (46%) felt some degree of cynicism towards school. On the one hand, engaged students used socio-digital technologies less intensively than the others. On the other hand, the students that were high and moderately high on cynicism reported using socio-digital technologies for educational purposes more intensively than the engaged students. Moreover, the students that were high and moderately high on cynicism reported that they would be more academically engaged and hardworking at school if they were able to make more use of information and communication technologies at school. These results indicate that one way to promote the engagement of cynical students might be to offer them the possibility to make greater use of socio-digital technologies at school. Finally, the authors discuss the implications of the study for Bildung-Psychology. They argue that socio-digital technology is one important tool for pre-adolescents to develop Bildung and to acquire knowledge acquisition practices.

This empirical paper can be placed in the cell 'Secondary school/ Research/ Microlevel' of the structural model of Bildung-Psychology (see Figure 1).

In the sixth paper, *Lüftenegger, Finsterwald, Klug, Bergsmann, van de Schoot, Schober, and Wagner* report evaluation results regarding the effectiveness of the TALK programme, an intervention to promote lifelong learning among adolescents. The concept of lifelong learning is in the core of the structural model of Bildung-Psychology as it comprises the whole Bildung-career (see Figure 1). The main goal of the TALK programme is to develop secondary school pupils' competencies for lifelong learning by optimizing teaching and enhancing competencies among teachers within a three semester teacher training. In this paper, the authors investigate whether the already proven gain in teacher competencies through the TALK programme also led to corresponding, perceptual changes in teaching and pupils' competencies for lifelong learning. To define lifelong learning two core factors are important: (1) an enduring motivation and appreciation for learning and education, and (2) those competencies that are needed to successfully realize this motivation through concrete learning activities (e.g., self-regulated learning). In order to evaluate the effectiveness of TALK, a pretest-posttest-follow up design including both training and control groups was utilized. Multivariate multilevel growth curve analyses showed the benefit in fostering lifelong learning competencies in schools on several levels. Effects were observed for pupils' perceptions of their classroom instruction (i.e., positive failure climate; a classroom climate more supportive of self-regulated-learning) and their individual motivation. The authors discuss the challenges to develop, implement and systematically evaluate a teacher training programme with the aim to foster pupils' competencies in different schools and classrooms. In addition, the evaluation study of the theoretically grounded intervention programme TALK is a best-practice example how to consider standards of evidence in the field of Bildung-Psychology.

This empirical paper can be placed in the cells 'Secondary school/Research, Intervention, Prevention, Counselling/Micro-, Mesolevel' of the structural model of Bildung-Psychology (see Figure 1).

In the seventh paper, *Solomontis-Kountouri, Gradinger, Yanagida, and Strohmeier* describe the implementation of the ViSC program in Cyprus. The ViSC program is a socio-ecological anti-bullying program which was developed, implemented and evaluated in Austria. To tackle bullying on different levels in the educational system, a cascaded train-the-trainer model has been realized. Nine permanent staff members of the Cypriot Ministry of Education were trained as multipliers by researchers. These multipliers trained teachers in three Cypriot schools and teachers trained their students. To investigate the effectiveness of the program, a quasi-experimental longitudinal study was conducted. Data from adolescents of three intervention and three control schools was collected via self-assessments at pre-test, post-test and follow-up. To investigate the program effectiveness regarding the reduction of victimization and aggressive behaviour, multilevel growth models were applied (time points at level 1, individuals at level 2, and classes at level 3). The analyses revealed that the program effects differed depending on the grade level of the students. Overall, the program was more effective for grade 7 compared to grade 8 students. In grade 8, bullying and victimization increased more in the intervention group compared with the control group at time 2, but also steeper decreased at time 3 indicating a sensitizing effect of the program. The authors point out that evidence-based bullying prevention in schools is a key area of Bildung-Psychology. The implementation of the ViSC program enables sustainable knowledge transfer between research and practice for the benefit of the well-being of Cypriot students.

This empirical paper can be placed in the cells 'Secondary school/Research, Intervention, Prevention, Counselling/Micro-, Mesolevel' of the structural model of Bildung-Psychology (see Figure 1).

In the eighth paper, *Koops, van den Kerkhof, Ostermeier, and van de Schoot* investigate the opinions and attitudes of young adults studying at Utrecht University (The Netherlands) regarding their main study motivations. The authors contrast two prototypical orientations: The 'McKinsey' orientation and the 'von Humbold' orientation. While the main motivation of the 'McKinsey' oriented students is the job market, Bildung is the most important goal for the 'von Humbold' oriented students. For this purpose, a new measure was developed. Students were asked about their opinion regarding the relevance of science, the aims of universities, the student's own general academic attitudes, and finally whether the participant is planning to make the choice for a research master or a professional master. Those who chose a research master were finally asked why they made this choice. The authors hypothesized to find a two-component structure of the measure referring to von Humboldt component (Bildung), and the McKinsey component (job market). They expected that students who already made the choice for special programmes that offer broader

BILDUNG-PSYCHOLOGY

intellectual formation will have higher scores on the von Humboldt component than on the McKinsey component, while in contrast their counterparts show the opposite pattern. Finally, they compared students who made the choice for applied and practical work and therefore choose a professional oriented master with students who choose a research master. They hypothesized that those students who make the choice for a research master will score higher on the von Humboldt orientation than on the McKinsey orientation, while the opposite was expected for academic master students. Results demonstrate that the two motivations are indeed important for university students. Students who pursue a research master's degree score higher on scientific and lower on economical motives than their counterparts. Opinions on the aim of the university also differed in the expected direction: students pursuing a research master scored lower on the factor of vocational education than their counterparts. Finally, for the questions on general opinions, those students who choose a research master score higher on the von Humboldt component and lower on the McKinsey component than the students who pursue an academic master.

This empirical paper can be placed in the cell 'Tertiary school/Research/Microlevel' of the structural model of Bildung-Psychology (see Figure 1).

3. Conclusion and outlook

In sum, this special issue shows the presence, importance and potential of Bildung-Psychology and its structural model. Bildung-Psychology incorporates theoretical ideas of developmental psychology by focusing on life-long learning (Bildung-career), five functional areas, and three activity levels. The eight papers which are presented in this special issue represent important examples of Bildung-Psychology, three with a theoretical focus, and five with an empirical one. All papers use clearly defined and integrative theoretical frameworks and have an explicit relation to the concept of Bildung-Psychology.

We hope that this special issue stimulates future studies in this field. In our view, the structural model of Bildung-Psychology demonstrates interfaces to other disciplines like, developmental psychology, life span sciences or educational science and identify possible inter- and multidisciplinary research approaches along the whole Bildung-career in different functional areas and activity levels.

But this special issue delivers not only an overview about activities in the field of Bildung-Psychology, it is also a 'tribute' to Christian Spiel as the main founder of Bildung-Psychology. Since many years, Christiane Spiel has conducted research and has worked as university teacher on a very high international level at the University of Vienna. Beyond that, she is holding many advisory capacities at the interface between science and society. She has been intensively promoting both the evidence-based practice and transfer of scientific knowledge to help resolve various societal challenges. Bildung-Psychology became Christiane Spiel's mission, for her Bildung-Psychology is more than the field she works in, Bildung-Psychology also comprises her basic attitudes as person and scientist, Bildung-Psychology is the Third Mission of universities in its pure form.

References

Baltes, P. B., Lindenberger, U., & Staudinger, U. M. (2006). Lifespan theory in developmental psychology. In R. M. Lerner (Ed.), *Theoretical models of human development. Volume 1 of handbook of child psychology* (pp. 569–664). Hoboken, NJ: Wiley.

Bronfenbrenner, U. (1979). *The ecology of human development – Experiments by nature and design.* Cambridge, MA: Harvard University Press.

Bronfenbrenner, U., & Morris, P. A. (2006). The bioecological model of human development. In R. M. Lerner (Ed.), *Theoretical models of human development. Volume 1 of handbook of child psychology* (pp. 793–828). Hoboken, NJ: Wiley.

Commission of the European Communities. (2000). *Memorandum on lifelong learning.* Brussels: Author.

European Commission. (2001). *Making a European area of lifelong learning a reality.* Brussels: Commission of the European Communities.

Greve, W. (2006). Bildungspsychologie – Alter Wein in neuen Schläuchen, notwendige Reform oder distraktiver Nebenkriegsschauplatz? [Bildung-Psychology – Old wine in new skins, necessary reform or distractive theatre?]. *Psychologische Rundschau, 57,* 45–46.

Lang, F. (2005). Bildungspsychologie – ein erfolgsversprechender neuer Zuschnitt? [Bildung-Psychology – A promising new concept?]. *Psychologische Rundschau, 56,* 296–297.

Leutner, D. (2005). 'Bildungspsychologie' als Ersatz für 'Pädagogische Psychologie'? [Bildung-Psychology – An alternative to educational psychology?]. *Psychologische Rundschau, 56,* 297.

Renkl, A. (2005). Bildungspsychologie: Ein Anzug, der in Teilen zu eng und in Teilen zu weit? [Bildung-Psychology: A suit – Partly too large and partly too small?]. *Psychologische Rundschau, 56,* 298–299.

Schober, B., Finsterwald, M., Wagner, P., Lüftenegger, M., Aysner, M., & Spiel, C. (2007). TALK – A training program to encourage lifelong learning in school. *Journal of Psychology, 215,* 183–193.

Silbereisen, R. (2005). Kommentar zur 'Bildungspsychologie' von Christiane Spiel & Ralph Reimann. [Comment to Bildung-Psychology developed by Christiane Spiel & Ralph Reimann]. *Psychologische Rundschau, 56,* 299–300.

Spiel, C. (2012). Bildung-Psychology: Concept and potential. In T. Wubbels, R. Abma, & J. Bos (Eds.), *Du choc, de botsing, the clash: du choc des opinions jaillit la lumiere. Liber Amicorum Willem Koops* (pp. 203–210). Amsterdam: SWP.

Spiel, C., & Reimann, R. (2005a). Bildungspsychologie [Bildung-Psychology]. *Psychologische Rundschau, 56,* 291–294.

Spiel, C., & Reimann, R. (2005b). Bildungspsychologie – auf dem Weg zum Erfolg? [Bildung-Psychology – On the road to success?]. *Psychologische Rundschau, 56,* 300–301.

Spiel, C., Reimann, R., Wagner, P., & Schober, B. (2008). Bildung-Psychology: The substance and structure of an emerging discipline. *Applied Developmental Science, 12,* 154–159.

Spiel, C., Schober, B., Finsterwald, M., Lüftenegger, M., Wagner, P., & Reimann, R. (2011). Bildungspsychologie: Konzeption und Potential [Bildung-Psychology: Concept and potential]. In E. Witte & J. Doll (Eds.), *Sozialpsychologie, Sozialisation und Schule* (pp. 53–76). Lengerich: Pabst Science.

Spiel, C., Schober, B., Wagner, P., & Reimann, R. (Eds.). (2010). *Bildungspsychologie* [Bildung-Psychology]. Göttingen: Hogrefe.

Spiel, C., Schober, B., Wagner, P., & Reimann, R. (2014). Das Strukturmodell der Bildungspsychologie – Ein analytischer Bezugsrahmen für moderne Pädagogik [Structural model of Bildung-Psychology – An analytical framework for modern education?]. In A. Ziegler & E. Zwick (Eds.), *Theoretische Perspektiven der modernen Pädagogik* (pp. 59–71). Münster: LIT-Verlag.

Spiel, C., Schober, B., Wagner, P., Reimann, R., & Strohmeier, D. (2011). Die Konzeption der Bildungspsychologie und das Potential ihres Strukturmodells [Concept of Bildung-Psychology and potential of its structural model]. *Die Deutsche Schule, 103,* 381–392.

Stokes, D. E. (1997). *Pasteur's quadrant: Basic science and technological innovation.* Washington, DC: Brookings Institution Press.

Petra Wagner

Dagmar Strohmeier

Barbara Schober

Overcoming the ivory tower: Transfer and societal responsibility as crucial aspects of the Bildung-Psychology approach

Barbara Schober, Laura Brandt, Marlene Kollmayer and Christiane Spiel

ABSTRACT
Strong evidence indicates the importance of successful education for individuals as well as for society as a whole; however, evidence-based knowledge from educational psychology is frequently not (successfully) transferred to decision-makers and practitioners. Besides, there is an increasing demand for transfer of academic knowledge in general to help resolve diverse societal challenges – codified as the obligation of universities to perform a *Third Mission*. This paper aims to demonstrate *Bildung-Psychology's* contribution to successful knowledge transfer. Two examples from Bildung-Psychology illustrate how teaching and research activities can contribute to fulfilling universities' Third Mission. By localizing these activities within the structure model of Bildung-Psychology, we aim to depict how this framework may serve as a role model for other scientific fields to build a firm basis for successful transfer.

The high relevance of progress in transfer in the field of education

Studies clearly indicate the importance of high-quality education for society as a whole and also for the individual. It is well established that education is one of the best predictors of health, job satisfaction and subjective success in life (e.g., Oreopoulos, Page, & Stevens, 2006; Oreopoulos & Salvanes, 2011). In addition, there is a significant positive effect of quality of education on economic growth (Hanushek & Kimko, 2000; Heckman, 2008). However, in educational practice, we witness many reforms that seem to be ill-designed 'education experiments' rather than sustainably planned processes of change. In many cases, this leads to unpredictable costs for individuals and for society (Woessmann & Piopiunik, 2009); see e.g., G8/G9 in Germany, i.e., reducing the number of school years until graduation in academic-track secondary schooling from nine to eight (Kühn, van Ackeren, Bellenberg, Reintjes, & im Brahm, 2013). Evidence-based knowledge from educational psychology and education economics – e.g., regarding causal effects of class size (Wilberg & Rost, 1997, 1999; Wild & Rost, 1995), the differential impact of polynomial school systems (Hanushek & Woessmann, 2007) or labor-market and student achievement outcomes of central school exit examinations (Jürgens, Schneider, & Büchel, 2005; Piopiunik, Schwerdt, & Woessmann, 2013) – seems to be frequently ignored by decision-makers and practitioners.

This theory-practice problem has long been a topic of debate in the field of education (e.g., Day, Fernandez, Hauge, & Møller, 2000; Usher & Bryant, 2014). However, the question inevitably arises as to whether the intersection of theory and practice necessarily represents a dilemma. As Kurt Lewin said: 'There's nothing more practical than a good theory' (Lewin, 1952, p. 169). This implies that theory and practice can go quite well together if a theory is understood as an (empirically testable and potentially falsifiable) model of causalities and relationships in a specific context. Thus, one might argue that the real problem lies not in an unhappy marriage of theory and practice, but in a lack of *transfer* from science, and in particular from universities – as the major producers of scientific knowledge – to society. In this view, despite all existing efforts to enhance transfer from science to educational systems (e.g., Gräsel, 2010), educational research is still trapped in the so-called *ivory tower*, which symbolizes 'the perceived detachment of universities from the real needs of real people in a real world' (Random House, 1993, p. 1017).

Since the year 2000, over 1000 papers including the term 'ivory tower' in their title have been published (according to a Google Scholar search). A large proportion of these publications focus on the field of education, indicating either that this scientific field suffers acutely from a lack of transfer from science to society or – put in more positive terms – that the field is particularly aware of this specific challenge for academia. In any case, the urgent need for new approaches to increase transfer from science to society in this context is obvious

This paper aims at demonstrating *Bildung-Psychology's* contribution to successful knowledge transfer in the context of increasing demand for transfer of academic knowledge to help resolve diverse societal challenges. Two examples were chosen to illustrate how teaching and research activities from the field of Bildung-Psychology can contribute to meet this need. By localizing these activities within the structure model of Bildung-Psychology, we aim to depict how this framework can serve as a model for other scientific fields in building a firm basis for successful transfer.

Bildung-psychology: transfer as an immanent characteristic

Indeed, there is not only strong evidence as mentioned before, but also wide consensus in the field of education that better transfer of scientific knowledge to society is important and needs to be accelerated (see e.g., the special issue *Understanding the Public Understanding of Science: Psychological Approaches*, Educational Psychologist, 2014; BMBF, 2016). However, addressing this concern remains elusive as long as initiatives aimed at ameliorating it are not systematized and interconnected, and thus cannot learn from each other. To date, research in educational psychology has been characterized by tension between its basic and its applied missions, leading to a fragmentation of the field (Pintrich, 2000; Scheurman, Heeringa, Rocklin, & Lohman, 1993): On the one hand, educational research aims at developing a *basic understanding* of learning, development, cognition, and motivation, with a focus on the individual learner. On the other hand, it is concerned with the *application* of evidence-based knowledge to improve educational contexts. Even though these two missions seemingly build well off of each other, in the broad field of education research, they are pursued disjointly. Hence, educational psychology lacks an integrative and compelling model or framework that allows for systematic representations and the interconnection of various activities (Spiel & Schober, in press).

Bildung-Psychology could contribute to overcoming this situation – it focuses on highly practice-oriented issues and is based on an integrative conceptual framework, designed to systematically bring together topics relevant to progress in transfer in the field of education (Spiel, Reimann, Wagner, & Schober, 2008). As described in the Editorial of this special issue (Wagner, Strohmeier, & Schober, 2016), Bildung-Psychology is explicitly concerned with all processes that contribute to the development of components constituting an individual's *Bildung* – consisting of occupational-technical qualifications and social-cultural competencies – as well as with all conditions and measures that can influence (i.e., initiate, maintain, support, and/or optimize) these processes (e.g., teachers' instructions, teacher education) (Spiel et al., 2008). The conditions and measures that can influence these processes (1) refer to the various age-specific *educational phases* of an individual, (2) require differential *functional areas* in the sense of concrete activities, and (3) refer to different *levels of activity*, which are defined in accordance with the ecological model presented by Bronfenbrenner (e.g., Bronfenbrenner & Morris, 2006). The systematic alignment of these three dimensions creates the structure model of Bildung-Psychology. Hence, Bildung-Psychology incorporates the core idea of lifelong learning (LLL), which has been gaining significance in European educational policies in recent years (e.g., Commission of the European Communities, 2000). LLL is represented in the structure model of Bildung-Psychology through the Bildung-career dimension, ranging from infancy to advanced adulthood.

Moreover, the conception of Bildung-Psychology is fundamentally grounded in a 'use-inspired basic research' approach (Stokes, 1997), which seeks to produce (basic) knowledge within the context of solving practical problems, and to analyze and directly change educational processes by explicitly addressing the dissemination of available knowledge to practitioners (Karoly, Boekaerts, & Maes, 2005). This use-inspired basic research approach is represented in the structure model of Bildung-Psychology through the different functional areas (research, counseling, prevention, intervention and monitoring/evaluation) and through the different levels of activity (micro/individual, meso/institutional, macro/systemic). Therefore, transfer is an explicit and immanent characteristic of the Bildung-Psychology approach.

While there are a range of transfer definitions and many different forms of transfer can be identified (e.g., Gräsel, 2010; Gräsel, Jäger, & Willke, 2006), within Bildung-Psychology, *transfer* is understood as an underlying basic orientation and structure for research which is not a unidirectional concept but rather a cycle: Societal problems come to (or are brought to) scientists' attention and are picked up by them (practice to science transfer), with scientists conducting research (ideally by including practitioners and policy-makers). Finally, attempts are made to implement the results of this research as sustainable solutions in practice (transfer from science to practice). This basic idea of an underlying structure for research – *not* just added as an afterthought – is also in line with new concepts demanding a systematic integration of intervention and implementation research (see the 'I³-Approach' by Spiel, Schober, and Strohmeier (2016).

Transfer is, however, not only a crucial premise for the implementation of successful education. There is a broader trend addressing the need for successful transfer from science to society to approach the growing public challenges of our time on a larger scale.

Transfer as an emerging challenge for universities

When debating universities' role in relation to society, reference is frequently made to the implicit social contract between science and society. Traditionally, this contract was based on the understanding that universities will provide research and teaching in return for public funding, with a high degree of institutional autonomy (Gibbons, 1999). This interpretation of the social contract dates back to the view of 'science as the endless frontier' (Bush, 1945). However, since the end of the last century, the necessity of re-negotiating the social contract has been voiced, against the backdrop of growing societal challenges:

> [T]he changed world of modern science and modern government means that it is imperative to search for and begin to define a new contract, or series of contracts, between the institutions of democracy and the institutions of science. The scientific community needs to reach out to justify its claim on public resources by demonstrating where and how it is relevant in solving public problems. (Guston & Keniston, 1994, p. 32)

This call has become increasingly louder, and – without questioning the high importance of basic research – experts have started to join together in order to (more) systematically disseminate knowledge to relevant actors in society on how to address growing societal challenges. Amongst other associations, the International Panel on Social Progress was formed in 2014 with the aim of 'uniting the world's leading researchers, sociologists, and economists in a single effort: Developing research-based, multi-disciplinary, non-partisan, action-driven solutions to the most pressing challenges of our time.' (International Panel on Social Progress, 2016). This panel will deliver a report (to be launched in 2017) addressed to all social actors, movements, organizations, politicians and decision-makers, in order to provide them with high-quality expert advice on questions of relevance to social change, authored by over 250 experts from various fields. Studies from Bildung-Psychology will contribute to this by specifically focusing on how education can promote social progress (Spiel, 2016).

The call for transfer to the 'outside world' is especially addressed to universities, which have long been perceived as an inward-looking Republic of Scholars (Bleiklie, Laredo, & Sörlin, 2007) – symbolized by the ivory tower. The emerging expectation that universities not only produce new knowledge but do so with social and economic perspectives in mind (e.g., European Commission, 2006), has been codified – and made into law in some countries – as the obligation of universities to perform a *Third Mission* (e.g., Bleiklie et al., 2007). To fulfill their Third Mission, universities are requested to use the results produced by their first (teaching) and second missions (research) to address growing social, economic and societal challenges. This implies taking responsibility, actively and consciously, for the society on whose behalf they are working (European Commission, 2011). The Third Mission has two key priorities: (1) targeted use and transfer of scientific knowledge to help resolve diverse societal challenges and (2) transfer of technologies and innovations in the form of cooperation with public and private enterprises.

It can be argued that not all scientific fields or universities have the same need to change or expand their focus with regard to these priorities. For example, applied universities or applied university programs are thematically better aligned with the Third Mission since their research per definition focuses on the development of applications, the majority of which are intended to meet societal demands. Indeed, it has been shown that applied universities that adapt their curriculum and research to the demands of their surrounding region have a high potential to fulfill the objectives of the Third Mission regarding regional knowledge transfer (Jaeger & Kopper, 2014; OECD, 2012a). In addition, many of the methods and approaches adopted in Third Mission activities appear to be little more than accentuations of more established paradigms such as action and participatory research, transdisciplinarity or technology transfer (Trencher, Yarime, McCormick, Doll, & Kraines, 2014). However, what appears new is the combination of these various modes into a *systematic* response to the growing public challenges. In this view, the lack of a distinct Third Mission profile, conceptualized as a deliberate and programmatic direction to face the high complexity of societal challenges, is not only applicable in the case of research universities but also many applied universities (Roessler, Duong, & Hachmeister, 2016).

Particularly at large universities, a rich variety of Third Mission activities are already being carried out in research or teaching; however, most of them have not been formally identified as such and are not interconnected. Therefore, a crucial first step in developing a successful Third mission strategy is to systematically structure and interconnect existing activities.

Bildung-Psychology integrates transfer from science to society as a basic approach, and thus has a high potential to contribute to the development of a successful Third mission strategy. The structure model of Bildung-Psychology allows for the mapping of all activities in educational psychology according to their functional area (from research to monitoring/evaluation), their activity level (from micro- to macrolevel) and the age-specific educational phase they impact (from infancy to advanced adulthood). As a result, the model does not only allow activities to be systematically structured but may also foster the interconnection of activities which operate on different functional and activity levels or impact different phases of the life course.

In the following, we seek to illustrate how teaching and research activities from the field of Bildung-Psychology can contribute to fulfilling universities' Third Mission. The first example takes an innovative approach to connect with society via teaching in higher education. This is highly relevant against the backdrop that students are the best agents for transfer when they are competent and committed to the ongoing acquisition of (the latest) scientific knowledge. The second example seeks to illustrate how taking responsibility in the educational field via specific ways of designing research activities may contribute to fulfilling the social contract. By localizing both activities on the structure model of Bildung-Psychology, we aim to demonstrate how this framework may serve as a model for making activities more visible.

Teaching: innovative approaches to ensure transfer

The central role of universities has long been to train students and prepare them for taking over professional activities not only in research but also in politics, economy and society (Laredo, 2007). Thus, academic teaching is one of the (major) means through which universities connect with society. Zgaga (2009) proposed four 'archetypal models' of understanding the purposes of higher education: The *Napoleonic Model*, which aims at training students for their multiple, diverse careers; the *Humboldtian Model*, which focuses on creating and maintaining a broad, advanced knowledge base and stimulating research and innovation; the *Newmanian Model* which seeks to enable students' personal development; and finally, the *Deweyan Model* which understands the purpose of

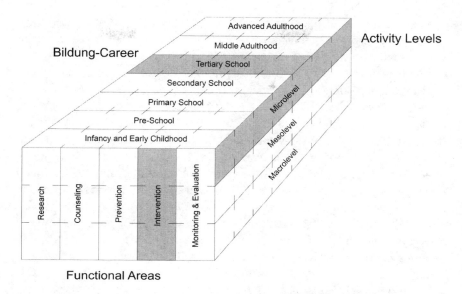

Figure 1. Localization of VEL within the structure model of Bildung-Psychology.

higher education as preparing students for a life as active citizens in a democratic society (Zgaga, 2009). But taping higher education's potential to contribute to successful and sustainable knowledge transfer necessitates the recognition of its 'full range of purposes' (London Communiqué, 2007).

In the following paragraphs, we will present the teaching concept Vienna E-Lecturing (VEL) as a concrete example of an innovative approach to teaching in higher education, focussing on at least some of these purposes (Schober, Wagner, Reimann, Atria, & Spiel, 2006; Schober, Wagner, Reimann, & Spiel, 2008). VEL addresses a (1) deep level of understanding regarding domain-specific knowledge as well as the sustainable promotion of (2) motivation, (3) self-regulated learning, (4) collaborative learning and (5) e-competence as basic determinants of LLL (see also Schober, Lüftenegger, Wagner, Finsterwald, & Spiel, 2013). The teaching concept is based on theories from motivational and instructional psychology (Pintrich & Schunk, 1996) and aims to impart relevant competencies to tomorrow's practitioners. VEL delivers a basal didactic framework for tertiary education, even if it is currently conceptualized as an intervention addressing students enrolled as psychology majors (tertiary sector, microlevel; see Figure 1). However, the specific content (relevant literature, exercises) of the imparted domain-specific knowledge remains dynamic; in other words, it can be adapted (also to other academic fields) and optimized. VEL supplies a structure founded in learning theory with a high degree of content flexibility, and has so far been implemented in a mandatory two-part course *Research Methods and Evaluation* for psychology majors at the University of Vienna for the past several years.

VEL is composed of 10 online modules and 11 face-to-face units taking place over the course of two semesters. The intervention was developed against the backdrop that university classes teaching the principles of methodology in psychology are in a difficult position: While methodological foundations are highly relevant for all students majoring in psychology, the popularity and perceived value of such methodology courses are significantly lower than those for subjects dealing with 'psychological content'. Students enrolled as psychology majors demonstrate negative attitudes toward methodology courses at the start of their studies, and these become even worse over the course of their studies (Giesler, 1998). This discrepancy between the importance and the esteem with which methodology courses are viewed made alternative teaching models necessary.

To achieve the five above introduced goals, VEL is based on two didactic principles: (1) networking and (2) optimal instructions. The principle of networking (1) is concerned with (a) the application of a blended learning approach, realized via the systematic combination of interrelated learning modules (online) and physical presence units (face-to-face), (b) the interlocking mediation of various learning goals, (c) the application of explicit and implicit forms of mediation, and (d) the inclusion of various types of knowledge: declarative, procedural, and conditional knowledge (Schober, 2002). Optimal instructions (2) are realized by systematically supplementing the learning material with specific exercises and by consistently assessing the results of these exercises via various types of feedback: (a) individual feedback (computer-generated), (b) group-specific feedback (written comments from the teacher, verbal comments from the teacher, written comments from peers), and (c) general feedback (written comments from the teacher). The feedback supplied in VEL is composed in such a way so as to encourage motivation (Schober, 2002): Strengths are highlighted, weaknesses are pointed out, and opportunities for improvement are brought up.

The evaluation of VEL was organized in a treatment-control group design (Schober et al., 2006; Wagner, Schober, Reimann, Atria, & Spiel, 2007). Evaluation results show that students who participated in VEL showed significantly higher motivation in the sense of higher competence beliefs regarding their factual knowledge, more competence in self-regulated learning, higher collaborative learning abilities and e-competence than students in the control group. Moreover, students in the treatment group achieve better performance in understanding and applying the imparted knowledge than students in the control group.

VEL represents a theory-based, systematically evaluated teaching concept, which addresses domain-specific knowledge as well as competences that are relevant for personal development, motivation and learning far beyond the context of the specific course. Considering that today's students are tomorrow's researchers, practitioners and policy-makers, adequate preparation – using high-quality teaching methods – for taking over positions of responsibility in politics, society and economy is the basis for a successful Third Mission.

Research: parameters for a basic approach to taking responsibility

In order to take societal responsibility in the educational field via research activities, scientists have to first and foremost tackle topics of high societal relevance. If this condition is met, their approaches need to meet additional demands, which are interconnected: (a) integrative theory development based on empirical measurement, (b) theory-based development and conducting intervention programs, (c) bringing interventions into the field (school/university), (d) involving stakeholders to guarantee sustainability, (e) conducting implementation research/transfer research, and (f) ensuring evaluation/quality assurance (for details see Schober & Spiel, in press).

In the following section, we will introduce the training program REFLECT – Gender Competence through Reflective Coeducation (Finsterwald et al., 2012; see also Kollmayer, Schober, & Spiel, 2016; Schultes, Jöstl, Finsterwald, Schober, & Spiel, 2015) as an example of a responsible research activity in the field of Bildung-Psychology. In terms of *demand (a)*, the training program REFLECT was developed against the empirical backdrop that the educational careers of women and men in Europe still differ dramatically – although gender equality in educational institutions is a central goal of the European Union (European Commission, 2015). Gender differences still exist in students' performance and motivation and in their vocational aspirations (OECD, 2012b, 2014), although there is no robust evidence for 'natural' gender differences in basic abilities or personality traits (Hyde, 2005). Teachers are considered a promising starting point for enacting change (e.g., Hattie, 2012), and teachers' attitudes and instructional practices are known to influence gender differences: For example, gender differences in classrooms decrease when teachers are able to foster aspects of individualization, autonomy and self-regulation in their students (Lüftenegger et al., 2012). Consequently, to move forward in promoting gender fairness in education, evidence-based training programs focusing on teachers' competences regarding reflective coeducation are needed. So far, the theoretical basis for reflective coeducation is rather weak – it is merely specified as teaching girls and boys together in a way that enables them to become aware of their individual competences and develop them without limitations arising from gender stereotypes. For this reason, REFLECT combines decisive theoretical determinants of successful reflective coeducation by integrating motivational theories and theories on self-worth, individualized teaching, action control and the mechanisms of stereotype development (see Finsterwald, Schober, Jöstl, & Spiel, 2013).

In terms of *demand (b),* the train-the-trainer program REFLECT (Finsterwald et al., 2012) is based on a current action theory in the field of intervention research – the actiotope model (Ziegler, Heller, Schober, & Dresel, 2006). REFLECT was conducted with the following goals: (1) expanding secondary school teachers' relevant objective action repertoire by providing them with the knowledge necessary to change their teaching (e.g., knowledge of the causes of gender differences, and of opportunities for fostering motivation in all students), (2) expanding teachers' subjective action space (e.g., enhancing their self-efficacy with regard to motivation enhancement in boys and girls), (3) promoting teachers' reflection on their own contributions to the formation of gender differences, resulting in changed teaching goals, and finally (4) reducing gender stereotypes among secondary school students.

In order to reach these goals, the program followed a course of four consecutive phases. In Phase 1, REFLECT was developed and organized by a group of researchers for a total of 38 teachers at 26 secondary schools distributed all over Austria. Thus, rather than being conducted within the limited context of few selected schools, REFLECT addresses a substantial number of actors in the field (*demand (c)*). Most participants simultaneously taught at pedagogical universities and were trained to subsequently take on a multiplication function (*demand (d)*). In Phase 2, the training was conducted over the course of seven months, blocked into four modules of two days each. Parallel to the training, a formative evaluation was carried out for its optimization. In Phase 3, teachers were supported in systematically integrating training contents into their teaching in the context of five-week projects in their classes. The class projects were developed and realized by the teachers themselves, and supervised by the REFLECT trainers (*demand (e)*). Phase 4 focused on evaluating the efficacy of REFLECT (*demand (f)*). The summative evaluation was carried out by means of a training-control group design with a multi-method, multi-informant approach. The results of the evaluation clearly show the effectiveness of the program: In comparison to the control group, participants' objective action repertoire increased, as did their subjective action space (Schober et al., 2012). Significant positive effects were also found among the students involved: their knowledge of gender issues increased during the program (Schultes et al., 2015). In the last phase of the program, a training manual was produced and distributed to all pedagogical universities.

In sum, the intervention program REFLECT was designed with the idea of transfer in mind at each step of the research progress: Competencies for reflective coeducation cannot be sustainably trained in isolated seminars, as they are closely connected to teachers' attitudes and to basic teaching principles. Therefore, a supervised transfer to the classroom is essential for practitioners (middle adulthood) to integrate and consolidate these competencies in daily school life (secondary school, microlevel; see Figure 2). Involving participants teaching at pedagogical universities as multipliers and producing and distributing a training manual are important steps to sustainably implement reflective coeducation in general teacher education (tertiary sector; see Figure 2).

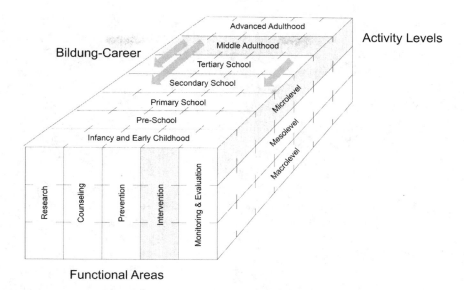

Figure 2. Localization of REFLECT within the structure model of Bildung-Psychology.

Conclusion

The emergence of universities' Third Mission as a clear directive to (finally) move beyond the ivory tower has generated tension due to concerns about excessive demands in addition to first and second mission activities. However, instead of requesting the design and development of completely new 'Third Mission activities', the Third Mission may be seen as a framework for activities which are relevant to society and/or the economy and *build on existing knowledge* from research and teaching. Such activities have been going on for a long time now in many scientific fields but have not been consolidated systematically. In order to be valued, activities need to be made (more) visible first. Bildung-Psychology, based on an integrative conceptual framework, may serve as a model for other scientific fields to make their activities more tangible. Localizing activities according to a structure model (see Figures 1 and 2) may also help to identify the specific strengths of a higher education institution and to develop of a clear profile.

Furthermore, identifying the specific levels on which a specific activity operates may facilitate the identification of opportunities to affect other levels. In the case of VEL, students (microlevel) may serve as transfer agents in the future (i.e., take action on the meso- or macrolevel). With regard to REFLECT, incorporating the training manual into general teacher education would be a crucial step to sustainably implementing reflective coeducation in educational systems (macrolevel). Thus, a clear localization of activities on the structure model may help to elucidate the full potential of research and teaching activities to fulfill universities' Third Mission by successfully transferring scientific knowledge to areas of need in society.

Only by taking responsibility, actively and consciously, not only for the society on whose behalf we are working but also for the scientific community in which we operate can a successful transfer cycle be assured. As demonstrated by the examples from Bildung-Psychology, this involves several steps. First, it must be assured that societal demand is identified and becomes the focus of research activities, which requires (an ongoing) exchange with practitioners (practice to science transfer). Second, adequate research designs must be developed by researchers within the context of the university, ideally by including practitioners, to produce high-quality evidence-based knowledge. This also implies actively getting involved in organizations concerned with promoting and improving scientific professions (e.g., the European Federation of Psychologists Associations, EFPA), and (increased) networking within the scientific community to ensure that research and teaching activities follow international best practice and the most current state of knowledge. Finally, to foster successful transfer of produced knowledge from science to society, it is not sufficient to make research results available to practitioners. To promote the implementation as sustainable solutions in practice, research results also have to be distributed to decision-makers.

Many challenges remain in developing concrete measures for sustainably implementing the transfer of scientific knowledge to society as one of the core missions of universities (Fixsen & Blase, 2009). However, making existing activities visible and structuring them is a crucial first step for universities in highlighting (the many) ongoing efforts and consequently in establishing *successful* transfer. This may also contribute to an increase in society's appreciation of science and research. The Bildung-Psychology framework can be seen as a convincing example of how a specific discipline can follow the inherent logic of scientific research, while integrating transfer from science to society as a basic approach and realizing a mission that definitely goes beyond the ivory tower.

Disclosure statement

No potential conflict of interest was reported by the authors.

Funding

Part of this research was funded by the Research Fund of the Austrian National Bank, [grant number 9956], and by the following Austrian Federal Ministries: Education, the Arts and Culture; Women and Public Service; Transport, Innovation and Technology; Labor, Social Affairs and Consumer Protection.

References

Bleiklie, I., Laredo, P., & Sörlin, S. (2007). Conclusion. *Higher Education Policy, 20*, 495–500.

BMBF. (2016). *Bildungsforschung 2020. Zwischen wissenschaftlicher Exzellenz und gesellschaftlicher Verantwortung* [Educational research 2020. Between academic excellence and social responsibility]. Berlin: Bundesministerium für Bildung und Forschung [German Federal Ministry of Education and Research].

Bronfenbrenner, U., & Morris, P. A. (2006). The bioecological model of human development. In R. M. Lerner (Ed.), *Theoretical models of human development, volume 1 of handbook of child psychology* (6th ed., pp. 793–828). Hoboken, NJ: Wiley.

Bush, V. (1945). Science: The endless frontier. *Transactions of the Kansas Academy of Science (1903-), 48*, 231–264.

Commission of the European Communities. (2000). *A memorandum for life-long learning, SEC(2000) 1832*. Brussels: Commission of the European Communities.

Day, C., Fernandez, A., Hauge, T. E., & Møller, J. (Eds.). (2000). *The life and work of teachers: International perspectives in changing times*. London: Falmer Press.

European Commission. (2006). Delivering on the modernisation agenda for universities: Education, research and innovation. *Communication from the commission to the council and the European Parliament, COM(2006) 208 Final*. Brussels: Commission of the European Communities.

European Commission. (2011). *A renewed EU strategy 2011–14 for corporate social responsibility*. Brussels: European Commission.

European Commission (2015). *Evaluation of the strengths and weaknesses of the Strategy for equality between women and men – A review of the situation and recent progress*. Brussels: Office for Official Publications of the European Communities.

Finsterwald, M., Jöstl, G., Popper, V., Hesse, N., Spiel, C., & Schober, B. (2012). *Abschlussbericht Reflect: Genderkompetenz durch Reflexive Koedukation* [Final report of reflect: gender competence through reflective coeducation]. (Unpublished report). University of Vienna.

Finsterwald, M., Schober, B., Jöstl, G., & Spiel, C. (2013). Reflexive Koedukation [Reflective coeducation]. In M. A. Wirtz (Ed.), *Dorsch – Lexikon der Psychologie* [Dorsch – Encyclopedia of psychology] (p. 837). Bern: Hogrefe.

Fixsen, D. L., & Blase, K. A. (2009). Implementation: The missing link between research and practice. *NIRN Implementation Brief, 1*. Chapel Hill, NC: The University of North Carolina, FPG, NIRN.

Gibbons, M. (1999). Science's new social contract with society. *Nature, 402*, C81–C84.

Giesler, J. M. (1998). Analysen zur Veränderung fachbezogener Interessen und Einstellungen von Studierenden des Fachs Psychologie in den beiden ersten Studiensemestern [Analysis of changes in subject-related interests and attitudes of psychology students in the first two study semesters]. In G. Krampen & H. Zayer (Eds.), *Psychologiedidaktik und Evaluation I. Konzepte, Erfahrungsberichte und empirische Untersuchungsbefunde aus Anwendungsfeldern der Aus-, Fort- und Weiterbildung* [Didactics and evaluation in psychology I. Concepts, opinions and empirical findings from application fields of education, training and education] (pp. 27–41). Bonn: Deutscher Psychologen Verlag.

Gräsel, C. (2010). Keyword: Transfer and transfer research in education science. *Zeitschrift für Erziehungswissenschaft, 13*, 7–20.

Gräsel, C., Jäger, M., & Willke, H. (2006). Konzeption einer übergreifenden Transferforschung unter Einbeziehung des internationalen Forschungsstandes [A conception of comprehensive transfer research involving the international state of research]. In R. Nickolaus & C. Gräsel (Eds.), *Innovation und Transfer. Expertisen zur Transferforschung* [Innovation and transfer. Expertises on transfer research] (pp. 445–566). Baltmannsweiler: Schneider Hohengehren.

Guston, D. H., & Keniston, K. (Eds.). (1994). *The fragile contract: University science and the federal government*. Cambridge, MA and London: MIT Press.

Hanushek, E. A., & Kimko, D. D. (2000). Schooling, labor-force quality, and the growth of Nations. *American Economic Review, 90*, 1184–1208. doi: 10.1257/aer.90.5.1184

Hanushek, E. A., & Woessmann, L. (2007). *The role of education quality for economic growth.* (World Bank Policy Research Working Paper, 4122).

Hattie, J. A. C. (2012). *Visible learning for teachers: Maximizing impact on learning*. London: Routledge.

Heckman, J. J. (2008). Schools, skills, and synapses. *Economic Inquiry, 46*, 289–324.

Hyde, J. S. (2005). The gender similarities hypothesis. *American Psychologist, 60*, 581–592.

International Panel on Social Progress. (2016). *Rethinking society for the 21st century.* Retrieved from https://www.ipsp.org/

Jaeger, A., & Kopper, J. (2014). Third mission potential in higher education: Measuring the regional focus of different types of HEIs. *Review of Regional Research, 34* 95–118.

Jürgens, H., Schneider, K., & Büchel, F. (2005). The effect of central exit examinations on student achievement: Quasi-experimental evidence from TIMSS Germany. *Journal of the European Economic Association, 3*, 1134–1155.

Karoly, P., Boekaerts, M., & Maes, S. (2005). Toward consensus in the psychology of self-regulation: How far have we come? How far do we have yet to travel? *Applied Psychology, 54*, 300–311.

Kollmayer, M., Schober, B., & Spiel, C. (2016). Gender stereotypes in eduactaion: Development, consequences, and interventions. *European Journal of Developmetal Psychology., 54*, 300–311.

Kühn, S. M., van Ackeren, I., Bellenberg, G., Reintjes, C., & im Brahm, G. (2013). How many years until abitur in German upper secondary schooling? – Taking stock in the context of current school duration debates. *Zeitschrift für Erziehungswissenschaft, 16*, 115–136.

Laredo, P. (2007). Revisiting the third mission of universities: Toward a renewed categorization of university activities? *Higher Education Policy, 20*, 441–456.

Lewin, K. (1952). *Field theory in social science: Selected theoretical papers by Kurt Lewin.* London: Tavistock.

London Communiqué. (2007). *Towards the European higher education area*. Communiqué of the Conference of European Ministers Responsible for Higher Education. Retrieved from http://www.ond.vlaanderen.be/hogeronderwijs/bologna/documents/MDC/London_Communique18May2007.pdf

Lüftenegger, M., Schober, B., van de Schoot, R., Wagner, P., Finsterwald, M., & Spiel, C. (2012). Lifelong learning as a goal – Do autonomy and self-regulation in school result in well prepared pupils? *Learning and Instruction, 22*, 27–36.

OECD. (2012a). *OECD territorial reviews: The Chicago tri-state metropolitan area, United States 2012*. Paris: Author.

OECD. (2012b). *PISA in focus: What kinds of careers do boys and girls expect for themselves?* (vol. 14). Paris: Author.

OECD. (2014). *PISA 2012 results: What students know and can do – Student performance in mathematics, reading and science* (Vol. 1, Revised ed.). Paris: Author.

Oreopoulos, P., Page, M. E., & Stevens, A. H. (2006). The intergenerational effects of compulsory schooling. *Journal of Labor Economics, 24*, 729–760.

Oreopoulos, P., & Salvanes, K. G. (2011). Priceless: The nonpecuniary benefits of schooling. *Journal of Economic Perspectives, 25*, 159–184.

Pintrich, P. R. (2000). Educational psychology at the millennium: A look back and a look forward. *Educational Psychologist, 35*, 221–226.

Pintrich, P. R., & Schunk, D. H. (1996). *Motivation in education: Theory, research and application*. Englewood Cliffs, NJ: Simon and Schuster.

Piopiunik, M., Schwerdt, G., & Woessmann, L. (2013). Central school exit exams and labor-market outcomes. *European Journal of Political Economy, 31*, 93–108.

Random House. (1993). *Webster's unabridged dictionary* (2nd ed.). New York, NY: Author.

Roessler, I., Duong, S., & Hachmeister, C. D. (2016). *Using various missions for positioning*. Gütersloh: CHE Centrum für Hochschulentwicklung.

Scheurman, G., Heeringa, K., Rocklin, T. R., & Lohman, D. F. (1993). Educational psychology: A view from within the discipline. *Educational Psychologist, 28*, 97–115.

Schober, B. (2002). *Entwicklung und Evaluation des Münchner Motivationstrainings (MMT)* [Development and evaluation of the muenchner motivationstraining (MMT)]. Regensburg: Roderer Verlag.

Schober, B., Finsterwald, M., Jöstl, G., Popper, V., Hesse, N., & Spiel, C. (2012, June). Development of gender differences: Current findings and evidence-based interventions in schools. *Paper presented at the International Conference on Research in Teaching and Teacher Education (EARLI – SIG 11)*, Bergen, Norway.

Schober, B., Lüftenegger, M., Wagner, P., Finsterwald, M., & Spiel, C. (2013). Facilitating lifelong learning in school – Age learners. *European Psychologist, 18*, 114–125.

Schober, B., & Spiel, C. (in press). Enabling improvements: Combining intervention and implementation research. In R. A. Scott, S. M. Kosslyn, & M. Buchmann (Eds.), *Emerging trends in the social and behavioral sciences*. Hoboken, NJ: Wiley.

Schober, B., Wagner, P., Reimann, R., Atria, M., & Spiel, C. (2006). Teaching research methods in an Internet-based blended-learning setting. *Methodology, 2*, 73–82.

Schober, B., Wagner, P., Reimann, R., & Spiel, C. (2008). Vienna e-lecturing (VEL): Learning how to learn self-regulated in an Internet-based blended learning setting. *International Journal on E- learning, 7*, 703–723.

Schultes, M.-T., Jöstl, G., Finsterwald, M., Schober, B., & Spiel, C. (2015). Measuring intervention fidelity from different perspectives with multiple methods: The Reflect program as an example. *Studies in Educational Evaluation, 47*, 102–112. doi: 10.1016/j.stueduc.2015.10.001

Spiel, C. (2016, February 11–13). How can education promote social progress? Basic issues for the contribution to the report of the international panel of social progress (IPSP). *Presentation at the Workshop on Education and Social Progress*, University of Vienna, Vienna.

Spiel, C., Reimann, R., Wagner, P., & Schober, B. (2008). Guest editorial: Bildung-psychology: The substance and structure of an emerging discipline. *Applied Developmental Science, 12*, 154–159. doi: 10.1080/10888690802199426

Spiel, C., Schober, B., & Strohmeier, D. (2016). Implementing intervention research into public policy – the 'I3-approach'. *Prevention Science, 17*(2), 1–10. doi: 10.1007/s11121-016-0638-3

Spiel, C., & Schober, B. (in press). Lessons learned for policy impact from research and interventions. In A. C. Petersen, F. Motto-Stafanidi, S. H. Koller, & S. Verma (Eds.), *Positive youth development in global contexts of social and economic change*. New York, NY: Taylor & Francis.

Stokes, D. E. (1997). *Pasteur's quadrant: Basic science and technological innovation*. Washington, DC: Brookings Institution Press.

Trencher, G., Yarime, M., McCormick, K. B., Doll, C. N., & Kraines, S. B. (2014). Beyond the third mission: Exploring the emerging university function of co-creation for sustainability. *Science and Public Policy, 41*, 151–179.

Usher, R., & Bryant, I. (2014). *Adult education as theory, practice and research: The captive triangle*. London: Routledge.

Wagner, P., Schober, B., Reimann, R., Atria, M., & Spiel, C. (2007). Vienna E-Lecturing: Trainingskonzept zum selbstregulierten Lernen im Studium [Vienna E-Lecturing: A program to enhance self-regulated learning at university]. In B. Schmitz & M. Landmann (Eds.), *Selbstregulation erfolgreich fördern. Praxisnahe Trainingsprogramme für effektives Lernen* [Promoting self-regulation successfully. Practical training-programs for effective learning] (pp. 290–311). Stuttgart: Kohlhammer.

Wagner, P., Strohmeier, D., & Schober, B. (2016). Bildung-psychology: Theory and practice of use inspired basic research. *European Journal of Developmental Psychology, 13*.

Wilberg, S., & Rost, D. H. (1997). Klassengröße und Geschichtskenntnisse [Class size and knowledge about history]. *Zeitschrift für Pädagogische Psychologie, 11*, 65–68.

Wilberg, S., & Rost, D. H. (1999). Große Klasse – kleine Leistung? [Large class – poor performance?]. *Zeitschrift für Entwicklungspsychologie und Pädagogische Psychologie, 31*, 138–143.

Wild, K. P., & Rost, D. H. (1995). Klassengröße und Genauigkeit von Schülerbeurteilungen [Class size and accuracy of student assessment]. *Zeitschrift für Entwicklungspsychologie und Pädagogische Psychologie, 27*, 78–90.

Woessmann, L., & Piopiunik, M. (2009). *Was unzureichende Bildung kostet. Eine Berechnung der Folgekosten durch entgangenes Wirtschaftswachstum* [The costs of insufficient education. A calculation of subsequent costs due to evaded economic growth]. Gütersloh: Bertelsmann Stiftung.

Zgaga, P. (2009). Higher Education and Citizenship: 'The full range of purposes'. *European Educational Research Journal, 8*, 175–188.

Ziegler, A., Heller, K. A., Schober, B., & Dresel, M. (2006). The actiotope: A heuristic model for the development of a research program designed to examine and reduce adverse motivational conditions influencing scholastic achievement. In D. Frey, H. Mandl, & L. V. Rosenstiel (Eds.), *Knowledge and action* (pp. 147–173). Göttingen: Hogrefe.

Social-emotional development: From theory to practice

Tina Malti and Gil G. Noam

ABSTRACT

This theoretical article aims to introduce a new conceptual framework for the understanding and enhancement of child and adolescent social-emotional development (SED). We first elaborate on a taxonomy to classify core dimensions of SED and make a case for its importance. Next, we introduce our developmental approach to the study of SED and elaborate as to why there is a need to connect developmental theory and research systematically with the use of social-emotional assessment tools. We briefly describe the holistic student assessment (HSA) as an example of such a tool through which children, teachers, and caregivers report on dimensions of SED. The HSA generates individual, classroom, and school-wide profiles of SED. How such profiles can be used to inform intervention planning and implement developmentally sensitive strategies to promote SED and intervene psychopathology will also be discussed. We conclude with reflections on how our developmental approach to understanding and assessing SED relates to Bildung-Psychology as we argue for a renewed focus on the 'whole child' and a broadened view of educational attainment.

Social-emotional development (SED) entails various dimensions of children's and adolescents' social and emotional development, and is widely recognized by researchers to be at the core of human development and growth (e.g., Collaborative for Academic, Social, and Emotional Learning [CASEL] 2013). As a result, there has been growing interest in deepening our understanding of SED and its enhancement in all children. There is also ample evidence on the importance of SED for academic achievement and mental health in childhood and adolescence (see Durlak, Domitrovich, Weissberg, & Gullotta, 2015). While much research on SED has been conducted and various evidence-based programs on social-emotional learning (SEL) have been widely implemented, there are still significant gaps in the research-practice connection.

This theoretical article aims to address parts of these gaps and will use the existing evidence on the beneficial role of SED in positive and productive outcomes as a starting point to introduce a developmental approach to conceptualizing and enhancing SED in children and adolescents. We introduce a taxonomy that classifies SED along its core dimensions and then provide a brief overview of a new developmental model to conceptualize and analyze SED. Next, we explain why there is a need not only to better understand, but also to assess SED systematically in all children. A selective review of current measurement approaches to assess SED for different ages and developmental levels is given. We then introduce our own SED tool, which is a school-based assessment through which children, adolescents, teachers, and caregivers report on children's SED. We illustrate how SED assessments can be used to inform intervention planning and support the implementation of preventative and treatment strategies in a way that addresses the target child's developmental needs and strengths. We conclude with reflections on how a developmental approach to SED relates to Bildung-Psychology as we argue for a renewed focus on the 'whole child' and a broadened view of educational attainment.

A taxonomical description of SED's core dimensions

SED is an umbrella term that describes individuals' various interpersonal and intrapersonal skills in the domain of social and emotional development (see Malti, 2011). In the applied literature, a commonly used, related umbrella term is social and emotional learning (SEL; see CASEL, 2013). Here, we use SED because of our theoretical perspective on developmental processes that underlie the formation, growth, and change of social and emotional skills across childhood and adolescence. SED includes understanding, regulating, and expressing emotions in a way that is appropriate for one's age and development, as well as the ability to establish, maintain, and develop healthy relationships with peers and adults (Eisenberg, 2000; Malti, Häcker, & Nakamura, 2009; Saarni, 1999). As such, SED presupposes an active, autonomous, and responsible stance towards the self in an interconnected social world. SED is central to navigating challenges in social interactions in everyday life and to adapting flexibly to situational demands.

In an effort to create a more coherent framework, we have recently discussed central dimensions of SED from an integrative conceptual perspective and created a taxonomy to systematize its core dimensions. Accordingly, SED entails (1) an individual's understanding of emotional experiences in the self and others, (2) the ability to express emotions in an age-appropriate way, and (3) emotion regulation capacities. These dimensions reflect the view of emotion as a multi-layered concept that is inherently linked to one's experiences of their own emotional responses (including bodily functions and physiological regulation), as well as responses to multifaceted social experiences and interactions (which involves both an understanding of others' emotions, as well as an age-appropriate expression of emotion). The first component, emotion understanding, is at the core of emotion theories (e.g., Saarni, 1999), as well as related theories on identity development. This is because an understanding of ourselves inevitably entails an increasing understanding of the other and the similarities and differences between his/her emotional experiences and our own (see Erikson, 1950–1963; Hoffman, 2000). The two last components, i.e., emotion expression and regulation of emotion, have been identified based on early theoretical accounts on ego/identity development and the description of temperamental dimensions that underlie the development of emotions, motivations, and behaviour (Block & Block, 1980; Malti, Sette, & Dys, in press; Noam & Malti, 2010).

While there is some agreement that SED components involve self-directed and other-oriented emotional skills, much more debate has evolved around the number of SED skills and subdimensions of SED. The literature has suggested various subsets of skills that are considered important for SED and its development across the lifespan (CASEL, 2013; Malti, 2011). In addition, numerous catalogues, lists, and classification schemes have been proposed to organize the various subskills that can be considered as parts of SED. For instance, the CASEL, has identified a set of five social and emotional learning competencies (see CASEL, 2013). These five core competencies, i.e., self-awareness, self-management, social awareness, relationship skills, and responsible decision-making, are interrelated and reflect a broad range of emotional, cognitive, and behavioural skills.

Thus, there is some consistency across the various attempts to describe the subdimensions of SED. Yet, there is less clarity about the existence of a set of core skills. Here, we argue that there are core skills that are necessary for any classification scheme, and that other less central skills are more interchangeable and can be flexibly used, depending on researchers' and practitioners' interests and needs (such as populations being served, availability of service structures, etc.). Thus, while it is important to identify subdimensions of SED, a first step to a fuller understanding of SED is to identify its core dimensions, as well as its structure and function. This core organizational structure can help identify central dimensions of SED, as well as various subdimensions that may be considered as part of SED.

Figure 1 shows a developmental taxonomy that we developed to provide a basic structure to organize core social-emotional skills along two continuous dimensions of self- and other- orientation, and over- and under-regulation of emotion and impulses. As can be seen, there are two core organizational principles to the structure and function of SED. The first is self- and other-orientation, an organizational principle to understand if the skill is (more) focused on the self (e.g., self-evaluative emotions), the other (e.g., other-oriented emotions such as sympathy), or both (social understanding requires an understanding of one's own and others' perspective) in a way that is adequate for the child's age

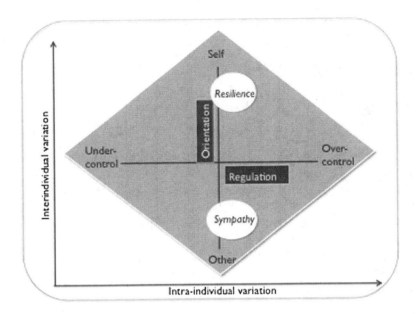

Figure 1. Taxonomy of social-emotional development.

and development. A balanced, age-appropriate development of self- and other-oriented skills is necessary to establish and maintain resilience (i.e., the ability to handle challenges) and being socially well adapted (i.e., the ability to express other-oriented skills and balance them with own needs in a responsible manner). This includes the core dimensions of emotion understanding and emotion expression. The second component, emotion regulation, is also a core dimension used to classify SED. Over- and under-regulation are organizational principles that help to identify the extent to which the individual is able to regulate and balance his/her own and others' emotions and impulses in a manner that is adequate for their age and development (Eisenberg, 2000). Central to this taxonomy is first, the integration of others' and self-perspectives that transcend one's own standpoint and ultimately lead to other-oriented sympathy (Malti & Ongley, 2014; see Hoffman, 2000), a core SED skill. Second, the taxonomy indicates that there is a basic human need to demonstrate emotional control and flexibility by regulating one's own emotions and impulses (see Block & Block, 1980) which leads to optimal resilience, the second core SED skill. In addition, there is both intra-individual and inter-individual variation in these two skills (i.e., they are subject to change), reflecting developmental processes of growth, decline, and transformation.

The importance of a better understanding of SED in children

Advancing our understanding of SED in children matters for several reasons. First, and most obviously perhaps, SED has been shown to be central for child and adolescent mental health and can help protect against psychopathology and risk across development (e.g., van Noorden, Haselager, Cillessen, & Bukowski, 2015). It has been shown that many children and adolescents across the globe suffer from mental health problems or are at risk of developing them, including anxieties, depression, attention problems, and aggressive behaviour disorders (Malti & Noam, 2008). As such, understanding the potential effects of psychological protective factors at different times in development is important. A plethora of research has also shown that mental health problems negatively affect academic motivation and functioning (e.g., Masten et al., 2005; Oberle, Schonert-Reichl, Hertzman, & Zumbo, 2014). Thus, understanding SED can also help researchers and practitioners alike to understand how a child's strengths and risks at any given time in development are associated with mental health and academic achievement, and, as such, inform strategies that address developmental needs and challenges. This approach is likely to create more effective outcomes (Malti et al., in press).

Taking this line of argument one step further, developmental psychologists have not only studied bidirectional relations between SED and mental health but have also studied *how* children's SED can serve as a protective factor, preventing children from developing or maintaining mental health problems. For example, recent research has shown that the capacity of children to regulate their own emotions plays a fundamental role for their subsequent psychological adaptation in peer relationships (Rubin, Bukowski, & Laursen, 2011). Such findings are hardly surprising, as related psychological research has provided much evidence that both under- and over- regulation are associated with various mental health problems (Eisenberg, Spinrad, & Eggum, 2010). Similarly, it has been shown that children's ability to feel and express other-oriented emotions, such as empathy, is positively associated with the developmental trajectories of prosocial behaviour and aggression and related behavioural problems (for reviews, see Eisenberg, Spinrad, & Knafo-Noam, 2015; Eisner & Malti, 2015). Given the well-documented role of SED in subsequent mental health outcomes, it appears important to (a) deepen our understanding of the dynamic processes underlying the links between various social-emotional skills, as well as with behavioural and emotional health, (b) utilize measures to assess SED in all children in a developmentally sensitive way, and (c) use these measures in contexts where all children can be reached to refine existing practices and make them more sensitive so that they fit the developmental needs and strengths of each child.

A developmental approach to SED

While much research on SED has been conducted and SEL programs have been implemented, many programs and assessment approaches still lack sufficient consideration of developmental theory and knowledge of both intra-individual and inter-individual differences in the various dimensions of

SED. A developmental taxnomony like ours is useful as it can inform practice by providing systematic approaches to the selection of SED subdimensions and related measurement choices. Vice versa, existing models on SED have often fallen short on translating their information into practice. Our own recursive developmental theory was developed over the past decade and attempts to provide a comprehensive model on SED (for a detailed overview, see Malti & Noam, 2008; Noam, Malti, & Karcher, 2013). One of its basic premises is that SED can be described as the leaves of a clover. The four leaves of the so-called 'Clover Model'—action, assertion, belonging, and reflection — describe the minimum dimensions required to understand the social-emotional skillsets and resiliencies of children and adolescents. An identification of these skills can be used to provide them with the right support and learning opportunities to engage and satisfy these needs.

Figure 2 depicts the Clover Model and the core developmental needs and strengths of individuals at each of the leaves. As can be seen, the action and belonging leaves reflect the central skills of emotion regulation, sympathy, and the related abilities to understand, communicate, and integrate emotions in one's self and in others. These self- and other-oriented dimensions of SED are at the core because they guide one's self- and other-oriented behaviour. In contrast, the two clover leaves of assertion and reflection are more strongly related to social-cognitive and motivational skills, most prominently perseverance (i.e., assertion), critical thinking, and high executive functioning (i.e., reflection).

The Clover model identifies measurable core dimensions of SED, such as emotion control and sympathy. Each of these dimensions are most typical in one specific clover leaf (e.g., high sympathy is expected to be part of the need to 'belong' because feeling with and for others creates bonds with them and often supports relationship quality and, as such, reflects a need to belong to others). We have elaborated in more detail how the various dimensions are associated with one core cloverleaf elsewhere (e.g., Noam et al., 2013). Importantly, each dimension can also occur in varying levels in other cloverleaves. For instance, the cloverleaf of belonging is characterized by high levels of sympathy, which is associated with a fundamental need to belong to (and care) for others. However, the cloverleaf of self-reflection can also (but does not need to) entail high levels of sympathy for others given the reflective, critical nature of this leaf. In addition to identifying these measurable core skills, the Clover Model assumes that SED skills are related to each other and associated with other life skills that are traditionally considered 'cognitive' skills in meaningful ways. For instance, emotion control is likely to be associated with the ability of attention allocation. The Clover Model assumes developmental plasticity and acknowledges that SED inherently varies across development and within any age group. For instance, the need to belong and the ability to feel empathic concern may remain relatively stable across childhood and adolescence, but its expression changes significantly with age and development. It may become

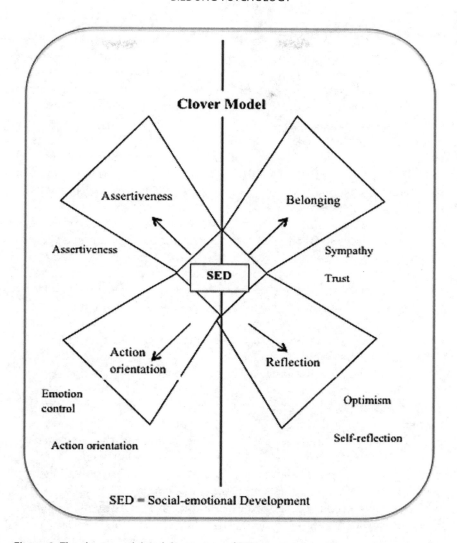

Figure 2. The clover model and dimensions of SED.

especially salient in adolescence, a time when peer relationships and group membership are important for identity formation and the development of a healthy balance between autonomy and interconnectedness. Importantly, the need to belong and the level of sympathy typically also varies substantially between children and adolescents of the same chronological age (Malti, Chaparro, Zuffianò, & Colasante, 2016). These within- and across-age variations in development are substantial when considering core dimensions of SED, and need to be reflected in any measurement approach that claims to be developmentally sensitive.

Measuring SED: From theory to practice

While it is clear that more research is needed to fully understand how development in the various subdimensions of SED occurs, how SED dimensions are interrelated over time, and how associated developmental needs change across time, assessing a core set of SED skills at any given time in development can substantially contribute to promoting their growth and learning. This is because educational practices that are rooted in an understanding of the normative and atypical trajectories of SED are more likely to fit the developmental needs of a child than practices that are not (Noam et al., 2013). Similarly to getting test scores from all children in schools, getting scores on SED skills can improve the planning and implementation of educational approaches and practices (Malti & Noam, 2008; Noam, Malti, & Guhn, 2012). More specifically, such tools can help practitioners choose the most effective strategies for promoting SED. For instance, if a tool reveals that a child has very low sympathy compared to his/her peer group and/or his/her age but relatively high levels of action orientation, intervention planning might involve the preparation of strategies that target the enhancement of sympathy in a developmentally sensitive way (i.e., strategies that are adequate for the child's developmental level), combined with the utilization of physical activity and action-oriented tasks that are likely to get the child engaged and enjoy these activities.

While SED assessment tools have been developed, there is a significant lack of consideration of knowledge that has been generated by theorizing and by developmental research in current discussions regarding assessment tools. Current discussions also neglect said knowledge in deciding if and how their use may add to intervention planning, implementation, and evaluation. In addition, the great majority of existing school-based assessments typically include questions either about strengths or risks only. Tools that are based in sound developmental theory and that include various components of SED are still relatively scarce. In addition, few of the existing instruments use multiple informants, and even fewer create individual, classroom, and school-based profiles for use in education planning. Lastly, information on developmental differences within and across grades is rarely considered comprehensively when making decisions about referrals and intervention strategies.

Nevertheless, several assessment tools for use in educational contexts have been developed (see Durlak et al., 2015). Three commonly used school-based instruments in childhood are the Devereux Student Strengths Assessment (DESSA), the Social-Emotional Assets and Resilience Scales (SEARS), and the Early Development Instrument/Middle Years Development Instrument (EDI/MDI). These instruments are strengths-based, mostly rely on other-reports, and do not assess risk factors. In addition, the EDI/MDI are population-level tools (Guhn & Goelman, 2011). Our own measure, the holistic student assessment (HSA) is rooted in our social-emotional developmental theory (Malti & Noam, 2008), and its main goal is to increase an understanding of SED to help teachers and practitioners assess the strengths and risks posed by the particular developmental setup of the child. It is comprised of both teacher-reported and self-reported rating scales designed to assess and guide intervention planning, and evaluate outcomes related to social-emotional strengths and challenges of middle school students. In its original version, the self-report and teacher/parent- report version of the HSA includes 61 items that tap into SED, as well as related life skills. There are seven core dimensions of SED in the self-report version, and we have recently shown that these seven dimensions can be represented by 32 items (for a more detailed description of the psychometric properties of the HSA/9-18, see Malti, Zuffiano, & Noam, 2016). The SED dimensions include action orientation (clover leaf: action orientation, e.g., 'I like being active'), emotion control (clover leaf: action orientation), assertiveness (clover leaf: assertiveness), sympathy (clover leaf: belonging, e.g., 'I feel sad for kids who are sad'), trust (clover leaf: belonging, e.g., 'I trust other people'), self-reflection (clover leaf: reflection, e.g., 'I try to understand the world I live in'), and optimism (clover leaf: reflection, e.g., 'I have more good times than bad times'; this dimension is the one that underlies all clover leaves to more or less an extent and, as such, it is harder to associate with one particular leaf). The SED items of the HSA have been adapted for use in the early years, i.e., HSA/3-8 (i.e., 3- to 8 years of age), and parent- and teacher versions are currently being used in Canadian kindergarten classes, schools, and in research laboratory and clinical settings.

Using SED tools: planning and implementing interventions

SEL programs operate under the premise that the enhancement of SED in children and adolescents will result in corresponding decreases in their problem behaviours, such as aggression, bullying, and attention deficit/hyperactivity problems (Durlak, Weissberg, Dymnicki, Taylor & Schellinger, 2011). Simultaneously, researchers have emphasized that there is a need to use developmental tailoring to fit the developmental level and needs of children and adolescents (Malti et al., 2016; Noam & Hermann, 2002; Ollendick, Grills & King, 2001; Weisz & Weersing, 1999; see Greenberg et al., 2003). While much progress has been made in the design of developmentally tailored SEL interventions for children and adolescents (Durlak et al., 2011), the systematic implementation of such approaches, including the use of screening and/or assessment tools is still much less (systematically) commonly used to plan, implement, and monitor outcomes and developmental processes (Malti et al., 2016). We argue that SED assessment tools can be used to improve current educational and intervention planning and implementation practices in several ways.

In the following, we illustrate this idea further by briefly discussing examples of the applicability of the HSA tool in practice. As mentioned above, the results of the HSA generate individual, classroom, and school-based profiles of the

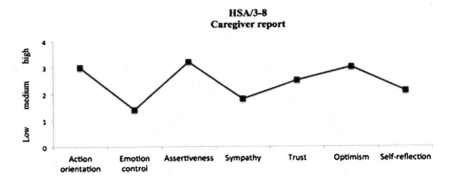

Figure 3. HSA/3–18 Caregiver report: sample profile for individual child.

social-emotional strengths and challenges of each student. These profiles summarize the individual (and/or group-based) results in an easy, accessible, and clear manner. For example, an individual profile summarizes the results of the HSA for a specific student and his/her social-emotional developmental strengths and challenges, as indicated by the level of each of the seven SED dimensions and related underlying Cloverleaf characteristics. His/her SED profile can be compared to his/her class average and/or other comparison data (e.g., all boys in a classroom, data of the entire grade in his/her school, etc.) as needed. A hypothetical individual sample profile for the HSA is illustrated in Figure 3. As can be seen, the mean scores of each SED dimension for a child, as rated by the primary caregiver, are shown. The profile highlights the social-emotional strengths and challenges for the child. In the example, the child exhibits relatively low levels of emotion control and relatively high levels of action orientation. This information can be used for intervention planning. For instance, a practitioner could use activities to promote this child's regulatory capacities and enhance emotion control by the use of strategies that are based in physical activities (which is part of an action orientation). In addition, one could compare this profile to the mean score of the classroom to see similarities and differences between the target child's score with a comparable peer group. Practitioners could use such a profile comparison to choose what dimensions to focus on when promoting SED in the classroom, what educational strategies to prioritize for some children, how to promote target skills, and with what intensity. Similarly, profiles for whole schools (or entire districts) can be generated when using SEL tools to inform principals about the level of SED in their school by classroom, grade, school, and district. Such group profiles can also help in the understanding of normative development of various SED dimensions (see Malti et al., 2016) and can potentially reveal differences and similarities between SED in a given school in comparison to larger populations. This is useful information for various reasons. An example would be to inform school principals and teachers about the SED in a classroom compared to other classrooms of the same grade or the SED in the whole school compared to district-wide data. Lastly, the profiles can be utilized by policy makers to derive information on how SED varies within and across communities.

These examples illustrate that SED assessment findings can be used for various purposes. One of our aims is to inform the planning, selection and delivery of developmentally tailored intervention strategies at the individual and/or classroom level. Clearly, individual profiles serve as a 'map' for individual prevention and treatment planning, go beyond a traditional risk focus, and have great potential to become more developmentally sensitive and responsive to the particular child's needs. While some social-emotional skills are easy to observe and may be easy to detect in everyday interactions, other skills (e.g., sympathy) might be harder to see. Assessment findings can therefore support our diagnostic accuracy and help inform best practices.

SED and Bildung-Psychology

SED and Bildung are not the same, but they are inseparably related (see Spiel, Reimann, Wagner, & Schober, 2008). After all, SED entails the lifelong process of learning, transformation, and transcendence of knowledge, a key element of Bildung in its most genuine sense. This is because cultivating our minds involves not only our thoughts and abstract reflection, but ultimately an equal emphasis on educating our emotions, natural instincts, and regulatory capacities in everyday social interactions. SED describes processes that contribute to the development of the Bildung of an individual over the lifespan, leading to an educated individual and a mature self (Spiel, Reimann, Wagner, & Schober, 2010, p. 11). Developmental models of SED emphasize a risk-and-resilience perspective because socioemotional skills can serve as protective factors, buffer psychological, contexual, and/or biological risks, and, as such, stimulate growth (Masten, 2014; Schonert-Reichl & Hymel, 2007). Bildung goes far beyond pure knowledge transfer and the acquisition and differentiation of cognitive and motivational skills. Rather, cultivating a reflected and respectful way to treat our own and others' emotions and impulses is at the core of the humane treatment of each other and of civilization. As such, our attempt to describe the SED of individuals as a core process and goal of human development across the lifespan fits well into the notion of Bildung.

While our notion that SED is inherently linked to Bildung reflects common humanistic accounts of Bildung, more empirical work is needed to explore the interrelatedness of SED and the process of Bildung across the lifespan. By arguing that lifelong learning is a pursuit of knowledge, growth, and individual development, this account paves the way for research that explores the role of emotions, cognitions, and behaviours across development and maturity in an integrated, comprehensive way. As Christiane Spiel and colleagues noted in 2008, Bildung focuses on life-long learning which in its entirety constitutes an individual's Bildung-career. SED undergoes life-long learning and change processes, and Bildung is not, and cannot, limit itself to changes in cognition and reflective thought, but inherently concerns individuals' emotions and social interactions in everyday life, and how they change in the dynamic interplay between cognition and affect.

Acknowledgement

We thank Akpene Kutuadu and Danah Elsayed, University of Toronto, for their editorial assistance with the manuscript.

Disclosure statement

No potential conflict of interest was reported by the authors.

Funding

The first author was funded, in part, by a New Investigator Award from the Canadian Institutes of Health Research (CIHR); the Social Sciences and Humanities Research Council of Canada (SSHRC).

References

Block, J. H., & Block, J. (1980). The role of ego-control and ego-resiliency in the organization of behavior. In W. A. Collins (Ed.), *Development of cognition, affect, and social relations: The Minnesota symposia on child psychology* (Vol. 13). Hillsdale, NJ: Erlbaum.

Collaborative for Academic, Social, and Emotional Learning. (2013). *CASEL school kit: A guide for implementing school wide academic, social, and emotional learning*. Chicago, IL: Author.

Durlak, J. A., Domitrovich, C. E., Weissberg, R. P., & Gullotta, T. P. (Eds.). (2015). *Handbook of social and emotional learning: Research and practice*. New York, NY: Guilford Press.

Durlak, J. A., Weissberg, R. P., Dymnicki, A. B., Taylor, R. D., & Schellinger, K. B. (2011). The impact of enhancing students' social and emotional learning: A meta-analysis of school-based universal interventions. *Child Development, 82*, 474–450. doi:http://dx.doi.org/10.1111/j.1467-8624.2010.01564.x

Eisenberg, N. (2000). Emotion, regulation, and moral development. *Annual Review of Psychology, 51*, 665–697. doi:http://dx.doi.org/10.1146/annurev.psych.51.1.665

Eisenberg, N., Spinrad, T. L., & Eggum, N. D. (2010). Emotion-related self-regulation and its relation to children's maladjustment. *Annual Review of Clinical Psychology, 6*, 495–525. doi:http://dx.doi.org/10.1146/annurev.clinpsy.121208.131208

Eisenberg, N., Spinrad, T. L., & Knafo-Noam, A. (2015). Prosocial development. In M. E. Lamb (Vol. Ed.) & R. M.Lerner(Series Ed.), *Handbook of child psychology and developmental science, Vol. 3: Social, emotional, and personality development* (7th ed., pp. 610–656). New York, NY: Wiley.

Eisner, M. P., & Malti, T. (2015). Aggressive and violent behavior. In M. E. Lamb (Vol. Ed.) & R. M. Lerner(Series Ed.). *Handbook of child psychology and developmental science, Vol. 3: Social, emotional and personality development* (7th ed., pp. 795–884). New York: Wiley.

Erikson, E. H. (1950–1963). *Childhood and society*. New York: Norton.
Greenberg, M. T., Weissberg, R. P., O'Brien, M. U., Zins, J. E., Fredericks, L., Resnik, H., & Elias, M. J. (2003). Enhancing school-based prevention and youth development through coordinated social, emotional and academic learning. *American Psychologist, 58,* 466–474. doi:http://dx.doi.org/10.1037/0003-066X.58.6-7.466
Guhn, M., & Goelman, H. (2011). Bioecological theory, early child development, and the validation of the population-level early development instrument. *Social Indicators Research, 103,* 193–217. doi:http://dx.doi.org/10.1007/s11205-011-9842-5
Hoffman, M. L. (2000). *Empathy and moral development: Implications for caring and justice.* New York, NY: Cambridge University Press. doi: http://dx.doi.org/10.1017/CBO9780511805851
Malti, T. (2011). Developing life skills in youth. In Jacobs Foundation (Ed.), *Jacobs Foundation guidelines on monitoring and evaluating life skills for youth development* (pp. 8–23). Zurich: Jacobs Foundation.
Malti, T., Chaparro, M. P., Zuffianò, A., & Colasante, T. (2016). School-based interventions to promote empathy-related responding in children and adolescents: A developmental analysis. *Journal of Clinical Child and Adolescent Psychology*. Early online publication, 18 February, 2016. doi:http://dx.doi.org/10.1080/15374416.2015.1121822
Malti, T., Häcker, T., & Nakamura, Y. (2009). *Sozial-emotionales Lernen in der Schule* [Social-emotional learning in schools]. Zurich: Pestalozzianum Verlag.
Malti, T., & Noam, G. G. (Eds.). (2008). Where youth development meets mental health and education: The RALLY approach. *New Directions for Youth Development, 120,* 1–194.
Malti, T., & Ongley, S. F. (2014). The development of moral emotions and moral reasoning. In M. Killen & J. Smetana (Eds.), *Handbook of moral development* (2nd ed., pp. 163–183). New York, NY: Psychology Press. doi:http://dx.doi.org/10.4324/9780203581957.ch8
Malti, T., Sette, S., & Dys, S. P. (in press). Social-emotional responding: A perspective from developmental psychology. In R. Scott, S. Kosslyn, & M. Buchmann (Eds.), *Emerging trends in the social and behavioral sciences.* Hoboken, NJ: John Wiley and Sons.
Malti, T., Zuffianò, A., Cui, L., Colasante, T., Peplak, J., & Bae, N. Y. (in press). Children's healthy social-emotional development in contexts of peer exclusion. In C. Spiel, N .J. Cabrera, & B. Leyendecker (Eds.), *Handbook of positive development of minority children.* Netherlands: Springer.
Malti, T., Zuffianò, A., & Noam, G. G. (2016). *Toward developmental assessment in psychological intervention: Understanding every child's social-emotional development.* Unpublished manuscript.
Masten, A. S. (2014). *Ordinary magic: Resilience in development.* New York, NY: Guilford.
Masten, A. S., Roisman, G. I., Long, J. D., Burt, K. B., Obradović, J., Riley, J. R., Boelcke-Stennes, K., & Tellegen, A. (2005). Developmental cascades: Linking academic achievement and externalizing and internalizing symptoms over 20 years. *Developmental Psychology, 41,* 733–746. doi:http://dx.doi.org/10.1037/0012-1649.41.5.733
Noam, G. G., & Hermann, C. A. (2002). Where education and mental health meet: Developmental prevention and early intervention in schools. *Development and Psychopathology, 14,* 861–875. doi:http://dx.doi.org/10.1017/S0954579402004108
Noam, G. G., & Malti, T. (2010). Ego development. In I. B. Weiner & E. Craighead (Eds.), *The Corsini encyclopedia of psychology* (Vol. 2, pp. 549–552). New York: Wiley. doi:http://dx.doi.org/10.1002/9780470479216.corpsy0296
Noam, G. G., Malti, T., & Guhn, M. (2012). From clinical-developmental theory to assessment: The holistic student assessment tool. *International Journal of Conflict and Violence, 6,* 201–213.

Noam, G. G., Malti, T., & Karcher, M. J. (2013). Mentoring relationships in developmental perspective. In D. DuBois & M. J. Karcher (Eds.), *Handbook of youth mentoring* (pp. 99–116). Thousand Oaks, CA: Sage.

Oberle, E., Schonert-Reichl, K. A., Hertzman, C., & Zumbo, B. (2014). Social-emotional competencies make the grade: Predicting academic success in early adolescence. *Journal of Applied Developmental Psychology, 35*, 138–147. doi:http://dx.doi.org/10.1016/j.appdev.2014.02.004

Ollendick, T. H., Grills, A. E., & King, N. J. (2001). Applying developmental theory to the assessment and treatment of childhood disorders: Does it make a difference? *Clinical Psychology and Psychotherapy, 8*, 304–314. doi:http://dx.doi.org/10.1002/cpp.311

Rubin, K. H., Bukowski, W., & Laursen, B. (Eds.). (2011). *Handbook of peer interactions, relationships, and groups.* New York, NY: Guilford Press.

Saarni, C. (1999). *The development of emotional competence.* New York, NY: Guilford Press.

Schonert-Reichl, K. A., & Hymel, S. (2007). Educating the heart as well as the mind: Why social and emotional learning is critical for students' school and life success. *Education Canada, 47*, 20–25.

Spiel, C., Reimann, R., Wagner, P., & Schober, B. (2008). Guest editorial: Bildung-Psychology: The substance and structure of an emerging discipline. *Applied Developmental Science, 12*, 154–159. doi:http://dx.doi.org/10.1080/10888690802199426

Spiel, C., Reimann, R., Wagner, P., & Schober, B. (2010). Bildungspsychologie – eine Einführung. In C. Spiel, B. Schober, P. Wagner, & R. Reimann (Eds.), *Bildungspsychologie* (pp. 11–20). Göttingen: Hogrefe.

van Noorden, T. H. J., Haselager, G. J. T., Cillessen, A. H. N., & Bukowski, W. M. (2015). Empathy and involvement in bullying in children and adolescents: A systematic review. *Journal of Youth and Adolescence, 44*, 637–657.

Weisz, J. R., & Weersing, V. R. (1999). Developmental outcome research. In W. K. Silverman & T. H. Ollendick (Eds.), *Developmental issues in the clinical treatment of children* (pp. 457–469). Needham Heights, MA: Allyn & Bacon.

Bildung-Psychology and implementation science

Dean L. Fixsen, Marie-Therese Schultes and Karen A. Blase

ABSTRACT
Bildung-Psychology encourages a long-term view of lifelong learning for individuals, educational organizations (e.g., schools), and systems (e.g., national education agencies). Learning on these levels does not happen independently from the other levels, as an individual's education is interrelated to characteristics of educational institutions and systems. Likewise, implementing educational innovations requires activities on all levels of the educational system. In this article we present a cascading logic model where an independent variable at one level is a dependent variable at the next level from the classroom to the federal government. In line with lifelong learning, implementation is a growing science built on research and evaluation of practices that unfold over years and decades. This article will summarize some of the major findings from implementation science as they have unfolded over the past 50 years. It points out similarities between the Bildung-Psychology framework and implementation science in order to build a theoretical base for a future research discourse.

Introduction

Based on Spiel, Reimann, Wagner, and Schober (2008), Bildung-Psychology is a new discipline of Psychology, which is in general concerned with the products and processes of learning and education as well as conditions and measures that can influence these products and processes. Accordingly, it attends to the factors influencing an individual's education with a focus on lifelong learning. The Bildung-Psychology framework proposed by Spiel and colleagues (2008) posits that lifelong learning is a product of (a) activities on an individual level, (b) organizations providing tools and environments that encourage those activities, and (c) political commitment and reforms to initiate, maintain, support, and optimize those environments and activities.

The framework further posits an integrated view. In this view, the subject matter of any one dimension (e.g., organization) is not isolated from that of the other two (individual, system) and the boundaries are weak, meaning that the components easily interact with one another. Spiel et al. (2008) also note that 'dissemination of available knowledge to practitioners' and 'a systematic procedure moving from fundamental principles to soundly evaluated programs and activities' are areas that have 'not yet been professionally addressed' (pp. 154, 156).

The purpose of this article is to focus on implementation science, which is the discipline that professionally researches the key factors of transferring knowledge, generated in laboratories, to the development and implementation of programs and activities that lead to intended effects in society. Implementation science is important to Bildung-Psychology. We will point out similarities between implementation frameworks and the Bildung-Psychology framework. A framework 'identifies a set of variables and the relations among them that are presumed to account for a set of phenomena' (Carpiano & Daley, 2006, p. 565). Frameworks are used to guide research in order to build a theoretical base for future research.

The integrated view offered by the Bildung-Psychology framework (Spiel et al., 2008) regarding lifelong learning as influenced by factors on the micro (individual)-, meso (institutional)-, and macro (system) level corresponds well to the findings from the developing field of implementation science. Developing implementation capacity – i.e., supporting the formation of resources and knowledge that are essential for successful implementation processes – in education and other human service settings involves lifelong learning and is the product of activities, organizations, and systems working in an integrated manner (Fixsen, Blase, Metz, & Van Dyke, 2013; Klingner, Boardman, & McMaster, 2013). In this sense, implementation science and Bildung-Psychology are based on similar assumptions. We will illustrate this by presenting a cascading logic model that guides implementation activities on the micro-, meso- and macrolevel. In order to provide the opportunity for individuals to benefit from educational innovations, all of the levels have to be considered when implementing educational innovations in practice.

The present theoretical paper addresses three goals: (1) to summarize some of the major findings from implementation science, (2) to point out similarities between Bildung-Psychology and implementation science, and (3) to build a theoretical base for a future research discourse. To achieve these goals, we provide a historical overview of the emergence of implementation science based on experiences with the implementation of a concrete intervention (the Teaching-Family Model), which developed over time into a systematic implementation approach covering different system levels (Teaching-Family Sites). The second section explores the importance of implementation science for the guidance of putting new and effective interventions into practice (e.g., through the use of the cascading logic model). In the third section Bildung-Psychology as a lifelong learning process and implementation science are associated through the use of PDSA (Plan-Do-Study-Act) cycles and supported by implementation teams.

Emergence of implementation science

Bildung-Psychology emphasizes active engagement in learning over a long period of time. Likewise, within implementation practice and science learning occurred through improvement cycles based on purposeful implementation experiences while transferring research-based innovations to real-world settings over the past 50 years. These decades of learning were necessary in order to gain the experiences that are the basis for current frameworks of systematic implementation. Such frameworks contain variables that should be considered when implementing interventions in organizations and how they can be addressed systematically. In this chapter we will illustrate a learning process leading to systematic implementation on the example of how we continuously improved implementing the 'Teaching-Family Model' in the U.S.

While the history of implementation science dates to an earlier time (Saetren, 2005), the Great Society programs that began in the 1960s in the U.S. mark the beginning of implementation science as a self-conscious set of activities and outcomes. The book on *Implementation* by Pressman and Wildavsky (1973) anticipates the later developments with its complete title *Implementation: How Great Expectations in Washington are Dashed in Oakland: or, Why It's Amazing that Federal Programs Work at All, This Being a Saga of the Economic Development Administration as Told by Two Sympathetic Observers Who Seek to Build Morals on a Foundation of Ruined Hopes*.

The omission of implementation science in social change efforts and the persistent lack of intended social benefit has been noted consistently over the decades (Kutner et al., 2007; Lipsey, 2009; Rossi & Wright, 1984). In 1967, as part of the Great Society programs, we (DF and KB) and our colleagues began the development of an evidence-based program called the Teaching-Family Model (Phillips, 1968; Phillips, Phillips, Fixsen, & Wolf, 1972). Research over the next three decades provided many opportunities to learn about evidence-based program development and about implementation methods.

The goals of the Teaching-Family Model were clear in 1967: establish a treatment program that is humane, effective, individualized, satisfactory to participants, cost efficient, and replicable. The Teaching-Family Model was developed as a family-style, group home (residential) treatment program for teenagers referred from the delinquency system. Married couples (called Teaching-Parents) lived in the group home and provided treatment services to five or six teenagers who lived with them. Key treatment components used by the Teaching

Parents are teaching appropriate alternative behavior as well as initializing motivation systems, self-government systems, and counseling (Phillips et al., 1972). Individualized treatment goals for youths include a variety of self-care skills, social skills, living with family, dealing with authority, and academic content and behavior at school (Bailey, Wolf, & Phillips, 1970; Eitzen, 1974; Fixsen, Phillips, & Wolf, 1973; Phillips, 1968; Phillips, Phillips, Fixsen, & Wolf, 1971; Werner et al., 1975). After four years of research and development the first few goals were being met at Achievement Place, the prototype group home treatment program. In 1971 the first attempt to replicate the successful Teaching-Family Model prototype failed after only nine months.

A great deal was learned before the replication group home failed. Fortunately, 'portable' video recording devices became available at that time and were used to videotape the Teaching-Parents in the replication group home and in the prototype group home. Analyses of the Teaching-Parent interactions on the tapes and direct observations in the replication group home led to hypotheses regarding the differences in interactions and outcomes with the youths. As we decided on a solution, we immediately provided *in vivo* modeling and training to try to improve the interactions among the Teaching-Parents and the teenagers in the replication group home. Looking back, we recognize our engagement in PDSA improvement cycles as we applied new learning as rapidly as we could (Fixsen, Blase, Duda, Naoom, & Van Dyke, 2010; Taylor et al., 2014). Progress was being made, but not soon enough to avoid having the group home close because of continuing problems.

The learning that occurred led to a redefinition of the Teaching-Family Model and improved methods for training staff (Wolf, Kirigin, Fixsen, Blase, & Braukmann, 1995). In addition, the process of comparing and contrasting the successful prototype program and the failed replication attempt led to the development of a way to assess fidelity of the use of the comprehensive and complex treatment program (Bedlington, Braukmann, Ramp, & Wolf, 1988; Braukmann et al., 1975). Thus, the process of attempting to replicate the successful prototype produced a deeper and more complete understanding of the intervention, improved methods for preparing staff, and a way to assess the presence and strength (fidelity) of the intervention in practice. For more information on major challenges and 'lessons learned' during the first replication of the Teaching-Family Model see Fixsen and Blase (1993) and Wolf et al. (1995).

Armed with better implementation methods the first successful replication occurred in 1972 when the Teaching-Parents met fidelity criteria. By 1977 there were over 100 Teaching-Family group homes in various states in the US. In 1973 a critical development occurred when three Teaching-Family staff members (and recent PhD graduates) left the University of Kansas (KU) and went to Western North Carolina to open eight Teaching-Family group homes (Maloney, Timbers, & Blase, 1977). The eight Teaching-Family group homes and staffing in Western North Carolina was soon recognized as the first example of a Teaching-Family

BILDUNG-PSYCHOLOGY

Site. A Teaching-Family Site is an organization that supports the functioning of four or more Teaching-Family group homes. The Site staff are accountable for developing the group homes (e.g., neighborhood entry, Board development, licensing), selecting staff, training staff, coaching staff, conducting fidelity assessments, working with local Boards of Directors to assure hospitable working conditions and administrative supports, and helping state bureaucracies fund the group homes at an acceptable level (Blase, Fixsen, & Phillips, 1984).

The success of the Teaching-Family Site in Western North Carolina was noticeable. Success was defined as sustainability of the group homes and the percent of Teaching-Parents meeting fidelity standards. The Teaching-Family homes in Western North Carolina were near the Site offices and were stable. In contrast, the group homes associated with KU were spread across the country and seemed to come and go as Teaching-Parents left, or Board leadership changed, or local regulations or funding changed. Discussions about these differences led to a proximity analysis that showed improved sustainability for those group homes within about three hours driving distance from the Site office in Kansas (60% within three hours vs. 15% more than three hours sustained for 5 + years). The difference linked to proximity for the KU related homes was sufficient evidence for us to change our approach to implementation. The focus shifted from training practitioners for individual group homes to training implementation teams to run organizations of group homes (i.e., Teaching-Family Sites). The Site Development approach improved 5 + year sustainability from 15% to about 80% (Blase et al., 1984) and confirmed the wisdom of changing strategies. The intervention (the Teaching-Family Model) was the same (fidelity standards being met) but sustainability was improved when the focus changed to Site Development (Fixsen & Blase, 1993).

Given the clear differences, scaling up the treatment model now required learning how to prepare implementation team members (Teaching-Family Site staff) who did not have the advantage of four or five years of graduate training at KU. Using the successful Teaching-Family Site in North Carolina as a model, three-person implementation teams were developed to staff new Sites. Staff selected for training as Site Directors, Directors of Training, and Directors of Evaluation were those who had worked in Teaching-Family group homes and had been Certified Teaching-Parents. This selection criterion meant that each person had high levels of content knowledge – they knew the Teaching-Family Model and all its nuances by virtue of having been a Certified Teaching-Parent for a year or more. They 'only' had to learn implementation skills related to how to conduct selection interviews, put on skill-based training workshops, develop the competencies to do coaching for competence, manage complex organizations, and so on. By 1977 there were over 100 Teaching-Family group homes and a steady supply of Certified staff who were interested in careers as Site staff.

In 1975 the Teaching-Family Association (TFA) was formed and in 1979 the first Site Certification evaluations were conducted. Whole organizations were Certified (or not) based on the rigorous criteria developed by TFA (the Association and the Certification of Teaching-Parents and Teaching-Family Sites continue to this day). From 1973 to 1995 attempts had been made to develop 60 TF Sites and 32 of those had met TFA Site Certification standards. The time from initiation of site development to meeting Site Certification standards was 4.3 years for all 32 Sites, with a mean of 5.9 years for the first 16 Sites and 2.8 years for the last 16 Sites. Effectiveness and efficiency improved with experience during those decades.

As an example of lifelong learning as proposed by the Bildung-Psychology framework, it took 28 years from starting research in one group home to having the strategies and methods in place to successfully expand the use of an evidence-based program. The treatment was effective (Kingsley, 2006; Kirigin, Braukmann, Atwater, & Wolf, 1982; Lipsey & Wilson, 1998; Roberts, 1996), but the approach to implementation and repeatable success took years to evolve (Blase et al., 1984; Fixsen & Blase, 1993; Fixsen, Blase, Timbers, & Wolf, 2001; Wolf et al., 1995). Throughout the 28 years data guided each step. In PDSA cycle fashion, as the work was being done the results were analyzed, strategies were changed, and the process was repeated. On the whole, the example of the Teaching-Family model shows that for successful implementation a systematic collaboration of different system levels is needed. The knowledge of how to systematically link individuals, organizations and systems took a long time to evolve. Current implementation efforts can benefit from these experiences that are now integrated into systematic frameworks of implementation.

Bildung-Psychology and implementations science

In this section we specify how implementation science can guide the successful use of educational innovations, i.e., interventions and programs that are new to an educational system, in practice. For this purpose, we present a cascading logic model that describes implementation activities targeting individuals, organizations, and systems (Fixsen et al., 2013; Klingner et al., 2013).

The lessons learned from the development and broad scale use of the Teaching-Family Model and other evidence-based programs have provided the means to understand implementation practice and science more fully. In the past decade many of those lessons – such as considering different system levels when implementing an evidence-based program – have been applied in education in the U.S. There are three considerations when moving from the laboratory to programs that are useful in society. These are summarized in the following formula:

Effective innovations × Effective implementation × Enabling contexts = Socially significant outcomes

Since the advent of the evidence-based movement in human services (Roberts, 1996; Sackett, Rosenberg, Gray, Haynes, & Richardson, 1996), the focus has been on the quality of the evidence in support of innovations. In this view, the quality of the evidence would compel potential practitioners to use the evidence-based innovation and would convince leaders and policy makers to support their uses in practice. While this quaint idea continues to be pursued (Haskins & Baron, 2011), the 'quality chasm' (Institute of Medicine, 2001) between evidence and practice grows wider. As shown in the Teaching-Family example, an effective innovation is important but not enough. No amount of evidence will produce self-actualizing innovations in the complex world of education (or other human services). On the contrary, attempts to use innovations (evidence-based or otherwise) routinely are crushed by the status quo (Braithwaite, Marks, & Taylor, 2014; Nord & Tucker, 1987).

Concerted, implementation informed efforts must be made on different system levels to counter the influence of the status quo. A cascading logic model has been developed within implementation science (Gane & Sarson, 1979; Metz & Bartley, 2012) to guide implementation capacity building in large and complex education systems. The cascade includes activities on the micro-, meso-, and macrolevel.

Table 1 outlines the cascading logic model. A distinguishing feature is that the input (independent variable) at one level is the output (dependent variable) at the next level. Beginning with the intended outcomes at the individual level (the top row), the next levels of organization and system inputs and outcomes are identified. Taking the example of a violence prevention program for schools, the intended outcome at the individual level could be for students to benefit from the program, e.g., by applying nonviolent strategies of conflict resolution. In order to achieve this goal, practitioners (e.g., school psychologists) have to skillfully teach students in applying such strategies. This requires an effective cooperation between practitioners and regular teachers, who first have to be convinced of the importance of the program by the school principal. For an incorporation of the program to the school's daily routine, principals need administrative support, which can be facilitated by district representatives. In order to know which kind of support is needed, implementation teams across regions need an infrastructure for communication, which can be provided by the ministry of education. As illustrated by this example, the model serves to answer two questions: (1) how does each level contribute to the intended outcomes for recipients and (2) who does the work at each level? For a more detailed applied example illustrating possible input and output variables in a cascading logic model see Metz and Bartley (2012).

The cascading logic model is based on implementation science as expressed in the active implementation frameworks (Blase, Van Dyke, Fixsen, & Wallace Bailey, 2012). These frameworks are guidelines for implementing evidence-based programs that can be applied in a variety of contexts. The active implementation frameworks are a product of a systematic examination of the best available scientific evidence regarding activities and processes that are relevant for

BILDUNG-PSYCHOLOGY

Table 1. Cascading logic model.

Population	Innovations (WHAT)	Innovation Outcomes
Recipients (e.g., students)	Skillful use of innovation methods when interacting with recipients (e.g., school psychologists skillfully teach students in evidence-based strategies of nonviolent conflict resolution)	Recipients benefit as intended (e.g., students apply nonviolent strategies of conflict resolution)
Population	**Implementation Strategies (HOW)**	**Implementation Outcomes**
Practitioners and Agencies (e.g., school psychologists)	Skillful use of evidence-based implementation methods by Local Implementation Team (LIT) (e.g., teachers effectively cooperate with school psychologists on the innovation, school psychologists are trained and continuously coached in teaching methods for strategies of nonviolent conflict resolution)	Skillful use of innovation methods when interacting with recipients
Schools & Districts	Skillful use of evidence-based implementation methods and Enabling change methods by District Implementation Team (DIT) (e.g., school principals incorporate the innovation into the schools' daily agenda and use effective leadership strategies in introducing the innovation to the teaching staff)	Skillful use of evidence-based implementation methods by Local Implementation Teams (LIT)
Districts and Regions	Skillful use of evidence-based implementation methods to develop DITs and supporting systems by Regional Implementation Team (RIT) (e.g., implementation teams across regions discuss innovation outcomes on a regular basis and communicate implementation challenges to district representatives, who facilitate its administration by providing the necessary resources)	Skillful use of evidence-based implementation methods and Enabling change methods by District Implementation Teams (DIT)
Regions and National Center	Work with the Minister and Executive Leadership to develop a state implementation infrastructure, manage change processes, and assess outcomes at all levels (e.g., the ministry provides a communication infrastructure for implementation teams and sets up a database for innovation outcomes)	Skillful use of evidence-based implementation methods to develop DITs and supporting systems by Regional Implementation Teams (RIT)

Notes. A cascading logic model for scaling innovations where the input (independent variable) at one level is the product (dependent variable) of the next level. Redundant implementation team roles, functions, and structures that avoid duplicating effort make scaling possible. In parentheses examples for each step are provided by applying the model to a violence prevention program for schools.

systematic implementation (Brownson, Colditz, & Proctor, 2012; Fixsen, Naoom, Blase, Friedman, & Wallace, 2005; Meyers, Durlak, & Wandersman, 2012; Tabak, Khoong, Chambers, & Brownson, 2012) and the experiences of those doing successful implementation work (Blase & Fixsen, 2003; Blase, Fixsen, Naoom, & Wallace, 2005; Bond et al., 2001; Schoenwald, Sheidow, & Letourneau, 2004). The active implementation frameworks are used to inform improved practices when practitioners are attempting to use evidence-based innovations (Bertram, Suter, Bruns, & O'Rourke, 2012; Horner et al., 2014; Metz et al., 2014; Ogden et al., 2012; Romney, Israel, & Zlatevski, 2014).

The active implementation frameworks make capacity development possible. Groups of people who are actively involved with implementation efforts – so-called implementation teams – at each level of the cascade need to possess

BILDUNG-PSYCHOLOGY

the same skill sets even though the skills are used for slightly different purposes. For more information on the formation and effectiveness of implementation teams see e.g., Fixsen et al. (2001) and Higgins, Weiner, and Young (2012). Scaled redundancy (Kluger, 2008) requires the development of repeatable structures, where skills are redundant but tasks are not (Morgan & Ramirez, 1983). For example, an implementation team includes members who are equally proficient as trainers, coaches, and organization change agents. While they have redundant skills, the team members divide the tasks so each of them is responsible for one area (e.g., training) when providing implementation supports for an evidence-based practice or other effective innovation. The idea of scaled redundancy is embedded in the Bildung-Psychology framework that has multiple links between activities, functional areas, and career as part of a long-term view of doing and learning (Spiel et al., 2008).

If completely different structures, roles, and functions were required for each level of the cascade, the Bildung-Psychology framework would require 105 unique sets (7 career levels × 3 activity levels × 5 functional areas). This would be highly improbable in practice. As professionals coordinating different educational activities for different age groups on different systems levels should share redundant knowledge about how to implement innovations effectively, the same is true for implementation teams. Implementation teams sharing redundant knowledge as outlined in the cascading logic model provide a basis for hope for making use of evidence-based programs and practices on a sufficient scale to promote lifelong learning for whole populations.

A theoretical base for the future

Implementation science is based on continuous learning and exchange of information. Bildung-Psychology also emphasizes lifelong learning. The purpose of this section is to underscore the importance of a lifelong learning process within implementation science as to further explore the theoretical base it shares with Bildung-Psychology. Concretely, we describe how lifelong learning is supported by implementation teams expanding their knowledge across system levels and how it is facilitated by the use of PDSA cycles as an opportunity to systematically learn and improve with experiences.

Kenneth Arrow (1996) won the Nobel Prize in 1972 for developing information economics. The premise is that in an information-based economy, knowledge expands with use. This is in contrast to an atom-based economy where resources (oil, minerals) are depleted with use. In effect, Arrow predicted the startling growth of the information age powered by connectivity among digital devices. Computers, smart phones, tablets and other digital devices have common hardware and software features that facilitate connectivity and, as such, represent the redundant components of an information-based economy.

This same growth is possible in education and human services with implementation teams as the redundant component. As implementation teams do the work they learn how to do the work more effectively and efficiently (e.g., with experience, Teaching-Family Sites were developed successfully in half the time). This information can be shared with other implementation teams within a system and across systems. This leads to exponential growth in learning as the knowledge base expands.

In the Bildung-Psychology framework, lifelong learning applies to individuals, organizations, and systems (the activity levels) across the lifespan. The active implementation frameworks include improvement cycles. They are based on the PDSA cycle. The PDSA cycle was invented at Bell Labs to reduce manufacturing defects for components of communication systems (Shewhart, 1931) and has been applied in many domains since then (Akin et al., 2013; Speroff & O'Connor, 2004; Taylor et al., 2014; Varkey, Reller, & Resar, 2007).

The basic idea is to get started and use the information from experience to get better. In the PDSA mode, every interaction every day presents opportunities for learning. Getting started down the path of lifelong learning often requires some form of facilitation. For example, parents facilitate the early social-emotional learning and language development of preschool children; educators and family members facilitate learning academic subjects; and employers and peers facilitate adult learning. Learning is a process and it begins with a shaky and incomplete performance before it matures into skillful accomplishments and contributions back to the knowledge base. The experience of learning produces opportunities to learn more.

In an implementation context, implementation team members facilitate teaching and learning processes. At the individual practitioner level, an implementation team facilitates learning by offering training, coaching, and regular fidelity assessments to practitioners who agree to participate in the learning process. As indicated in the cascading logic model, an implementation team holds itself accountable for the outcomes it produces. Thus, teachers are not asked to do anything they are not prepared to do. If the preparation is inadequate (i.e., the teachers are not able to meet fidelity criteria and produce intended student outcomes), it is up to the implementation team to engage in PDSA cycle problem solving to develop improved content and instruction methods. In this way, an implementation team has the opportunity to improve the supports for teachers every month. The PDSA logic applies at the organization and system levels as well. In these cases, an implementation team notes any impediments to lifelong learning and brings those impediments to the attention of leaders and managers. In this way, leaders have the opportunity to change organizations and systems to improve supports for teachers and student learning (Fixsen et al., 2013).

Conclusions

Both Bildung-Psychology and implementation science strive for an effective use of educational innovations in practice. The goals of the present paper were (1) to summarize important findings from implementation science, (2) to point out similarities between Bildung-Psychology and implementation science, and (3) to build a theoretical base for a future research discourse. Based on experiences with the implementation of the Teaching-Family Model, we described how knowledge for systematic implementation developed over time. With the emergence of frameworks of systematic implementation, it became clear that considering different system levels is a necessity for the effective implementation of educational innovations and that the integration of system levels can be substantially supported by implementation teams. The significance of interacting system levels is also promoted by the Bildung-Psychology framework. Based on this important similarity, we presented a cascading logic model that guides putting new and effective interventions into practice by considering implementation variables on multiple system levels. Finally, we connected Bildung-Psychology and implementation science through a lifelong-learning point of view, which is also inherent to both disciplines. This approach was specified on the examples of PDSA cycles and of implementation teams supporting the expansion of knowledge.

In order to achieve an effective use of evidence-based practice in education, continuous learning and exchange of knowledge among individuals, organizations and systems is necessary. Implementation science and the cascading logic model can serve as a systematic guide for the development of implementation capacity to achieve an effective use of the activities described in the Bildung-Psychology framework in practice. Implementation capacity is developed by virtue of implementation teams at national/state, regional, district, and local levels. Implementation teams are the redundant structures essential for successful use of innovations on a scale useful in society. Implementation team members have considerable knowledge about innovations and how to support their use in practice. Integrating activities on the micro-, meso-, and macrolevel as they work with leaders and others to change organizations and systems can more fully support and sustain evidence-based innovations.

Disclosure statement

No potential conflict of interest was reported by the authors.

Funding

This work was supported by US Department of Education [grant number H326K120004-14], Project Officer, Jennifer Coffey. However, the contents do not necessarily represent the policy of the US Department of Education, and endorsement by the Federal Government should not be assumed.

References

Akin, B. A., Bryson, S. A., Testa, M. F., Blase, K. A., McDonald, T., & Melz, H. (2013). Usability testing, initial implementation, and formative evaluation of an evidence-based intervention: Lessons from a demonstration project to reduce long-term foster care. *Evaluation and Program Planning, 41*, 19–30.

Arrow, K. (1996). The economics of information: An exposition. *Empirica, 23*, 119–128. doi: http://dx.doi.org/10.1007/BF00925335

Bailey, J. S., Wolf, M. M., & Phillips, E. L. (1970). Home-based reinforcement and the modification of pre-delinquents' classroom behavior1. *Journal of Applied Behavior Analysis, 3*, 223–233.

Bedlington, M. M., Braukmann, C. J., Ramp, K. A., & Wolf, M. M. (1988). A comparison of treatment environments in community-based group homes for adolescent offenders. *Criminal Justice and Behavior, 15*, 349–363.

Bertram, R. M., Suter, J. C., Bruns, E. J., & O'Rourke, K. E. (2012). Implementation research and wraparound literature: Building a research agenda. *Journal of Child and Family Studies, 20*, 713–715. doi:http://dx.doi.org/10.1007/s10826-010-9430-3

Blase, K. A., & Fixsen, D. L. (2003). *Evidence-based programs and cultural competence*. National Implementation Research Network. Retrieved from http://nirn.fpg.unc.edu/resources/evidence-based-programs-and-cultural-competence-reaching-consensus

Blase, K. A., Fixsen, D. L., Naoom, S. F., & Wallace, F. (2005). *Operationalizing implementation: Strategies and methods*. Tampa, FL: University of South Florida, Louis de la Parte Florida Mental Health Institute.

Blase, K. A., Fixsen, D. L., & Phillips, E. L. (1984). Residential treatment for troubled children: Developing service delivery systems. In S. C. Paine, G. T. Bellamy, & B. Wilcox (Eds.), *Human services that work: From innovation to standard practice* (pp. 149–165). Baltimore, MD: Paul H. Brookes Publishing.

Blase, K. A., Van Dyke, M., Fixsen, D., & Wallace Bailey, F. (2012). Implementation science: Key concepts, themes, and evidence for practitioners in educational psychology. In B. Kelly & D. Perkins (Eds.), *Handbook of implementation science for psychology in education* (pp. 13–34). London: Cambridge University Press.

Bond, G. R., Becker, D. R., Drake, R. E., Rapp, C. A., Meisler, N., Lehman, A. F., ... Bell, M. D. (2001). Implementing supported employment as an evidence-based practice. *Psychiatric Services, 52*, 313–322.

Braithwaite, J., Marks, D., & Taylor, N. (2014). Harnessing implementation science to improve care quality and patient safety: A systematic review of targeted literature. *International Journal for Quality in Health Care, 3*, 321–329. doi:http://dx.doi.org/10.1093/intqhc/mzu047

Braukmann, C. J., Fixsen, D. L., Kirigin, K. A., Phillips, E. A., Phillips, E. L., & Wolf, M. M. (1975). Achievement Place: The training and certification of teaching-parents.In W. S. Wood (Ed.), *Issues in evaluating behavior modification* (pp. 131–152). Champaign, IL: Research Press.

Brownson, R. C., Colditz, G. A., & Proctor, E. K. (Eds.). (2012). *Dissemination and implementation research in health*. New York, NY: Oxford University Press.

Carpiano, R. M., & Daley, D. M. (2006). A guide and glossary on postpositivist theory building for population health. *Journal of Epidemiology and Community Health, 60*, 564–570.

Eitzen, D. S. (1974). Impact of behavior modification techniques on locus of control of delinquent boys. *Psychological Reports, 35*, 1317–1318.

Fixsen, D. L., & Blase, K. A. (1993). Creating new realities: Program development and dissemination. *Journal of Applied Behavior Analysis, 26*, 597–615.

Fixsen, D. L., Blase, K. A., Duda, M., Naoom, S., & Van Dyke, M. (2010). Implementation of evidence-based treatments for children and adolescents: Research findings and their implications for the future. In J. Weisz & A. Kazdin (Eds.), *Implementation and dissemination: Extending treatments to new populations and new settings* (2nd ed., pp. 435–450). New York, NY: Guilford Press.

Fixsen, D. L., Blase, K. A., Metz, A., & Van Dyke, M. (2013). Statewide implementation of evidence-based programs. *Exceptional Children, 79*, 213–230.

Fixsen, D. L., Blase, K. A., Timbers, G. D., & Wolf, M. M. (2001). In search of program implementation: 792 replications of the Teaching-Family Model. In G. A. Bernfeld, D. P. Farrington, & A. W. Leschied (Eds.), *Offender rehabilitation in practice: Implementing and evaluating effective programs* (pp. 149–166). London: Wiley.

Fixsen, D. L., Naoom, S. F., Blase, K. A., Friedman, R. M., & Wallace, F. (2005). *Implementation research: A synthesis of the literature.* Tampa, FL: University of South Florida, National Implementation Research Network.

Fixsen, D. L., Phillips, E. L., & Wolf, M. M. (1973). Achievement place: Experiments in self-government with pre-delinquents1. *Journal of Applied Behavior Analysis, 6*, 31–47.

Gane, C., & Sarson, T. (1979). *Structured systems analysis: Tools and techniques.* New York, NY: Prentice Hall.

Haskins, R., & Baron, J. (2011). *Building the connection between policy and evidence: The Obama evidence-based initiatives.* London. Retrieved from www.nesta.org.uk

Higgins, M., Weiner, J., & Young, L. (2012). Implementation teams: A new lever for organizational change. *Journal of Organizational Behavior, 33*, 366–388. doi: http://dx.doi.org/10.1002/job.1773

Horner, R. H., Kincaid, D., Sugai, G., Lewis, T., Eber, L., Barrett, S., ... Johnson, N. (2014). Scaling up school-wide positive behavioral interventions and supports: Experiences of seven states with documented success. *Journal of Positive Behavior Interventions, 16*, 197–208. doi: http://dx.doi.org/10.1177/1098300713503685

Institute of Medicine. (2001). *Crossing the quality chasm: A new health system for the 21st century.* Washington, DC: National Academy Press.

Kingsley, D. E. (2006). The teaching-family model and post-treatment recidivism: A critical review of the conventional wisdom. *International Journal of Behavioral and Consultation Therapy, 2*, 481–497.

Kirigin, K. A., Braukmann, C. J., Atwater, J. D., & Wolf, M. M. (1982). An evaluation of Teaching-family (Achievement Place) group homes for juvenile offenders. *Journal of Applied Behavior Analysis, 15*(1), 1–16.

Klingner, J. K., Boardman, A. G., & McMaster, K. L. (2013). What does it take to scale up and sustain evidence-based practices? *Exceptional Children, 79*, 195–211.

Kluger, J. (2008). *Simplexity: Why simple things become complex (and how complex things can be made simple).* New York, NY: Hyperion.

Kutner, M., Greenberg, E., Jin, Y., Boyle, B., Hsu, Y., & Dunleavy, E. (2007). *Literacy in everyday life: Results from the 2003 National Assessment of Adult Literacy (NCES 2007–480).* Washington, DC: US Department of Education, National Center for Education Statistics.

Lipsey, M. W. (2009). The primary factors that characterize effective interventions with juvenile offenders: A meta-analytic overview. *Victims and Offenders, 4*, 124–147. doi: http://dx.doi.org/10.1080/15564880802612573

Lipsey, M. W., & Wilson, D. B. (1998). Effective intervention for serious juvenile offenders: Synthesis of research. In R. Loeber & D. P. Farrington (Eds.), *Serious and violent juvenile offenders: Risk factors and successful interventions* (pp. 313–345). Thousand Oaks, CA: Sage Publications, Inc.

Maloney, D. M., Timbers, G. D., & Blase, K. A. (1977). The bringing it all back home project: Regional adaptation of the teaching-family model group home for adolescents. *Child Welfare, 56*, 787–796.

Metz, A., & Bartley, L. (2012). Active implementation frameworks for program success. *Zero to Three, 32*, 11–18.

Metz, A., Bartley, L., Ball, H., Wilson, D., Naoom, S., & Redmond, P. (2014). Active implementation frameworks (AIF) for successful service delivery: Catawba county child wellbeing project. *Research on Social Work Practice, 25*, 415–422. doi:http://dx.doi.org/10.1177/1049731514543667

Meyers, D. C., Durlak, J. A., & Wandersman, A. (2012). The quality implementation framework: A synthesis of critical steps in the implementation process. *American Journal of Community Psychology, 50*, 462–480. doi:http://dx.doi.org/10.1007/s10464-012-9522-x

Morgan, G., & Ramirez, R. (1983). Action learning: A holographic metaphor for guiding social change. *Human Relations, 37*(1), 1–28.

Nord, W. R., & Tucker, S. (1987). *Implementing routine and radical innovations*. Lexington, MA: D. C. Heath and Company.

Ogden, T., Bjørnebekk, G., Kjøbli, J., Patras, J., Christiansen, T., Taraldsen, K., & Tollefsen, N. (2012). Measurement of implementation components ten years after a nationwide introduction of empirically supported programs – A pilot study. *Implementation Science, 7*, 49. doi: http://dx.doi.org/10.1186/1748-5908-7-49

Phillips, E. L. (1968). Achievement place: Token reinforcement procedures in a home-style rehabilitation setting for "pre-delinquent" boys1. *Journal of Applied Behavior Analysis, 1*, 213–223.

Phillips, E. L., Phillips, E. A., Fixsen, D. L., & Wolf, M. M. (1971). Achievement place: Modification of the behaviors of pre-delinquent boys within a token economy123. *Journal of Applied Behavior Analysis, 4*, 45–59.

Phillips, E. L., Phillips, E. A., Fixsen, D. L., & Wolf, M. M. (1972). *The teaching-family handbook* (1st ed.). Lawrence: University of Kansas Printing Service.

Pressman, J. L., & Wildavsky, A. (1973). *Implementation: How great expectations in washington are dashed in Oakland: Or, why it's amazing that federal programs work at all, this being a Saga of the economic development administration as told by two sympathetic observers who seek to build morals on a foundation of ruined hopes*. Berkeley: University of California Press.

Roberts, M. C. (Ed.). (1996). *Model programs in child and family mental health Mahwah*. NJ: Lawrence Erlbaum Associates.

Romney, S., Israel, N., & Zlatevski, D. (2014). Exploration-stage implementation variation. *Zeitschrift für Psychologie, 222*, 37–48. doi:http://dx.doi.org/10.1027/2151-2604/a000164

Rossi, P. H., & Wright, J. D. (1984). Evaluation research: An assessment. *Annual Review of Sociology, 10*, 331–352.

Sackett, D. L., Rosenberg, W. M. C., Gray, J. A. M., Haynes, R. B., & Richardson, W. S. (1996). Evidence based medicine: What it is and what it isn't. *British Medical Journal, 312*, 71–72.

Saetren, H. (2005). Facts and myths about research on public policy implementation: Out-of-fashion, allegedly dead, but still very much alive and relevant. *Policy Studies Journal, 33*, 559–582.

Schoenwald, S. K., Sheidow, A. J., & Letourneau, E. J. (2004). Toward effective quality assurance in evidence-based practice: Links between expert consultation, therapist fidelity, and child outcomes. *Journal of Clinical Child and Adolescent Psychology, 33*, 94–104.

Shewhart, W. A. (1931). *Economic control of quality of manufactured product*. New York, NY: D. Van Nostrand.

Speroff, T., & O'Connor, G. T. (2004). Study designs for PDSA quality improvement research. *Quality Management in Health Care, 13*, 17–32.

Spiel, C., Reimann, R., Wagner, P., & Schober, B. (2008). Guest editorial: Bildung-Psychology: The substance and structure of an emerging discipline. *Applied Developmental Science, 12*, 154–159.

Tabak, R. G., Khoong, E. C., Chambers, D. A., & Brownson, R. C. (2012). Bridging research and Practice. *American Journal of Preventive Medicine, 43*, 337–350.

Taylor, M. J., McNicholas, C., Nicolay, C., Darzi, A., Bel, D., & Reed, J. E. (2014). Systematic review of the application of the plan–do–study–act method to improve quality in healthcare. *British Medical Journal of Quality and Safety, 23*, 290–298.

Varkey, P., Reller, M. K., & Resar, R. K. (2007). Basics of quality improvement in health care. *Mayo Clinic Proceedings, 82*, 735–739.

Werner, J. S., Minkin, N., Minkin, B. L., Fixsen, D. L., Phillips, E. L., & Wolf, M. M. (1975). "Intervention package": An analysis to prepare juvenile delinquents for encounters with police officers. *Criminal Justice and Behavior, 2*, 55–84.

Wolf, M. M., Kirigin, K. A., Fixsen, D. L., Blase, K. A., & Braukmann, C. J. (1995). The teaching-family model. *Journal of Organizational Behavior Management, 15*, 11–68.

Gender role self-concept at school start and its impact on academic self-concept and performance in mathematics and reading

Ilka Wolter and Bettina Hannover

ABSTRACT

This research investigates children's self-ascriptions of feminine and masculine attributes (gender role self-concept) and whether they predict academic self-concepts and performance in gendered subject domains in their early Bildung-career. We suggest that as children incorporate gender stereotypes into their self-concept, perceptions of their competence (cognitive component of academic self-concepts), their affective-motivational reactions (affective component of academic self-concepts), as well as their performance in reading and mathematics are shaped accordingly. In a sample of 113 first graders we (1) measured gender role self-concept, and (2) analyzed its impact on children's academic self-concepts and performance in mathematics and reading half a year later. As expected, girls ascribed comparatively more feminine and boys comparatively more masculine-stereotyped behaviors to themselves. Furthermore, the more feminine children described themselves the better was their reading performance half a year later, while no indirect effects, mediated via the academic self-concept, appeared. Also, the more masculine children described themselves, the higher were their mathematics related ability self-concepts half a year later, however, mathematics achievements were unrelated to any of the other variables. We discuss that future research needs to more systematically study the variables investigated in this research in children as they move from school start into third grade when the gender role self-concept as well as differences between girls and boys in their academic self-concepts, their liking for different school subjects, and their skills are well established.

Our research, studying children in an early phase of their Bildung-career, is placed in the cell 'Research-Primary School-Microlevel' of the cube describing the structure of Bildung-Psychology (Spiel, Reimann, Wagner, & Schober, 2008, p. 155). The Bildung-Psychology approach describes and categorizes educational processes that are important for the development of educational components, as well as the prerequisites and interventions that influence those processes (cf., Spiel, Reimann, Wagner, & Schober, 2010). Against this background, the present study reflects on the incorporation of gender stereotypes as a relevant factor in explaining educational trajectories with respect to gender differences in subject domains. We aim to investigate the assumption that gender differences in academic self-concepts – comprising ability perceptions and affective-motivational reactions – as well as in performance outcomes in mathematics and reading, go back to children incorporating gender stereotypes into their selves. We posit that to the extent that girls and boys ascribe gendered attributes to themselves (gender role self-concept), their academic self-concepts and performances are consistent with gender stereotypes half a year later, at the end of first grade in primary school. More specifically, to the extent that children describe themselves with feminine attributes they should (a) perceive their reading related abilities as higher, (b) enjoy reading more, and (c) reach higher reading related performance scores. By the same token, to the extent that they ascribe masculine attributes to themselves they should (a) perceive their mathematics related skills as higher, (b) enjoy mathematics more, and (c) reach higher scores in a mathematics related test.

As early as primary school girls are on average more confident of their ability to read, are more interested in reading, and reach higher reading skills than boys (e.g., Bos, Bremerich-Vos, Tarelli, & Valtin, 2012; Niklas & Schneider, 2012). Boys on the other hand are more assured of their mathematics related skills, enjoy mathematics more than girls, and are overrepresented among the strong performers in mathematics (e.g., Mullis, Martin, Foy, & Arora, 2012; Niklas & Schneider, 2012). We assume that these gender differences reflect children's incorporation of gender stereotypes into their self-concepts, the starting point for gendered educational trajectories throughout children's school careers.

Development of gender stereotypes

As mentioned there are differences in ability perceptions, affective-motivational reactions, and performances of boys and girls which are consistent with gender stereotypes. *Gender stereotypes* are socially shared beliefs about which characteristics male and female persons have or should have (e.g., Eagly, Wood, & Diekman, 2000), i.e., *associations between gender and attributes* (e.g., 'mathematics is rather for boys'; Tobin et al., 2010). Among many other things, gender stereotypes suggest that varying subject domains are differentially related to males and females. Several studies found that even in primary school children associate high capabilities and motivation in mathematics with men and boys, but high capabilities and motivation in reading with girls and women. For instance, using an Implicit Association Test, Cvencek, Meltzoff, and Greenwald (2011) found in first grade children that boys more quickly associated mathematics with their own gender (than the other gender) and girls with the other gender (than their own gender). Similarly, Steffens, Jelenec, and Noack (2010) observed implicit math-gender stereotypes and implicit affinity to language in nine-year old girls. Dwyer (1974) reported that from second grade onwards children of either gender think of reading as a feminine activity. Similarly, Pottorff, Phelps-Zientarski, and Skovera (1996) found that from second grade onwards both boys and girls associated reading books with mothers rather than fathers, and considered girls as better able to read books than boys.

Incorporation of gender stereotypes into the self: the gender role self-concept

Around the time when children are two and a half years old, they typically learn to connect themselves with a gender category, i.e., a *gender identity* is established (*association between self and gender*; e.g., 'I am a girl', Tobin et al., 2010). It is much later (varying strongly between children), at about the age of three to seven, that children accomplish *gender constancy*, i.e., an understanding of the permanence of categorical gender ('I am a boy and will always be a boy') (see Halim & Ruble, 2010; for an overview on gender development). Developmental research also shows that as early as toddler years children start to acquire gender stereotypes (e.g., Halim & Ruble, 2010). Once children have reached a full understanding of gender constancy they are particularly responsive to gender-related information, and are inclined to ascribe attributes associated with their own gender to themselves. That is, they incorporate stereotypes about their own gender into their self (Martin & Halverson, 1981): a *gender role self-concept* evolves, with girls ascribing feminine-typed attributes, and boys ascribing masculine-typed attributes to themselves (*association between self and gendered attributes*, e.g., 'I (as a girl) do not like mathematics'; Tobin et al., 2010). *Ability related self-concepts*, i.e., assumptions about how strong one's capabilities are in different academic domains, start to develop at about the age of school entry (e.g., Ruble, 1994; Ruble, Eisenberg, & Higgins, 1994).

The gender role self-concept as an individual difference variable

The first goal of our research was to investigate the assumption that children at school start differ in their gender role self-concept, i.e., in the extent to which they have incorporated gender stereotypes into their selves. Since children in general already have considerable knowledge about gender stereotypes before they enter school, we predicted that they would differ in their gender role self-concepts, i.e., in the extent to which they associate themselves with these stereotypes (cf. Tobin et al., 2010): while some girls and boys in first grade of primary school should (almost) fully perceive all attributes associated with their own gender group as self-descriptive, others may endorse fewer same-gender attributes and also adopt some other-gender attributes.

The gender role self-concept is supposed to consist of two latent dimensions: masculinity and femininity respective instrumentality and expressivity (e.g., Athenstaedt, 2003). Typically, the gender role self-concept is measured by having research participants describe themselves with gender-typed attributes, i.e., personality traits or behaviors that are observed or assumed to vary with gender.

As stable gender differences in the self-ascription of gender-typed attributes typically appear from middle childhood onwards, i.e., when children are at least eight years old, gender role self-concept has almost exclusively been investigated in older children. In fact, the vast majority of studies have been conducted with adults, either using the Bem Sex Role Inventory (BSRI, Bem, 1974) or the Personal Attribute Questionnaire (PAQ, Spence, Helmreich, & Stapp, 1974). To measure the extent to which individuals have incorporated gendered attributes into their selves, these scales provide them with a variety of trait terms which – according to gender stereotypes – are more strongly associated with males (e.g., active) or with females (e.g., emotional). As gender stereotypes do not only comprise female and male gender-typed personality traits but also gendered behaviors, more recent measures additionally include behavior related items (e.g., do repair work, sew on a button; e.g., Gender Role Behavior Scale by Athenstaedt, 2003; Sex Role Behavior Scale by Orlofsky & O'Heron, 1987).

Research on the gender role self-concept in young children is scarce and outdated. The few studies investigating children at about the age of school entry neither found consistent self-ascriptions of gendered attributes nor consistent differences between boys and girls. For instance, Inoff, Halverson, and Pizzigati (1983) found no systematic gender differences in the strength with which kindergartners, and first and second graders endorsed masculine (e.g., assertiveness, boastfulness) and feminine personality traits (e.g., nurturance, gentleness) as self-descriptive. Cowan and Hoffman (1986) had three- and five-year-old children describe themselves on pairs of gender-typed traits (e.g., strong-weak, nice-mean), and two pairs of terms relating to gendered activities (doll-truck, baseball-sweeping). Results revealed that self-ascriptions of gendered terms (with boys and girls more likely ascribing the masculine or feminine term to themselves respectively) was greater than chance (Chi-square analyses), but only regarding the two behavioral items. Biernat (1991) asked kindergartners (mean age 5.4 years), third-, seventh-, and tenth-graders as well as college students to describe themselves using gendered physical features (e.g., muscular, pretty smile), personality traits (e.g., makes decisions easily, emotional), behaviors (plays baseball, babysits), and future occupations (truck driver, schoolteacher). Results showed that overall, female participants more likely described themselves with feminine than masculine gender-typed attributes and vice versa for male participants, unfortunately, however, neither subscale-specific nor age-specific findings are reported (see footnote on p. 361).

More clear-cut results emerge from studies investigating older samples, from mid-childhood onwards. Building on the BSRI, Boldizar (1991) developed a scale to measure gender role self-concept in middle childhood and adulthood. In a sample of third, fourth, sixth, and seventh graders she found girls to ascribe feminine traits and behaviors more strongly to themselves and boys to endorse masculine traits and behaviors as more self-descriptive than girls (with no age differences for the masculine items, and the gender difference on the feminine subscale being the largest among the youngest and oldest groups of children). Interestingly, trying to validate the newly developed scale, Boldizar (1991) found children's self-ascriptions of feminine and masculine traits to most strongly correlate with a questionnaire measuring proxies of gendered behaviors, i.e., toy and activity preferences (Perry, Perry, & Hynes, 1990, cited from Boldizar, 1991). In a sample of eight-11-year-olds (fourth to sixth grade), and using Boldizar`s (1991) scale, McGeown, Goodwin, Henderson, and Wright (2012) found girls to endorse more feminine trait terms as self-descriptive than boys and boys more masculine trait terms than girls. Investigating fourth- and eighth-graders, Egan and Perry (2001) found that as compared to their male class-mates, girls ascribed significantly more feminine trait terms (e.g., showing emotions, expressing concern when others need help), and significantly fewer masculine trait terms (e.g., being a leader among friends, getting others to do what they want them to do), more feminine behavior related items (e.g., babysitting or looking after younger kids, jump rope or gymnastics), and fewer masculine behavior related items (e.g., using tools to make things, playing video games) to themselves.

Against the background of these somewhat inconsistent findings, in our own study we measured children's gender role self-concept at school start using both, behavior related and trait like items. Due to general principles of cognitive development, children first acquire gender stereotypes relating to concrete concepts such as physical characteristics or behaviors. The concept of personality traits is learned much later, starting at about second grade in primary school, when the child gains an understanding of a latent and stable variable underlying repeated manifestations of behaviors (Ruble, 1994; Ruble et al., 1994). Hence, it makes sense to assume that in the gender role self-concept of young children gender stereotypes about concrete behaviors prevail, while gender stereotypes pertaining to personality traits become integrated as children grow older. We therefore expected that with respect to behavior-based items, and possibly also with respect to trait-based items, boys more likely endorse masculine gender-typed attributes than girls, while girls more likely endorse feminine gender-typed attributes than boys.

Even if children as young as at school start may not yet have developed an understanding of gender stereotypes about personality traits, they should already have acquired behavior related gender stereotypes and may have incorporated them into their selves. Possibly, this may even explain the inconsistencies in the above-reported findings of previous studies: results were clearer cut when behavior related attributes were included than if children had only been provided with trait terms to describe themselves.

The gender role self-concept at school start as a predictor of gendered ability perceptions, affective-motivational reactions, and performances in mathematics and reading

The second goal of our research was to show that individual differences in the gender role self-concept at school start are predictive of the extent to which children's academic self-concepts and skills in reading and mathematics, two gendered subject domains, develop in consistency with gender stereotypes. We hypothesized that the gender role self-concept predicts the degree to which children's academic self-concepts – comprising ability perceptions and affective-motivational reactions – as well as their performances in reading and mathematics, are consistent with gender stereotypes, i.e., for children describing themselves more feminine higher in reading, and for children describing themselves more masculine higher in mathematics.

Academic self-concepts in mathematics and reading at school start comprise two components: children's self-perceived competence (cognitive component; i.e., 'I am good at math') and their affective–motivational reactions (affective component; e.g., 'I enjoy reading'; Arens & Hasselhorn, 2015; Arens, Yeung, Craven, & Hasselhorn, 2011; Marsh, Craven, & Debus, 1999). Shavelson, Hubner, and Stanton (1976) declared that self-concept should include both evaluative and descriptive components, although more recent research has found both factors to be empirically distinguishable (e.g., Arens et al., 2011). We expected that the more strongly children associate themselves with attributes that – according to gender-stereotypes – are associated with their own (biological) gender, the more their self-perceived competence and their affective-motivational reactions towards mathematics and reading would also be consistent with gender stereotypes.

Consider, for instance, a boy in first grade presented with the choice of reading a story or working on a mathematics task, with the teacher's assistance. Suppose that he is aware of the gender stereotype that 'math is for boys' and 'reading is for girls' (e.g., Steffens & Jelenec, 2011; Steffens et al., 2010), based on his gender identity ('I am a boy', Tobin et al., 2010) he will think that 'math tasks are for me' and 'reading a story is not for me' (cf. Martin & Halverson, 1981, p. 1120). To the extent that he endorses masculine attributes as self-descriptive (gender role self-concept), he should anticipate to enjoy working on the mathematics task more than reading a story (affective component of academic self-concept), and assume that he will do better on the mathematics task than on the reading task (cognitive component of academic self-concept). Moreover, as a result, he should more likely engage in the mathematics task than the reading task, thus training his skills in mathematics related tasks rather than reading related tasks.

Indirect evidence for these assumptions comes from the extended research showing positive relations between levels of gender constancy (as explained above, studies investigating children at school start age have typically not measured their gender role self-concept, but rather the extent to which children have reached gender constancy) and gendered preferences or behaviors. For instance, children who accomplished gender constancy (but not children of the same age who have not yet developed gender constancy) are more attentive to same-gender than other-gender models, and are more likely to prefer gender-typed clothing, same-gender peers and to engage in gender-typed activities (see Martin, Ruble, & Szkrybalo, 2002, for a review).

More direct evidence comes from previous studies using older samples and investigating interrelations between the gender role self-concept on the one hand and ability self-perceptions or motivation related variables on the other. Several studies found higher ability self-concepts and motivation in mathematics and sciences the more individuals ascribed masculine attributes to themselves (Anderson, 2004 for ninth grade students; Handley & Morse, 1984 for adolescents; Hannover, 2002; for university students). Using Implicit Association Tests, Nosek, Banaji, and Greenwald (2002) found that associating the self with female and math with male attributes made it difficult for women to associate mathematics with the self. McGeown et al. (2012) found that the more strongly their eight to 11 years old research participants ascribed feminine trait terms to themselves the more motivated they were to read, while the self-ascription of masculine traits did not matter very much. Pajares and Valiante (2001) found that all gender differences favoring girls in writing motivation and achievement in middle school turned insignificant when self-ascriptions of feminine attributes (what they call a feminine orientation) were controlled for.

While these studies investigating older samples suggest that the gender role self-concept is predictive of ability self-perceptions and affective-motivational reactions in mathematics vs. reading related academic realms, it is not entirely clear whether the academic self-concept of children at school start is already differentiated according to subject domain. For instance, investigating four- and five-year-olds, Marsh, Ellis, and Craven (2002) found that while the children differentiated between academic and nonacademic facets of their self-concepts, their mathematics and reading related self-concepts were strongly correlated with $r = .73$ (p. 384), suggesting that they did not differentiate between the two academic domains. Also, Marsh et al. (2002) found gender neither to be correlated with children's mathematics nor their reading related self-concept, suggesting that the gender stereotypes about mathematics and reading were not yet fully acquired. In their hierarchical, multifaceted model of the self, Shavelson et al. (1976) suggest that children of that age group have a generalized (and highly positive) self-concept which becomes increasingly multifaceted as they learn about their relative weaknesses and strengths in different school subjects. It is only at the end of primary school that children's ability self-concept is reliably differentiated according to subject domains, evident in different self-concept facets being only moderately correlated, and, at the same time, being significantly correlated with external indicators of competence (e.g., Arens et al., 2011; Marsh & Shavelson, 1985). As the children of our sample were older than the one's studied by Marsh et al. (2002) (but younger than the one's studied by Arens & Hasselhorn, 2015; or Arens et al., 2011), we hoped to find their self-concepts to be differentiated by domain and to be predictive of achievements in the respective domain.

To summarize, we expected that as early as first grade, children differ in their gender role self-concepts, at least with respect to behavior-based items: boys ascribe more masculine and girls more feminine attributes to themselves. In addition, we expected children's gender role self-concept to predict academic self-concepts and achievements in mathematics and reading: to the extent that children describe themselves with feminine attributes, their ability self-perceptions, their affective-motivational reactions, and their skills in reading should increase, while to the extent that children ascribe masculine attributes to themselves, ability self-perceptions, affective-motivational reactions, and skills in mathematics should increase.

Method

Research participants

Participants were 113 children ($n = 52$ boys, $n = 61$ girls) who participated in a longitudinal study and therefore were recruited before entering primary school from different preschools in Berlin.[1] Out of the 113 children $n = 109$ children participated at $t1$ and $n = 107$ participated at $t2$, with $n = 103$ children participating at both $t1$ and $t2$. Since the sample was conducted within a broader longitudinal study some children were only present at one of the two measurement points that are presented here. Most of the temporary drop-outs were due to time restraints or failed attempts to reach the families. In total, missing values are rather infrequent, and not related to constructs included in this research which is why they are considered as missing at random. At $t1$, children were aged $M = 78.42$ months, SD = 3.3, *range:* 72–85 months. 44.9% of the children had one sibling, 17.3% had two siblings, 6.3% had three or more siblings and 31.5% had no brothers or sisters.

---

[1] The slightly uneven distribution of children's gender resulted from our longitudinal design: 65 boys and 70 girls sampled from 117 different preschools in Berlin, Germany, had first been investigated in kindergarten, where only one child had been sampled per kindergarten group. Those children were then followed up into their first grade in primary school, however, some of the children dropped out of the study (in most cases because they could no longer be reached), and were not included in the analyses for the present study (for a detailed description of the sampling strategy see Wolter, Glüer, & Hannover, 2014).

Every child was investigated in an individual session. Children's gender role self-concept was tested in the midst of first grade ($t1$). Academic self-concepts and achievements in mathematics and reading were measured at the end of first grade ($t2$), on average 5 months after the first measurement, Min = 4 months, Max = 6 months.

Research instruments

Gender role self-concept

To measure children's gender role self-concept, we wanted to generate behavior based and trait term based attributes viewed as either feminine or masculine by children of our age group. To that end, partly using items from extant questionnaires (e.g., the Children's Sex Role Inventory by Boldizar, 1991), in a pilot study we presented 21 items to 10 preschoolers (between five and six years old), asking them to describe whether they were typical for girls, for boys, or for girls and boys alike. Six trait terms ('strong', 'brave', 'cry when hurt', 'friendly/ nice', 'care about others', 'share with others') and 6 behavior-based terms ('do dangerous things', 'fighting in play', 'make clothes dirty when playing', 'like to dress up in smart clothes', 'like to watch oneself in the mirror', 'play to pretend as if, e.g. shopping') which had consistently been jugded as either typical of girls or typical of boys were used in our main study. Children were asked to indicate how much each description applied to themselves on a 4-point Likert scale (from 1 = not at all to 4 = very much).

The four subscales measuring children's gender role self-concept yielded satisfactory internal consistencies, given that they consisted of only three items each, and that they intended to measure a rather broad, general construct which usually is measured with substantially more items: $a = .53$ for behavior-based masculinity, $a = .53$ for trait-based masculinity, $a = .56$ for trait-based femininity, $a = .64$ for behavior-based femininity.

Academic self-concepts: cognitive and affective components

To measure the cognitive and the affective component of children's academic self-concepts, we translated and slightly adapted the *Self-Description Questionnaire for Preschoolers* (Marsh et al., 2002) into German. To grasp the cognitive component, children were asked whether they are good at reading (e.g., 'Bist du gut im Lesen? [Are you good at reading?]') or math related tasks (e.g., 'Kennst du viele Zahlen? [Do you know many numbers?]'). The affective component is defined by items asking the children whether they like, are interested in, or enjoy working with reading (e.g., 'Hörst du dir gerne Geschichten an? [Do you like to listen to stories?]') or math related tasks (e.g., 'Zählst du gerne? [Do you like counting?]').

Children had to respond to the items on 4-point answering scales (1 = not at all to 4 = very much). For each child we calculated mean scores across the three items of the cognitive and the two items of the affective subscales for both mathematics and reading (Wolter & Hannover, 2014). The internal consistencies of all four subscales were: $a = .44$ for the cognitive component of the mathematics self-concept, $a = .53$ for the cognitive component of the reading self-concept, $a = .61$ for the affective component of the mathematics self-concept, and $a = .65$ for the affective component of the reading self-concept. Thus, reliabilities were rather low but satisfactory considering that the scales consisted of only two or three items each.

Academic achievements
To investigate children's reading competence at the end of first grade in primary school ($t2$), we used the 'Würzburger LeiseLeseprobe', WLLP (Küspert & Schneider, 1998), a one scale speed-test of silent reading. The test consists of a maximum of 140 items, actual tests scores of the children of our sample ranged between 13 and 106, $M = 42.34$, SD = 18.09. Test scores of our sample were comparable to norm values for this age group (norm sample from item development: $N = 646$, $M = 42.82$, SD = 17.15; $t(779) = 0.082$, n.s.). The reliability of the scale was very good (Kuder-Richardson formula for dichotomous items: .96).

The HRT 1-4, 'Heidelberger Rechentest' (Haffner, Baro, Parzer, & Resch, 2005), was used to measure children's mathematics competence at the end of first grade. The standardized test has norm values for first to fourth graders and tests both, children's arithmetic and visual-spatial skills. The test consists of nine subscales such as addition and subtraction as well as sequences of numbers and cube rotation tasks. Children's test scores (corresponding to the number of correct answers calculated across all tasks) were on average $M = 130.76$, SD = 35.34. The reliability of this scale was satisfactory with Cronbach's alpha $a = .74$. Test scores of our sample (transformed into T-values to compare with norm sample, $M = 50.27$, SD = 0.94) were comparable to norm values for this age group (norm sample from item development: $N = 2262$, $M = 50$, SD = 10; $t(2373) = 0.31$, n.s.).

Analyses – path models
To test our hypothesis that children's gender role self-concept influences their academic self-concepts and achievements, we conducted manifest path models using Mplus (Muthén & Muthén, 1998–2012), modeling gender role self-concept's direct and indirect effects on reading and mathematics achievement. The level of significance of the indirect effects was determined by confidence intervalls via bias-corrected bootstraps with 1000 bootstrap-samples for each path model. Compared to other resampling methods or joint significance tests (cf., Baron & Kenny, 1986) this method secures higher statistical power but a slight increase in alpha error (Taylor, MacKinnon, & Tein, 2008; Williams & MacKinnon, 2008). Missing data were handled as missing at random (cf., Lüdtke, Robitzsch, Trautwein, & Köller, 2007) using the full information maximum likelihood estimation.

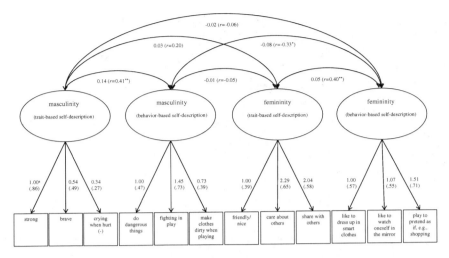

Figure 1. Factors of the gender role self-concept with unstandardized factor loadings and factor covariances (correlations between factors, and standardized factor loadings in brackets).
Note: [a]Factor loadings of the first items of the latent scales are fixed at 1 by default in Mplus.

Table 1. Means and standard deviations for cognitive and affective components of self-concepts for mathematics and reading, for children's gender role self-concept and achievements in mathematics and reading.

	Boys M (SD)	Girls M (SD)	Mean diff. t(111)
Trait-based masculinity	3.29 (0.57)	2.63 (0.61)	5.91***
Behavior-based masculinity	2.37 (0.76)	2.04 (0.62)	2.54*
Trait-based femininity	3.29 (0.54)	3.39 (0.51)	1.01
Behavior-based femininity	2.50 (0.69)	3.23 (0.67)	5.69***
Cognitive reading self-concept	3.55 (0.53)	3.63 (0.44)	0.88
Affective reading self-concept	3.35 (0.80)	3.73 (0.44)	3.19**
Cognitive mathematics self-concept	3.84 (0.30)	3.85 (0.26)	0.19
Affective mathematics self-concept	3.16 (0.77)	3.33 (0.69)	1.24
Reading achievement	39.16 (15.98)	46.56 (18.54)	2.25*
Mathematics achievement	130.62 (38.08)	130.67 (33.92)	−0.00

***$p < .001$; **$p < .01$; *$p < .05$.

Results

Gender role self-concept

We conducted a confirmative factor analysis and found the expected four factor structure (cf. Athenstaedt, 2003) with a satisfactory-to-good model fit, $\chi^2 = 48.833$, $df = 48$, $p = .439$; CFI = .993; TLI = .991; RMSEA = .013, $p = .845$; SRMR = .067: a trait-based and a behavior-based self-description for both femininity and masculinity. Figure 1 displays the final factor structure, together with unstandardized and standardized factor loadings and latent correlation coefficients between factors.

Further, we tested whether our measures of gender role self-concept were invariant across the genders by comparing measurement models. For the behavior-based scales fully scalar invariance was confirmed with a model fit of $x^2 = 24.234$, $df = 26$, $p = .563$, CFI = 1.00, TLI = 1.05; RMSEA = .000, 90%CI .000–.098; SRMR = .089, and an insignificant x^2 difference to the prior metric model, $\Delta x^2 = 1.137$, $df = 4$, $p = .888$. Similar findings emerged for the trait-based scales: femininity and masculinity scales were fully scalar invariant with a model fit of $x^2 = 24.670$, $df = 26$, $p = .538$, CFI = 1.00, TLI = 1.04; RMSEA = .000, 90%CI .000–.100; SRMR = .104, and an insignificant x^2 difference to the prior metric model, $\Delta x^2 = 1.065$, $df = 4$, $p = .899$. As depicted in Table 1 and validated in the latent mean differences, as expected boys endorsed the items of both the behavior and the trait-based masculinity subscales to a stronger extent than girls, Masc-trait: $b_{(diff)} = -0.707$, SE = 0.267, $z = -2.648$, $p < .01$; Masc-behavior: $b_{(diff)} = -0.648$, SE = 0.279, $z = -2.325$, $p < .05$. Also as expected, girls endorsed the behavior-based items of the femininity subscale to a stronger extent than boys, $b_{(diff)} = 1.462$, SE = 0.307, $z = 4.760$, $p < .001$. However, no gender difference was observed on the trait-based femininity subscale, $b_{(diff)} = 0.249$, SE = 0.257, $z = 0.966$, n.s. Hence, girls ascribed more feminine behavior-based descriptions, but not more feminine trait-based items to themselves than boys did.

As expected, the more strongly boys and girls endorsed feminine behavior-based items the less they endorsed masculine behavior-based items ($r = -.33$, $p < .05$). However, the two trait-based subscales were uncorrelated ($r = .20$, n.s.). Together with our finding that the genders did not differ on the trait-based femininity scale, our results are in line with previous studies investigating children of our age group which neither found stereotype consistent self-ascriptions of gendered trait terms nor stereotype consistent differences between boys and girls. It seems, children at age six still have not yet fully acquired the abstract concept of a personality trait and therefore could not make use of the trait terms to describe themselves. While the trait-based items may prove useful in future research investigating older children, we decided to only include the behavior-based items of the femininity and the masculinity scale in our further analyses.[2]

Cognitive and affective components of academic self-concepts

As depicted in Table 1, children reported very positive academic self-concepts overall: All means were between the answering categories 'much' (3) and 'very much' (4), i.e., irrespective of domain and their gender, children thought of their abilities and described their liking of the subjects as very high. Most notably,

---

[2]All path models were also calculated including children's trait-based self-descriptions. The results of the models remained the same, however, the model fits were somewhat lower, confirming our decision not to include the trait-based items.

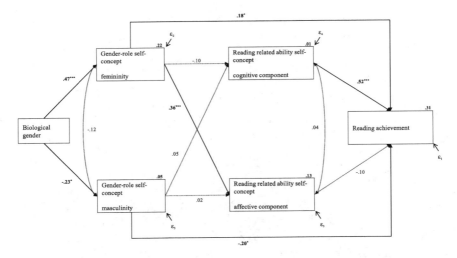

Figure 2. Path model of direct and indirect effects of gender role self-concept and ability self-concept on reading achievements at the end of first grade.
Note: Standardized path coefficients are displayed, ***$p < .001$, **$p < .01$, *$p < .05$, +$p < .10$.

the mean of the cognitive mathematics related self-concept was almost at the maximum of the scale, $M = 3.85$, coinciding with quite small variance, $SD = 0.28$. No gender differences appeared, with the exception of the affective component of the reading related self-concept: girls described their interest and enjoyment of reading as significantly stronger, $M = 3.73$, than boys, $M = 3.35$; $t(111) = 3.19$, $p < .01$ (cf. Wolter & Hannover, 2014). The self-concept subcomponents were correlated across the subject domains mathematics and reading: $r = .79$, $p < .001$, for the cognitive component, and $r = .58$, $p < .001$, for the affective component.

Academic achievements

There was a significant gender difference in children's academic achievement in reading at the end of first grade in primary school. Girls, $M = 46.56$, $SD = 18.54$, outperformed boys, $M = 39.16$, $SD = 15.98$; $t(111) = 2.25$, $p < .05$, in reading, whereas both genders performed equally well in mathematics; boys: $M = 130.62$, $SD = 38.08$; girls: $M = 130.67$, $SD = 33.92$, $t(111) = -0.00$, n.s.

Prediction of reading achievements at the end of first grade from academic self-concepts and gender role self-concept

To predict children's reading achievements at the end of first grade, we conducted a path analysis (see Figure 2). Biological gender, the behavior-based feminine subscale of the gender role self-concept measured at $t1$, cognitive and affective components of the reading related academic self-concept and reading achievements measured at $t2$ were included. Also, the behavior-based masculine subscale of the gender role self-concept was included as a control. With $\chi^2 = 6.048$, $df = 3$, $p = .109$, CFI = .965, TLI = .825, RMSEA = .095, $p = .194$, SRMR = .044, the model was well fitted. With only three degrees of freedom our model is rather restricted. In combination with a fairly small sample size for this kind of analysis this fact might explain the slightly lower TLI in this model fit. However, since the TLI depends on the average size of correlations in the data, and the additional model fit indices are good, we decided to accept this model.

Direct effects

The path analysis yielded a significant effect for the feminine behavior-based subscale of the gender role self-concept, $b = 4.11$, SE = 1.96, $\beta = .18$, $p < .05$, $d = 0.36$, on reading achievement at the end of first grade. As expected, the more feminine children described their behavior to be half a year after school start, the better their reading achievements were at the end of first grade. Furthermore, there was a significant direct negative effect of the masculine subscale of the gender role self-concept, $b = -5.03$, SE = 2.05, $\beta = -.20$, $p < .05$, $d = -0.41$, on reading achievement: the more masculine children described themselves the worse they performed in reading half a year later.

Further, the path model revealed a direct effect of self-ascribed femininity on the affective component of the reading self-concept, $b = 0.31$, SE = 0.10, $\beta = 0.36$, $p < .01$, $d = 0.55$, with children liking reading more the more feminine they had described themselves half a year earlier. In contrast, femininity did not impact the cognitive component of the reading self-concept, $b = -0.06$, SE = 0.05, $\beta = -0.10$, n.s. Children's self-ascribed masculinity was neither related to their cognitive, $b = 0.03$, SE = 0.07, $\beta = 0.05$, n.s., nor their affective self-concept in reading, $b = 0.02$, SE = 0.09, $\beta = 0.02$, n.s.

The cognitive component of the reading self-concept was a significant predictor of reading achievement, $b = 19.00$, SE = 3.54, $\beta = 0.52$, $p < .001$, $d = 0.89$: the stronger children described their reading skills to be, the better their actual performance was. In contrast, the affective component of the reading related self-concept was unrelated to later reading performance, $b = -2.77$, SE = 2.34, $\beta = -0.10$, n.s.

Indirect effects

Deviating from our expectations, there were no mediated effects of children's self-ascription of femininity on later reading achievements. Neither did femininity impact reading achievements via the affective component of the reading self-concept, $b = -0.85$, SE = 0.71, $\beta = -0.04$, n.s., nor via the cognitive reading self-concept, $b = -1.20$, SE = 1.01, $\beta = -0.05$, n.s. (Also, masculinity neither impacted reading achievements via the affective component, $b = -0.06$, SE = 0.33, $\beta = -0.00$, n.s., nor via the cognitive component of the reading self-concept, $b = 0.61$, SE = 1.41, $\beta = 0.02$, n.s.). Hence, while there were direct

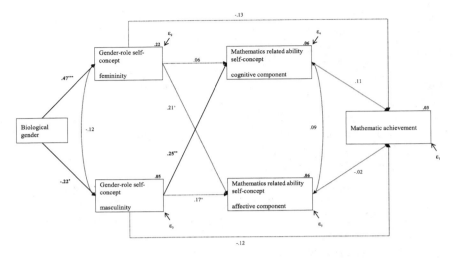

Figure 3. Path model with direct and indirect effects of gender role self-concept and ability self-concept on achievement in mathematics at the end of first grade.
Note: standardized path coefficients are displayed; *** p < .001, ** p < .01, * p < .05, +p < .10.

effects of femininity and masculinity on reading achievements, these effects were not mediated via the reading related academic self-concept.

To summarize, the path model showed that the more feminine and the less masculine children had described themselves half a year earlier, the better they were in reading at the end of first grade. While high femininity also predicted strong liking for reading, the academic self-concept did not mediate the gender role self-concept's impact on reading achievements.

Prediction of mathematic achievements at the end of first grade from academic self-concepts and gender role self-concept

To predict children's math achievements at the end of first grade, we also conducted a path analysis (see Figure 3). Analogous to the procedure in the domain of reading, biological gender, the masculine component of the gender role self-concept measured at $t1$, cognitive and affective components of the mathematics related academic self-concept and mathematic achievements measured at $t2$ were included. Also, the feminine component of the gender role self-concept was included as a control. With $\chi^2 = 1.525$, $df = 3$, $p = .677$, CFI = 1.00, TLI = 1.13, RMSEA = .000, $p = .762$, SRMR = .021, the model was well fitted.

Direct effects

As expected, the more masculine children described themselves the more competent they perceived themselves to be in mathematics, $b = 0.10$, SE = 0.04, $\beta = 0.25$, $p < .01$, $d = 0.47$, and also – but only marginally significantly so – the more positive their affective-motivational reaction towards mathematics was, $b = 0.18$, SE $= 0.10$, $\beta = 0.17$, $p = .06$, $d = 0.33$, half a year later. However, children's gender role self-concept did not predict their later mathematic achievements (for femininity $b = -6.13$, SE $= 4.90$, $\beta = -0.13$, n.s., for masculinity $b = -5.91$, SE $= 6.08$, $\beta = -0.12$, n.s.). Moreover, children's academic self-concept did not have a significant impact on their later achievement in mathematics (cognitive component: $b = 14.02$, SE $= 14.16$, $\beta = 0.11$, n.s.; affective component: $b = -0.93$, SE $= 5.48$, $\beta = -0.02$, n.s.)

Indirect effects
There were no mediation effects from the masculine component of children's gender role self-concept on their mathematic achievement (cognitive component: $b = 1.40$, SE $= 1.57$, $\beta = 0.03$, n.s.; affective component: $b = -0.17$, SE $= 1.14$, $\beta = -0.00$, n.s.).

To summarize, as expected, the more masculine children described themselves, the higher they thought of their mathematics skills and – by trend – the more they liked mathematics half a year later. However, the academic self-concept was uncorrelated with children's achievement in mathematics.

Discussion

In this research we investigated children's gender role self-concept at school start and whether it can contribute to an explanation of the development of gendered cognitive and affective academic self-concepts and skills in mathematics and reading. While there is a large extent of research on academic self-concepts being strongly gendered early on, even after controlling for the impact of actual performance levels (e.g., Niklas & Schneider, 2012), to our knowledge no previous studies have investigated children's gender role self-concept at school start as a precursor of gendered academic self-concepts and skills.

From the time children identify themselves as either a girl or a boy (i.e., gender identity; Tobin et al., 2010) they are inclined to incorporate stereotypes about their own gender into their self (Martin & Halverson, 1981), with the emerging gender role self-concept thus containing more attributes regarded as feminine in girls and more attributes regarded as masculine in boys. The few studies having looked at the gender role self-concept in children as young as six years old did not find consistent gender differences on trait-based items (Inoff et al., 1983), but only on behavior-based ones (Cowan & Hoffman, 1986), while studies investigating older children found both trait-based and behavior-based attributes applicable to them (Biernat, 1991; Boldizar, 1991; Egan & Perry, 2001; McGeown et al., 2012). To gain a clearer picture as to when children start to reliably associate their self with gendered attributes (cf., Tobin et al., 2010), in our research we had six to seven year old children describe themselves using both, trait-term based and behavior-based attributes, either stereotyped as feminine or as masculine.

In line with the findings of previously published studies (e.g., Biernat, 1991; Cowan & Hoffman, 1986), a reliable pattern emerged for the behavior-based items only. In our sample girls were significantly more likely to describe themselves via feminine-stereotyped behaviors than boys, and boys with masculine-stereotyped behaviors than girls. Also, the more feminine-stereotyped behaviors children considered as self-descriptive, the fewer masculine-stereotyped behaviors they endorsed. In contrast, children's self-ascriptions of trait-based feminine and masculine terms were uncorrelated and it was only for the masculine (but not the feminine) component of the gender role self-concept that a gender difference in accordance with gender stereotypes was observed. It seems, the children had already incorporated gender stereotypes into their selves, however, at this early age concrete characteristics, like behaviors, prevail in their views of the genders, while abstract concepts, such as gendered personality traits, seem to not yet be fully understood. As Martin and Halverson (1981) put it, 'children are not aware of the more subtle personality traits associated with each of the sexes until 10 or 11 years of age ... Very young children do know, however, many of the behaviors ... appropriate to each sex' (p. 1120). Future research may want to investigate the applicability of our scale, consisting of both behavior- and trait-based items in older groups of children, to find out when exactly the gender role self-concept comprises not only concrete behavior-based, but also abstract concepts, like personality traits. The early emergence of differentiated gender role self-concepts highlights the importance of research regarding educational trajectories that starts before children enter school. As also stated in the Bildung-Psychology-Model by Spiel and colleagues (e.g., Spiel, Reimann, Wagner & Schober, 2010) with its focus on lifelong educational pathways, the consideration of preschool years of children's Bildung-careers seem inevitable when further investigating the emergence and incorporation of gender stereotypes in children's self-concept development. We are not aware of any studies having investigated the potential role that children's gender role self-concepts at school start may play in the later development of gendered academic self-concepts and skills: when children as early as in first grade describe their abilities and their liking of mathematics and reading in consistency with what gender stereotypes predict (e.g., Niklas & Schneider, 2012), can this (partly) be explained by the extent to which they have incorporated gender stereotypes into their gender role self-concept?

Results from our path analyses revealed that biological gender predicted femininity and masculinity gender role self-concepts as expected. In addition, children's gender role self-concept predicted their skill development in reading, however, this deviated from our expectation in that this was not mediated via children's academic self-concepts but rather directly: children's reading skills were higher, the more feminine they had described themselves half a year earlier. Going beyond our research hypotheses, but not inconsistent with our theorizing, we additionally found a direct negative impact of the masculine component of children's gender role self-concept on their reading skills: the more masculine children had described themselves, the lower their reading skills were half a year later. This finding suggests that children not only profited from the incorporation of the feminine gender stereotype into their gender role self-concept for their skill development in a subject domain regarded as feminine, such as reading, but also had a disadvantage from the incorporation of the masculine gender stereotype into their gender role self-concept.

While high femininity also predicted strong liking of reading, it did not strengthen children's ability perceptions towards reading. At the same time, only the cognitive component but not the affective component of children's reading related academic self-concept was correlated with children's reading achievements, hence, our hypothesis that the impact of the gender role self-concept on skill development would be mediated via children's academic self-concept was not supported.

While our assumption that children's behavior-based gender role self-concept predicts skill development in reading was partly supported, for mathematics, the only reliable effect emanated from the masculinity self-concept on the cognitive component of the mathematics related academic self-concept: As expected, the more masculine children had described themselves half a year earlier, the more convinced they now were of their mathematics-related skills. However, children's ability perceptions were unrelated to their mathematics achievements.

A possible interpretation as to why we obtained (partial) support for our assumptions for reading but not for mathematics is that while children are already involved in reading related activities long before school start (e.g., parents or preschool teachers reading to them; cf., Artelt et al., 2007; Baumert & Stanat, 2010), the concept of mathematics as a subject domain is less clearly developed in children as young as six years old. The finding might also be explained by the fact that children's educational development does not only take place during their institutional learning. As the Bildung-Psychology-Model also states, education is considered a continuous process which neither starts nor ends with formal schooling (cf. Spiel, Reimann, Wagner & Schober, 2010). Furthermore, it is hoped that the particular relevance of our research to the issues of prevention and intervention is apparent.

A further reason why our hypotheses, for both reading and mathematics, were only weakly supported is that six-year-olds have not yet developed reliable and subject specific academic self-concepts. In our sample, only children's perception of their ability in reading correlated substantially with their reading skills, whereas no such covariation was observed for mathematics. Also, the affective components of children's academic self-concepts did not correlate with their achievements, neither in reading nor in mathematics. At the same time, the cognitive components of children's academic self-concepts were particularly strongly correlated across domains, suggesting that they did not clearly differentiate between their reading and mathematics related skills. These findings parallel those reported by Marsh et al. (2002) from their sample of four- and five-year-olds, whose mathematics and reading related self-concepts were comparably strongly correlated as in our sample of six- to seven-year-olds. It seems, children's general ability self-concept is reliably differentiated into domain specific self-concepts only at a later stage, indicated by the specific self-concepts being only moderately correlated among each other and, at the same time, reliably correlated with performances in the respective domains, as, for instance, Arens et al. (2011) found in their sample of third graders.

Compared to the very strong covariation between our research participants' ability perceptions in mathematics and reading, children's liking varied more strongly between the two subject domains (cf., Wolter & Hannover, 2014). A possible interpretation is that children's general academic self-concept starts to differentiate into domain-specific sub-concepts via the affective component: liking or enjoyment of an activity (for instance being read a book or working on a mathematics related task) is a behavior-based and concrete concept, in contrast to the concept of an ability whose acquisition presupposes both an understanding that achievements are manifestations of an inner, abstract ability, and an understanding that ability is quite stable over time. This interpretation is consistent with the fact that the only gender difference we found in children's academic self-concepts related to an affective component: girls reported to enjoy reading more than boys did, while no gender differences appeared for children's liking of mathematics, or children's reading and mathematics related ability perceptions (Wolter & Hannover, 2014).

Limitations of our study

With the research reported in the paper, we tried to add to the scarce and out-dated studies investigating the extent to which children at school start describe themselves by attributes that, according to gender-stereotypes, are either typical of girls or of boys. We also wanted to find out whether these early indicators of a gender role self-concept predict the development of academic self-concepts and skills in gendered performance domains. There are a few limitations to our study that should be considered in future research on this topic. We only had two measurement points, and therefore academic self-concept and achievement were measured cross-sectionally. Therefore, any kind of conclusions about the causality of the relationships between those constructs are unverifiable. Our findings suggest that investigating the development of children's gender role self-concepts over a longer period should also be considered in future research.

In summarizing our findings, they provide only very preliminary support for the assumption that children's gender role self-concept at school start is

– among other things not investigated in our study – a precursor of gendered academic self-concepts and skill development. As we were interested in finding out more about when exactly children's gender role self-concept and gendered academic self-concepts start to emerge, we used measurement instruments which to our knowledge no previous research has ever (successfully) applied in samples as young as six- to seven-year-olds. As a result, only one of the two subscales of our measure of children's gender role self-concept turned out to be appropriate and the scales that intended to measure the cognitive and affective components of children's academic self-concepts seemed to not reliably differentiate between the subject domains of mathematics and reading, and did not covary substantially with children's achievements. Also, while our predictions regarding children's gender role self-concept and how this would impact their achievement development were the same for mathematics and reading, our empirical findings varied between the two domains. As we could not rely on previous research to predict whether our measures would be appropriate for the age group investigated in our study, we cannot decide whether these differences should be interpreted as substantial or are simply due to our measures being differentially reliable, depending on the subject domain. This is particularly true as our sample was only quite small, such that all of our findings certainly need to be replicated before they can be considered reliable. Nevertheless, more importantly for our purposes, the internal consistency of our gender role self-concept scales shows a considerable correlation of the items which all contribute some unique information to the scales. Gender-role self-concept usually is considered a broad, more generic construct which is measured by a higher number of items in adults, but this was not our aim nor within the scope of our study.

Even so, we consider our findings thought provoking and stimulating for future research as they suggest that children's incorporation of gender stereotypes into their selves, starting long before school entry, may channel them into lifelong gendered academic pathways. As previous studies have consistently found gendered patterns of domain-specific academic self-concepts and skills from mid childhood onwards, future research should more systematically follow up children's gender role self-concepts and academic self-concepts from school entry until third grade, and to relate these to their achievements in gender stereotyped and gender neutral subject domains.

Disclosure statement

No potential conflict of interest was reported by the authors.

Funding

This research was supported by a grant from the *Deutsche Forschungsgemeinschaft* allocated to the second author, Bettina Hannover [HA 2381/8-1; 8-2].

References

Anderson, B. S. (2004). The relation between sex-typed traits and perceptions of academic ability in gifted 9th grade students. *Dissertation Abstracts International Section A, 65,* 407. Retrieved July 5, 2015, from PsycINFO, Ipswich, MA.

Arens, A. K., & Hasselhorn, M. (2015). Differentiation of competence and affect self-perceptions in elementary school students: Extending empirical evidence. *European Journal of Psychology of Education, 29,* 1–15.

Arens, A. K., Yeung, A. S., Craven, R. G., & Hasselhorn, M. (2011). The twofold multidimensionality of academic self-concept: Domain specificity and separation between competence and affect components. *Journal of Educational Psychology, 103,* 970–981.

Artelt, C., McElvany, N., Christmann, U., Richter, T., Groeben, N., Köster, J., ... Ring, K. (2007). *Förderung von Lesekompetenz. Expertise.* [Promotion of reading competence. Expertise] Bundesministerium für Bildung und Forschung [Federal Ministry of Education and Research] (Bildungsforschung, Bd. 17).

Athenstaedt, U. (2003). On the content and structure of the gender role self-concept: Including gender-stereotypical behaviors in addition to traits. *Psychology of Women Quarterly, 27,* 309–318.

Baron, R. M., & Kenny, D. A. (1986). The moderator-mediator variable distinction in social psychological research: Conceptual, strategic, and statistical considerations. *Journal of Personality and Social Psychology, 51,* 1173–1182.

Baumert, J., & Stanat, P. (2010). Internationale Schulleistungsvergleiche [International comparative academic achievement studies]. In D. H. Rost (Hrsg.) (Ed.), *Handwörterbuch Pädagogische Psychologie* [Concise dictionary educational psychology] (4th ed., pp. 324–335). Weinheim: Beltz.

Bem, S. (1974). The measurement of psychological androgyny. *Journal of Consulting and Clinical Psychology, 42,* 155–162.

Biernat, M. (1991). Gender stereotypes and the relationship between masculinity and femininity: A developmental analysis. *Journal of Personality and Social Psychology, 61,* 351–365.

Boldizar, J. P. (1991). Assessing sex typing and androgyny in children: The Children's Sex Role Inventory. *Developmental Psychology, 27,* 505–515.

Bos, W., Bremerich-Vos, A., Tarelli, I., Valtin, R. (2012). Lesekompetenzen im internationalen Vergleich. In W. Bos, I. Tarelli, A. Bremerich-Vos, & K. Schwippert (Hrsg.). IGLU 2011. *Lesekompetenzen von Grundschulkindern in Deutschland im internationalen Vergleich.* (S.91–136). Münster: Waxmann.

Cowan, G., & Hoffman, C. D. (1986). Gender stereotyping in young children: Evidence to support a concept-learning approach. *Sex Roles, 14,* 211–224.

Cvencek, D., Meltzoff, A. N., & Greenwald, A. G. (2011). Math-gender stereotypes in elementary school children. *Child Development, 82,* 766–779.

Dwyer, C. (1974). Influence of children's sex role standards on reading and arithmetic achievement. *Journal of Educational Psychology, 66,* 811–816.

Eagly, A. H., Wood, W., & Diekman, A. B. (2000). Social role theory of sex differences and similarities: A current appraisal. In T. Eckes & H. M. Trautner (Eds.), *The developmental social psychology of gender* (pp. 123–174). Mahwah, NJ: Lawrence Erlbaum Associates.

Egan, S., & Perry, D. (2001). Gender identity: A multidimensional analysis with implications for psychosocial adjustment. *Developmental Psychology, 37,* 451–463.

Haffner, J., Baro, K., Parzer, P., & Resch, F. (2005). *Heidelberger Rechentest (HRT 1–4). Erfassung mathematischer Basiskompetenzen im Grundschulalter* [Diagnosis of mathematical

BILDUNG-PSYCHOLOGY

basic competence in elementary school age: The Heidelberger Rechentest (HRT)]. Göttingen: Hogrefe.

Halim, M. L., & Ruble, D. N. (2010). Gender identity and stereotyping in early and middle childhood. In J. Chrisler & D. McCreary (Eds.), *Handbook of gender research in psychology* (pp. 495–525). New York, NY: Springer.

Handley, H. M., & Morse, L. W. (1984). Two-year study relating adolescents' self-concept and gender role perceptions to achievement and attitudes toward science. *Journal of Research in Science Teaching, 21*, 599–607.

Hannover, B. (2002). Auswirkungen der Selbstkategorisierung als männlich oder weiblich auf Erfolgserwartungen gegenüber geschlechtskonnotierten Aufgaben [Effects of self-categorization as male or female on expected success in gender-connotated tasks]. In B. Spinath & E. Heise (Eds.), *Pädagogische Psychologie unter gewandelten gesellschaftlichen Bedingungen* (pp. 37–51). Hamburg: Kovac.

Inoff, G. E., Halverson, C. F., & Pizzigati, K. A. L. (1983). The influence of sex-role stereotypes on children's self-and-peer-attributions. *Sex Roles, 9*, 1205–1222.

Küspert, P., & Schneider, W. (1998). *Würzburger Leise Leseprobe (WLLP)* [Wuerzburger Silent Reading-test]. Göttingen: Hogrefe.

Lüdtke, O., Robitzsch, A., Trautwein, U., & Köller, O. (2007). Umgang mit fehlenden Werten in der psychologischen Forschung [Handling of missing data in psychological research]. *Psychologische Rundschau, 58*, 103–117.

Marsh, H. W., Craven, R. G., & Debus, R. (1999). Separation of competency and affect components of multiple dimensions of academic self-concept: A developmental perspective. *Merrill-Palmer Quarterly, 45*, 567–601.

Marsh, H. W., Ellis, L. A., & Craven, R. G. (2002). How do preschool children feel about themselves? Unraveling measurement and multidimensional self-concept structure. *Developmental Psychology, 38*, 376–393.

Marsh, H. W., & Shavelson, R. (1985). Self-concept: Its multifaceted, hierarchical structure. *Educational Psychologist, 20*, 107–123.

Martin, C. L., & Halverson, C. F. (1981). A schematic processing model of sex typing and stereotyping in children. *Child Development, 52*, 1119–1134.

Martin, C. L., Ruble, D. N., & Szkrybalo, J. (2002). Cognitive theories of early gender development. *Psychological Bulletin, 128*, 903–933.

McGeown, S., Goodwin, H., Henderson, N., & Wright, P. (2012). Gender differences in reading motivation: does sex or gender identity provide a better account? *Journal of Research in Reading, 35*, 328–336.

Mullis, I., Martin, M., Foy, P., & Arora, A. (2012). *TIMSS 2011 – International results in mathematics.* Chestnut Hill, MA: IEA Publishing.

Muthén, L. K., & Muthén, B. O. (1998–2012). *Mplus user's guide* (7th ed.). Los Angeles, CA: Muthén & Muthén.

Niklas, F., & Schneider, W. (2012). Die Anfänge geschlechtsspezifischer Leistungsunter-schiede in mathematischen und schriftsprachlichen Kompetenzen [The beginning of gender-specific performance differences in mathematics and linguistic competencies]. *Zeitschrift für Entwicklungspsychologie und Pädagogische Psychologie, 44*, 123–138.

Nosek, B. A., Banaji, M. R., & Greenwald, A. G. (2002). Math = male, me = female, therefore math ≠ me. *Journal of Personality and Social Psychology, 83*, 44–59.

Orlofsky, J. L., & O'Heron, C. A. (1987). Stereotypic and nonstereotypic sex role trait and behavior orientations: Implications for personal adjustment. *Journal of Personality & Social Psychology, 52*, 1034–1042.

Pajares, F., & Valiante, G. (2001). Gender differences in writing motivation and achievement of middle school students: A function of gender orientation? *Contemporary Educational Psychology, 26*, 366–381.

Perry, L. C., Perry, D. G., & Hynes, J. (1990). The relation of sex-typing to the outcomes children expect for sex-typed behavior. Unpublished manuscript, Florida Atlantic University, Boca Raton.

Pottorff, D. D., Phelps-Zientarski, D., & Skovera, M. E. (1996). Gender perceptions of elementary and middle school students about literacy at school and home. *Journal of Research and Development in Education, 29*, 203–211.

Ruble, D. N. (1994). A phase model of transitions: Cognitive and motivational consequences. In M. P. Zanna & M. P. Zanna (Eds.), *Advances in experimental social psychology* (Vol. 26, pp. 163–214). San Diego, CA: Academic Press.

Ruble, D. N., Eisenberg, R., & Higgins, E. T. (1994). Developmental changes in achievement evaluation: Motivational implications of self-other differences. *Child Development, 65*, 1095–1110.

Shavelson, R. J., Hubner, J. J., & Stanton, G. C. (1976). Self-concept: Validation of construct interpretations. *Review of Educational Research, 46*, 407–441.

Spence, J., Helmreich, R., & Stapp, J. (1974). The personal attributes questionnaire: A measure of self-role stereotypes and masculinity-femininity. *JSAS: Catalog of Selected Documents in Psychology, 4*, 43–44.

Spiel, C., Reimann, R., Wagner, P., & Schober, B. (2008). Bildung-psychology: The substance and structure of an emerging discipline. *Applied Developmental Science, 12*, 154–159.

Spiel, C., Reimann, R., Wagner, P., & Schober, B. (2010). Bildungspsychologie – eine Einführung [Bildung-Psychology – an introduction]. In C. Spiel, B. Schober, P. Wagner, & R. Reimann (Eds.), *Bildungspsychologie* [Bildung-Psychology] (pp. 11–20). Göttingen: Hogrefe.

Steffens, M. C., & Jelenec, P. (2011). Separating implicit gender stereotypes regarding math and language: Implicit stereotypes are self-serving for boys and men, but not for girls and women. *Sex Roles, 64*, 324–335.

Steffens, M. C., Jelenec, P., & Noack, P. (2010). On the leaky math pipeline: Comparing implicit math-gender stereotypes and math withdrawal in female and male children and adolescents. *Journal of Educational Psychology, 102*, 947–963.

Taylor, A. B., MacKinnon, D., & Tein, J.-Y. (2008). Tests of the three-path mediated effect. *Organizational Research Methods, 11*, 241–269.

Tobin, D. D., Menon, M., Menon, M., Spatta, B. C., Hodges, E. V. E., & Perry, D. G. (2010). The intrapsychics of gender: A model of self-socialization. *Psychological Review, 117*, 601–622.

Williams, J., & MacKinnon, D. P. (2008). Resampling and distribution of the product methods for testing indirect effects in complex models. *Structural Equation Modeling: A Multidisciplinary Journal, 15*, 23–51.

Wolter, I., & Hannover, B. (2014). Kognitive und affektive Fähigkeitsselbstkonzepte zu Schulbeginn. Domänenspezifische Differenzierung und Geschlechtsunterschiede [Cognitive and affective ability self-concepts at beginning of school. Domain-specific differentiation and gender differences]. In C. Theurer, C. Siedenbiedel & J. Budde (Eds.), *Lernen und Geschlecht* [Learning and Gender] (pp. 151–171). Immenhausen: Prolog Verlag.

Wolter, I., Glüer, M., & Hannover, B. (2014). Gender-typicality of activity offerings and child-teacher relationship closeness in German "Kindergarten". Influences on the development of spelling competence as an indicator of early basic literacy in boys and girls. *Learning and Individual Differences, 31*, 59–65.

School burnout and engagement profiles among digital natives in Finland: a person-oriented approach

Katariina Salmela-Aro, Joona Muotka, Kimmo Alho, Kai Hakkarainen and Kirsti Lonka

ABSTRACT

Applying a person-oriented approach, this study set out to examine what profiles of school engagement and school burnout (i.e., exhaustion, cynicism, inadequacy) can be identified among elementary school children at age 12, a generation also often referred to as the generation of digital natives. We compared the group memberships in their use of socio-digital technologies and related functioning as we expected to find a gap between some digital natives and current educational practices which do not include socio-digital technology in feelings of cynicism towards school. Latent profile analysis identified five groups: *Engaged* (50%) students, who formed the majority; *Stressed* (4%) students, who reported high exhaustion and high inadequacy as a student; Students *High in cynicism (burnout group)* (5%) with high scores on all the components of school burnout, particularly cynicism, but also on exhaustion and inadequacy as a student; students *Moderate in Cynicism* (15%), whose cynicism was directed in particular towards studying and school; and, finally, students *Emerging Cynicism (bored group)* (26%), whose feelings of cynicism were nevertheless elevated. These results thus revealed that almost half (46%) of the elementary students felt some degree of cynicism towards school, thereby supporting our gap hypothesis: these groups of cynical students reported that they would be more engaged at school if socio-digital technologies were used at school. These results indicate that one way to promote the engagement of cynical students might be to offer them the possibility to make greater use of socio-digital technologies at school.

The current generation, sometimes referred to as the generation of digital natives (Prensky, 2001; also Bennett, Maton, & Kervin, 2008; Palfrey & Gasser, 2011; Veen & Vrakking, 2008), is highly experienced in working with socio-digital technologies and media, such as integrating mobile devices, computers, social media and the Internet, outside of school on an everyday basis (Gee & Hayes, 2011; Ito et al., 2010; OECD, 2015). In the context of the model by Christiane Spiel on Bildung-Psychology, the new digital generation uses new ways to engage them in "bildung". However, information and communication technologies (ICTs) are relatively seldom used in the school context in Finland. There appears to be a widening gap between adolescents' practices of using socio-digital technologies and the practices of their schools. Might this be related to disengagement from school and possible school-related cynical attitudes among the digital native generation in Finland? Finnish students have been highly ranked academically in the Program for International Assessment (PISA; OECD, 2009) assessments. However, recent PISA (OECD, 2013) results revealed that Finnish students are less likely to be engaged and to like school than adolescents in most of the other countries: Finland was ranked 60th among the 65 countries on the item measuring students' liking of school. The present study examines digital natives' school engagement and disengagement profiles and how these are related to their use of socio-digital technologies at school in a large representative sample of Finnish elementary school students.

While the definitions and characteristics of engagement continue to vary in the literature, school engagement is typically described as a construct that comprises affective, cognitive and behavioural aspects (e.g., Appleton, Christenson, & Furlong, 2008; Wang & Peck, 2013). The *affective* component refers to students' enjoyment and interest in school-related challenges, the *cognitive* component refers to their cognitive investment in school and the *behavioural* component is often described in terms of involvement. More recently, engagement in schoolwork has also been examined as a positive, ful-filling study-related state of mind (Salmela-Aro & Upadyaya, 2012). In line with this recent approach, we define elementary school students' school engage-ment as a combination of energy, dedication and absorption, thereby high-lighting the affective component of school engagement. In this framework, *energy* refers to high levels of vigour and energy while studying. *Dedication* is characterized by a positive cognitive attitude towards studying in general, a perception of studying as meaningful, and experiencing a sense of signif-icance, enthusiasm, challenge and inspiration. *Absorption* is characterized by being fully concentrated and happily engrossed in one's studying so that time passes quickly. These dimensions have been found to correlate highly with each other (Salmela-Aro & Upadyaya, 2012). Increasingly, researchers have begun to consider engagement and disengagement as separate con-cepts that should be measured on separate scales (Skinner, Furrer, Marchand, & Kinderman, 2008). Recent psychometric work suggests that the positive and negative features of emotional engagement are both consequential and structurally distinguishable. Thus, disengagement is not considered solely to reflect the absence of engagement, but rather, it is a separate and distinct psychological process that contributes uniquely to student outcomes in school settings. Consequently, disengagement has recently been approached in the context of school burnout (Salmela-Aro, Kiuru, Leskinen, & Nurmi, 2009), which comprises three separate dimensions: exhaustion due to school demands, a cynical and detached attitude towards school, and feelings of inadequacy as a student (Salmela-Aro et al., 2009). Exhaustion refers to being tired, ruminating on school-related issues and sleep problems. Cynicism is manifested as an indifferent or distal attitude towards studying in general, a loss of interest in studying and not seeing studying as meaningful. Sense of inadequacy refers to a diminished feeling of competence, achievement and accomplishment as a student.

Studies have rarely examined emotional engagement and school burnout simultaneously (for exceptions, see Salmela-Aro & Upadyaya, 2014; Tuominen-Soini & Salmela-Aro, 2014; Wang, Chow, Hofkens, & Salmela-Aro, 2015), despite research results indicating that positive and negative emotional processes are distinct and may have differential effects on adolescents' academic and emotional well-being (Janosz, Archambault, Morizot, & Pagani, 2008). Earlier studies have shown that high school students display different patterns of academic and socio-emotional functioning and that adjustment problems in school appear to cluster in a minority of adolescents (e.g., Li & Lerner, 2011; Roeser et al., 2008), whereas most students are engaged (Tuominen-Soini & Salmela-Aro, 2014). Wang and Peck (2013) recently identified five groups among high school students in the USA: highly, moderately and minimally engaged, emotionally and cognitively disengaged, whereas Tuominen-Soini and Salmela-Aro (2014) found four groups among Finnish high school students: engaged, engaged-exhausted, burnout and cynical. A recent study using the demands-resources model in the school context revealed that school burnout predicted decrease in school engagement later on (Salmela-Aro & Upadyaya, 2014). Study-related demands, such as demanding education goals and workload, predicted school burnout, whereas both personal (self-efficacy) and school-related resources (support) predicted school engagement (Salmela-Aro & Upadyaya, 2014). Gendered pathways indicate that girls are more likely to suffer from exhaustion or inadequacy (Salmela-Aro & Tynkkynen, 2012), and boys from cynicism (Bask & Salmela-Aro, 2013).

The present study is one of the first to examine both school engagement and burnout and related profiles among early adolescents (born in 2000) at the end of elementary school. These adolescents are often described as digital natives (Prensky, 2001; Palfrey & Gasser, 2011) on account of the fact that the rapid development of socio-digital technologies has transformed their lives, for example in their use of mobile devices and social media for keeping in constant touch and hanging out with an extended network of peers. Nevertheless, young people's patterns of socio-digital participation are heterogeneous, and only some of them are pursuing their interests through cultivating advanced computer or media skills and actively participating in various network communities (Gee & Hayes, 2011; Ito et al., 2010). Sometimes intensive socio-digital participation is driven by harmonious passions (Vallerand et al., 2007) that lead adolescents to develop their skills and competencies and engage in gradually more complex activities (Ito et al., 2010). In other cases, young people may develop an obsessive passion (Vallerand et al., 2007), or even addiction, involving repeated participation in monotonous and compulsive activities related to computer gaming. Most Finnish students appear to use various technologies daily outside of school, but considerably less for learning inside school (e.g., European Commission, 2013): in Finnish schools, most students are still being presented with traditional learning tasks, the accomplishment of which does not require in-depth knowledge, collaboration or creative use of technology. Thus, drawing on this framework and on the observations that outside school many students engage in socio-digital participation in informal contexts (Ito et al., 2010), we outline our gap hypothesis: those digital natives who use socio-digital tools outside school may feel cynical or disengaged in the school context because in school context the use of technology for studying is rare. However, studies on simultaneous school engagement and burnout in relation to early adolescents' patterns of using socio-digital technologies in the school context, however, are largely absent.

In the present study, our aim was to examine simultaneous school burnout and engagement profiles among digital natives and to examine how these profiles differ in their reported socio-digital participation and competence. Following a person-oriented approach, we focused on classifying students into homogenous profiles of school engagement and school burnout symptoms, viz. exhaustion, cynicism and inadequacy, to examine what kinds of school engagement and school burnout profiles can be identified (Tuominen-Soini & Salmela-Aro, 2014; Wang & Peck, 2013), and then how these profiles differ with respect to the use of socio-digital technologies and related engagement at school (Ito et al., 2010; Murdock, 2013). In line with previous studies conducted among high school students (Tuominen-Soini & Salmela-Aro, 2014), we expected to find engaged, exhausted, cynical and burnout groups. With respect to gender differences, we hypothesized, in line with earlier studies (Salmela-Aro & Tynkkynen, 2012), that in particular boys would outnumber girls in groups characterized by high cynicism (Bask & Salmela-Aro, 2013). Moreover, we assumed that a mismatch would emerge between the school's practices with respect to the deployment of socio-digital technologies in teaching and the intensity of the use and mastery of these technologies by some digital natives. Therefore, we expected to find groups of cynical students who would appraise themselves as more engaged when able to make use of ICT in their learning at school (Ito et al., 2010).

Method

The Mind-the-Gap Survey 2013 target population consisted of 6th grade elementary school students, born in 2000 from the Metropolitan area of Helsinki. It comprised 759 elementary school students from 33 schools (males = 336, females = 423). The participants (12–13 years) completed a questionnaire, which took about an hour during school hours. Participation was voluntary, and informed consent forms were collected from both the students and their parents. The study protocol was approved by the Ethics Committee of the University of Helsinki.

Measures

School engagement was assessed by using the Schoolwork Engagement Inventory (EDA; Salmela-Aro & Upadyaya, 2012). The EDA consists of items measuring *energy* (3 items, e.g., "When I study, I feel that I am bursting with energy"), *dedication* (3 items, e.g., "I am enthusiastic about my studies") and *absorption* (3 items, e.g., "Time flies when I'm studying") in relation to school. Participants rated all items on a 7-point Likert-type scale ranging from 0 (*Never*) to 6 (*Every day*). The sum score of school engagement was used, and yielded a Cronbach's α reliability of .90.

School burnout was assessed by using the School Burnout Inventory (SBI; Salmela-Aro et al., 2009). The inventory consists of three subscales: *exhaustion* (4 items, e.g., "I feel overwhelmed by my studies"), *cynicism towards the meaning of studying* (3 items, e.g., "I feel that I am losing interest in my studies") and *sense of inadequacy as a student* (2 items, e.g., "I often have feelings of inadequacy in my studies"). Participants rated all items on a 6-point Likert-type scale ranging from 1 (*Completely disagree*) to 6 (*Completely agree*). Composite scores were computed separately for the three subscales. The Cronbach α reliabilities were between .85 and .92.

Intensity of socio-digital participation was elicited by 10 items on how often the respondent used ICTs, such as when reading news, or reading blogs, each rated on a 7-point Likert-type scale ranging from 1 (*Never*) to 7 (*All the time*) (Cronbach α = .85). *Advanced socio-digital competency* was elicited by 5 items such as "I am maintaining a blog or website", "I am editing videos", each rated on a 5-point Likert-type scale from 1 (*Not at all*) to 5 (*Very skilful*) (Cronbach α = .85). *Intensity of educational use of socio-digital technologies* was elicited by 10 items on how often they use ICT at school, such as when writing, doing school tasks, doing homework and in asking for and giving help in schoolwork, rated on a 7-point Likert-type scale ranging from 1 (*Never*) to 7 (*All the time*) (Cronbach α = .90). *School engagement when using socio-digital technologies* was elicited by the following three items: "I would like to use ICT more in doing schoolwork", "I am more engaged at school when I can use ICT" and "I am more hardworking at school, when I can use ICT at school", each rated on a 5-point Likert-type scale ranging from 1 (*Completely disagree*) to 5 (*Completely agree*) (Cronbach $\alpha = .88$). Gender was coded.

Data analyses

Latent profile analysis

Using a person-oriented approach, students with similar patterns of school engagement and school burnout were identified through latent profile analysis (LPA; Vermunt & Magidson, 2002). LPAs were conducted using the composite scores of the scales assessing school engagement and school burnout. LPA is a probabilistic or model-based variant of traditional cluster analysis (Vermunt & Magidson, 2002). The goal of LPA is to identify the smallest number of latent groups that adequately describe the associations among the observed continuous variables, and it provides fit indices that enable comparison between different numbers of classes and the number of underlying classes. For choosing the best-fitting model, the Bayesian Information Criterion (BIC) and Vuong–Lo–Mendell–Rubin (VLMR) and adjusted Lo–Mendell–Rubin likelihood ratio tests were used as the statistical criteria. The model with the lowest BIC value is considered to provide a better fit to the data, while a p value higher than .05 for VLMR and LMR indicates that the model with one less class should be rejected in favour of the estimated model (Lo, Mendell, & Rubin, 2001). In addition, classification quality, usefulness, the interpretableness of the latent classes and the reasonableness of the solutions in relation to the model and to previous research findings are considered when comparing different models.

Comparison of groups

For categorical variables, we carried out crosstabs with groups, and for continuous variables we carried out a one-way ANOVA and subsequent Tukey HSD *post hoc* pairwise comparisons in order to validate the emergent profiles by comparing them on various criterion variables. Methods of LPA were implemented by *Mplus* 6.1 (Muthén & Muthén, 1998–2010), ANOVAs by PASW 18. Missing values in the clustering variables were imputed by the expectation–maximization (EM) algorithm as implemented in the PASW program. Only about .5% of the item scores measuring engagement and burnout were missing.

Table 1. Information criteria values for different class solutions.

Number of classes	Sample size adjusted BIC	p_{VLMR}	p_{LMR}	Entropy	Group sizes
1	8911.257	–	–	–	759
2	8761.889	<.0001	<.0001	.828	597/162
3	8690.227	.0416	.0452	.855	201/506/52
4	8619.357	.0085	.0095	.869	390/212/118/39
5	*8591.025*	*.2577*	*.2683*	*.870*	*402/24/35/112/186*
6	8563.992	.3706	.3759	.875	31/406/18/190/95/19

Results

The first aim was to examine what kinds of school engagement and burnout profiles can be identified. The results from a series of LPAs (Table 1 for fit indices) showed that the BIC value decreased when additional latent classes were added, whereas the VLMR and LMR tests and interpretation provided support for the five-group solution. In addition, classification quality, usefulness, the interpretableness of the latent classes and the reasonableness of the solutions in relation to the model supported the five-class solution. These groups were labelled, according to the score mean profiles, as *engaged, stressed, high cynicism, moderate cynicism* and *emerging cynicism* (Table 2). Figure 1 presents the *z*-score means on the clustering variables by profiles. The largest group (50%) was formed by those *engaged* in school. They scored moderate on school engagement and relatively low on all three school burnout dimensions. The second group was labelled *stressed* (4%), as they reported very high levels of exhaustion and inadequacy. Further, we identified three groups of students who reported feeling cynical towards school. Those in the *high cynicism (burnout)* group (5%) were characterized by high levels of exhaustion and inadequacy, but especially of cynicism. They were in risk of school burnout. Those in the *moderate cynicism (15%)* and *emerging cynicism* (bored) groups (26%) showed similar profiles with high cynicism group but of a gradually decreasing magnitude. These results showed that almost half (46%) of these young people felt cynical towards school. The results showed only a small statistically significant gender difference $\chi^2(4) = 11.610, p = .021$: the moderate *cynicism* group contained relatively more boys (adjusted residual = 3.0) than girls (adjusted residual = -3.0).

Second, we examined differences between these five profiles in socio-digital participation, competence and school engagement when using ICT (Tables 3 and 4). The results for intensity of socio-digital participation revealed statistically significant difference between intensity and group. Post hoc pairwise comparisons revealed differences between the engaged and the other profiles: engaged students used socio-digital technologies less intensively than the others. The results revealed a statistically significant difference between advanced socio-digital competence and group. Pairwise comparisons revealed differences between the engaged and moderate cynicism groups: those in the moderate cynicism group gave higher appraisals of their socio-digital competencies than those in the engaged group. Next, we examined between-group differences in intensity of educational use of socio-digital technologies. Pairwise comparisons revealed differences between engaged and high or moderate cynicism groups: the high and moderate cynicism groups reported using socio-digital technologies for educational purposes more intensively than the engaged. The results revealed differences in engagement when using socio-digital technologies at school and group. Pairwise comparisons revealed differences between the engaged and high and moderate cynicism groups: the high and moderate

Table 2. Mean differences in variables between groups.

Variable	1. Engaged $n = 402, M$	SD	2. Stressed $n = 24, M$	SD	3. Highly cynical $n = 35, M$	SD	4. Moderately cynical $n = 112, M$	SD	5. Emerging cynicism $n = 186, M$	SD	F(df1,df2)	p	η_p^2	Pairwise comparisons
Engagement	5.10	1.15	4.12	1.50	3.24	1.67	3.51	1.25	3.95	1.29	60.06(4,752)	<.001	.24	2,3,4,5 < 1 3,4 < 5
Exhaustion	2.02	.75	4.91	.69	3.91	1.31	3.29	1.03	2.76	.81	134.23(4.752)	<.001	.42	1 < 2,3,4,5 5 < 2,3,4 4 < 2,3 3 < 2
Cynicism	1.32	.37	2.33	.46	5.44	.41	3.94	.42	2.68	.34	1894.66(4,751)	<.001	.91	1 < 2,3,4,5 2 < 3,4,5 5 < 3,4 4 < 3
Inadequacy	1.94	.93	4.48	1.24	4.49	1.23	3.56	1.14	2.82	1.05	117.17(4,749)	<.001	.39	1 < 2,3,4,5 5 < 2,3,4 4 < 2,3

Note: Pairwise comparisons column shows which group differences are statistically significant at $p < .05$ (with Bonferroni correction).

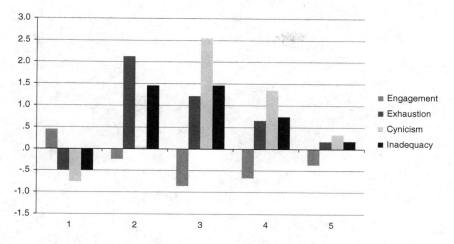

Figure 1. Standardized means on the clustering variables by profiles.

cynicism students reported that they would be more academically engaged and hardworking at school if they were able to make more use of ICT at school.

Discussion

Our results demonstrate that, already in elementary school, students display diverse patterns of simultaneous school engagement and burnout. Our results show that most of the young people are engaged to "bildung". However, we argue some of them; in particular, those cynical towards school might need new practices in schools, such as new technology, in which to engage in "bildung". As expected, and consistent with earlier research (e.g., Tuominen-Soini & Salmela-Aro, 2014), diverse groups representing different combinations of school engagement and burnout, emerged from the data. Half of the sample was engaged. However, compared with the earlier study among high school students (Tuominen-Soini & Salmela-Aro, 2014), in the present study the engaged group was only moderately rather than highly engaged. The results showed that socio-digital technologies appeared to play only a minor role in the free time and school activities of this engaged group. Compared with the engaged students, the stressed students were more exhausted and felt inadequate as a student. In the earlier study on high school students, the stressed group was also quite high in engagement (Tuominen-Soini & Salmela-Aro, 2014). Among the present study however, the stressed group was extremely high in exhaustion and inadequacy as a student and low in engagement. Moreover, the present stressed group was quite small, accounting for only about 4%. Interestingly, three groups emerged in which cynicism towards school was elevated. These groups were named high, moderate and emerging cynicism. The three groups had similar profiles but

Table 3. Correlations, means and standard deviations.

Variable	1	2	3	4	5	6	7	8	Mean	SD
Intensity of socio-digital participation									3.74	1.21
									3.47	1.20
School engagement when using socio-digital technologies	.30**									
Intensity of educational use of socio-digital technologies	.39**	.26**							2.25	.88
Advanced socio-digital competence	.35**	.14**	.32**						2.00	1.04
Engagement	−.10**	−.15**	.04	−.20					4.47	1.42
Exhaustion	.25**	.20**	.23**	.10*	−.24**				2.57	1.10
Cynicism	.23**	.22**	.16**	.15**	−.50**	.59**			2.27	1.24
Inadequacy	.28**	.20**	.17**	.14**	−.34**	.65**	.64**		2.59	1.30

*Correlation is significant at the .05 level (2-tailed).
**Correlation is significant at the .01 level (2-tailed).

Table 4. Mean differences in variables between groups.

Variable	1. Engaged $n = 402$, M	SD	2. Stressed $n = 24$, M	SD	3. Highly cynical $n = 35$, M	SD	4. Moderately cynical $n = 112$, M	SD	5. Emerging cynicism $n = 186$, M	SD	F(df1,df2)	p	η_p^2	Pairwise comparisons
Intensity of socio-digital participation	3.49	1.17	4.55	.87	4.41	1.30	3.94	1.16	3.91	1.22	11.73(4,735)	<.001	.06	1 < 2,3,4,5
School engagement when using socio-digital technologies	3.27	1.23	3.59	1.15	4.07	1.17	3.89	1.00	3.53	1.15	8.45(4,713)	<.001	.05	1 < 3,4
Intensity of educational use of socio-digital technologies	2.13	.73	2.45	1.11	2.66	1.45	2.46	1.07	2.22	.83	4.89(4,719)	.001	.03	1 < 3,4
Advanced socio-digital competence	1.88	.96	2.14	.97	2.36	1.40	2.28	1.14	2.02	1.03	4.34(4,713)	.002	.02	1 < 4

Note: Pairwise comparisons column shows which group differences are statistically significant at $p < .05$ (with Bonferroni correction).

differed in the relative magnitudes of the dimensions of exhaustion, cynicism and inadequacy. In these profiles, cynicism was the dominant dimension. The high cynicism group—which was in risk of burnout—was the smallest, comprising 5% of the students, while the moderate cynicism contained 15%, and the emerging cynicism group 26% of the students. Importantly, almost half of the students at the end of the elementary school had a profile characterized by feelings of high cynicism towards school.

One of the reasons behind this cynicism towards school may be that these particular students experience the current modes of learning and instruction at school as disengaging. If so, this could indicate the existence of a gap between certain segments of the digital native generation and school practices. The newest generations of digital natives are used to active personal and collaborative participation in the use of socio-digital technologies, whereas educational practices in Finland tend to use traditional media in the context of teacher-controlled working with narrow textbook-based tasks (Hakkarainen et al., 2000). Moreover, the recent PISA (OECD, 2013), which revealed that Finland was ranked among the bottom five countries on the item of liking school, can also be related to this widening gap between prevailing educational practices and the new digital native generation. These observations need to be taken seriously, if we are not to have a cynical digital generation at risk for dropping out, first from school, and then from society as a whole. We argue that disengaged students, such as cynical students, might be more engaged if they are able to make more intensive use of socio-digital technologies as facilitators in their educational activities (Wang et al., 2015). Importantly, the cynical students in our sample reported that they would be more engaged if they could make greater use of ICT at school. Schools need to develop new pedagogical methods and practices that will engage the new digital generations. These issues need to be addressed in the ongoing educational reform in Finland through the promotion of student-centred and project- and phenomenon-based projects capitalizing on the collaborative use of socio-digital technologies. As digital natives are highly familiar with self-directed and collaborative activities, various forms of game-based learning could provide novel pedagogical possibilities for engaging these individuals. Educational activities mediated by socio-digital technologies would be likely to motivate those who are already deeply involved in socio-digital participation. The possible widening gap between digital natives and the practices of their schools needs to be taken seriously.

Our results are quite consistent with earlier studies conducted in the high school context (e.g., Li & Lerner, 2011; Roeser & Peck, 2003) suggesting that the majority of young people stay academically quite engaged, remain psychologically healthy, and respond rather well to the multiple challenges associated with their studies. However, our results also revealed that 26% of the elementary students were in the emerging cynicism group, a profile which suggested that these students are disengaging and bored at school (Wang & Peck, 2013).

Moreover, 5% of the students already in the end of elementary school were burned out and 15% were in risk of burnout which should be taken seriously. In similar vein, Roeser, Eccles, and Sameroff (1998) have argued that adolescents who show signs of psychological distress during their high school years are also those who begin to disengage from school later on, although some young people will continue to function well despite experiencing feelings of emotional distress. Recognizing the fact that students show different patterns of combined school engagement and burnout in elementary school is important in order to effectively consider alternative ways of responding to their varying needs. Schools should foster engagement in cynical students and so reduce their risk of alienation from school. We should also not ignore stressed students, who are susceptible to exhaustion, feelings of inadequacy and fear of failure. Adequate student welfare services and a learning environment that does not highlight social comparison and competition might promote well-being and academic functioning among this group. Schools should pay special attention to students with different types of adjustment problems and risks, not only in order to support their well-being in school but also to promote their long-term educational attainment and adjustment.

Limitations and future research

This study was conducted in Helsinki and thus one must be cautious about generalizing the results to elementary schools in Finland or in other countries. Additional studies are needed to replicate these findings in other countries, in different educational contexts, and among more heterogeneous populations to further understand patterns of engagement and burnout among early adolescents. Here, we report only cross-sectional results. All the variables were assessed using student self-reports, and hence information on students' attendance and adherence to school rules, along with sociometric information from peers and teachers and interviews is lacking. While the purpose was specifically to look into adolescents' own experiences of and feelings about their academic and emotional functioning, the inclusion of control variables might have reduced self-report bias. Moreover, interviews and teacher, parent or peer data could be used in future research to supplement self-report data. Because adolescents' participation in using socio-digital technologies is often hyper intensive in nature, retrospective assessment of usage patterns should be complemented with media use diaries. Socio-digital technologies have emerged rapidly and adolescents' ways of using them are in flux. Some of the measures employed here have not been used before, and the measures of socio-digital competence, in particular, could involve self-report bias.

Despite these limitations, this study has several strengths. By linking various dimensions of academic functioning and by utilizing analytical approach, which examines the person as a whole, we were able to focus on individual differences in engagement and burnout. New inventories assessing the constructs of school burnout and engagement were used. By including recent data, we also gained some information about the current situation and about the challenges that face early adolescents who are members of the new digital generation.

Implications

This study has several implications for educational and bildung-psychology. First, in Finnish schools technology is either not used or is used in an encapsulated way that does not promote students' interests, bildung and engagement. Outside school, however, these new digital generations engage with a diversity of novel information technologies. We would argue that familiarity with these new technologies may also cause adolescents to develop bildung and knowledge acquisition practices that conflict with the often more traditional practices emphasized in school. Further, the fact that these informal settings provide infinite learning opportunities carries the risk that formal education institutions will inadvertently engender cynicism towards school among some students. It is important to acknowledge the value of these informal learning contexts and instead of seeking to combat them, blaming technology or, even worse, labelling students as incapable, try to bridge this gap. To be able to capitalize on the use of educational technologies, it would be important to build on the novel learning practices made possible by the introduction of socio-digital technologies in the school context. Intensive engagement in socio-digital activities competes with after-school resources that should be deployed on other activities. If a student makes excessive use of ICT to the extent that it takes up time that would otherwise be allocated to other important areas of life, it is likely to have negative effects on school engagement and may also lead to symptoms of burnout. Also, spending most of their leisure hours engaged in ICT will leave students struggling to find the time to do everything else required by the school. Moreover, the pressure of being online and keeping up with one's media feed is inevitably a continuous distraction, and challenges a students' ability to engage in their studies. This may cause students to feel that they are in a constant hurry, leading to feelings of exhaustion and inadequacy. In these cases, the educational sector may need to find ways of providing students with adequate scaffolding and support to develop practices that enable them to critically evaluate and regulate their use of time.

Conclusions

In conclusion, our results demonstrate that students in elementary school display diverse patterns of school engagement and burnout. The results indicate that early adolescence is not consistently a time of either school engagement and well-being or disengagement and distress. Most students are engaged and thrive at school, some students are stressed and exhausted, some students are disengaged but still get along quite well, while a small minority of students display both low engagement and school adjustment problems. However, their engagement might be enhanced by employing socio-digital technologies that support inquiry-, phenomenon- and project-based pedagogical practices that could make school education a more engaging experience.

Disclosure statement

No potential conflict of interest was reported by the authors.

Funding

This study is part of ongoing Mind-the-Gap between Digital Natives and Educational practices project (Academy of Finland 265528). It has also been supported by Riksbankens Jubileumsfond's grant to Kimmo Alho and Academy of Finland project 273872 (TULOS program) to Katariina Salmela-Aro.

References

Appleton, J. J., Christenson, S. L., & Furlong, M. J. (2008). Student engagement with school: Critical conceptual and methodological issues of the construct. *Psychology in the Schools, 45*, 369–386. doi:10.1002/pits.20303

Bask, M., & Salmela-Aro, K. (2013). Burned out to drop out: Exploring the relationship between school burnout and school dropout. *European Journal of Psychology of Education, 28*, 511–528. doi:10.1007/s10212-012-0126-5

Bennett, S., Maton, K., & Kervin, L. (2008). The 'digital natives' debate: A critical review of the evidence. *British Journal of Educational Technology, 39*, 775–786.

European Commission. (2013). *Survey of schools: ICT in education*. Belgium: European Union.

Gee, J. P., & Hayes, E. R. (2011). *Language and learning in the digital age*. London: Routledge.

Hakkarainen, K., Ilomäki, L., Lipponen, L., Muukkonen, H., Rahikainen, M., Tuominen, T., … Lehtinen, E. (2000). Students' skills and practices of using ICT: Results of a national assessment in Finland. *Computers & Education, 34*, 103–117.

Ito, M., Baumer, S., Bittandi, M., Boyd, D., Cody, R., Herr-Stephenson, B., … Tripp, L. (2010). *Hanging out, messing around, and geeking out*. Cambridge, MA: MIT Press.

Janosz, M., Archambault, I., Morizot, J., & Pagani, L. S. (2008). School engagement trajectories and their differential predictive relations to dropout. *Journal of Social Issues, 64*, 21–40. doi:10.1111/j.1540-4560.2008.00546.x

Li, Y., & Lerner, R. M. (2011). Trajectories of school engagement during adolescence: Implications for grades, depression, delinquency, and substance use. *Developmental Psychology, 47*, 233–247. doi:10.1037/a0021307

Lo, Y., Mendell, N. R., & Rubin, D. B. (2001). Testing the number of components in a normal mixture. *Biometrika, 88*, 767–778. doi:10.1093/biomet/88.3.767

Murdock, K. (2013). Texting while stressed: Implications for students' burnout, sleep, and well-being. *Psychology of Popular Media Culture, 2*, 207–221. doi:10.1037/ppm0000012

Muthén, L. K., & Muthén, B. O. (1998–2010). *Mplus user's guide* (6th ed.). Los Angeles, CA: Author.

OECD. (2009). *Education at glance*. Paris: Author.

OECD. (2013). *PISA 2012 results: Ready to learn (Volume III) students' engagement, drive and self-beliefs*. Paris: Author.

OECD. (2015). *The ABC of gender equity in education*. Paris: Author.

Palfrey, J., & Gasser, U. (2011). Reclaiming an awkward term: What we might learn from "Digital Natives". In M. Thomas (Ed.), *Deconstructing digital natives: Young people, technology, and the new literacies* (pp. 186–204). London: Routledge.

Prensky, M. (2001). Digital natives, digital immigrants. *The New Horizon, 9*(5), 1–6.

Roeser, R., & Peck, S. (2003). Patterns and pathways of educational achievement across adolescence: A holistic-developmental perspective. *New Directions for child and adolescent development, 101*, 39–62.

Roeser, R. W., Eccles, J. S., & Sameroff, A. J. (1998). Academic and emotional functioning in early adolescence: Longitudinal relations, patterns, and prediction by experience in middle school. *Development and Psychopathology, 10*, 321–352. doi:10.1017/S0954579498001631

Roeser, R. W., Galloway, M., Casey-Cannon, S., Watson, C., Keller, L., & Tan, E. (2008). Identity representations in patterns of school achievement and well-being among early adolescent girls: Variable- and person-centered approaches. *The Journal of Early Adolescence, 28*, 115–152. doi:10.1177/0272431607308676

Salmela-Aro, K., Kiuru, N., Leskinen, E., & Nurmi, J.-E. (2009). School burnout inventory (SBI): Reliability and validity. *European Journal of Psychological Assessment, 25*, 48–57. doi:10.1027/1015-5759.25.1.48

Salmela-Aro, K., & Tynkkynen, L. (2012). Gendered pathways in school burnout among adolescents. *Journal of Adolescence, 35*, 929–939. doi:10.1016/j.adolescence.2012.01.001

Salmela-Aro, K., & Upadyaya, K. (2012). The schoolwork engagement inventory: Energy, dedication and absorption (EDA). *European Journal of Psychological Assessment, 28*, 60–67. doi:10.1027/1015-5759/a000091

Salmela-Aro, K., & Upadyaya, K. (2014). School burnout and engagement in the context of demands-resources model. *British Journal of Educational Psychology, 84*, 137–151. doi:10.1111/bjep.12018

Skinner, E., Marchand, G., Furrer, C., & Kinderman, T. (2008). Engagement and disaffection in the classroom: A part of a larger motivational dynamic? *Journal of Educational Psychology, 100*, 765–781.

Tuominen-Soini, H., & Salmela-Aro, K. (2014). Schoolwork engagement and burnout among Finnish high school students and young adults: Profiles, progressions and educational outcomes. *Developmental Psychology, 50*, 649–662.

Vallerand, R. J., Salvy, S.-J., Mageau, G. A., Elliot, A. J., Denis, P. L., Grouzet, F. M., & Blanchard, C. (2007). On the role of passion in performance. *Journal of Personality, 75*, 505–534.

Wang, M.-T., Chow, A., Hofkens, T., & Salmela-Aro, K. (2015). The trajectories of student emotional engagement and school burnout with academic and psychological development: Findings from Finnish adolescents. *Learning and Instruction, 36*, 57–65.

Wang, M.-T., & Peck, S. C. (2013). Adolescent educational success and mental health vary across school engagement profiles. *Developmental Psychology, 49*, 1266–1276. doi:10.1037/a0030028

Veen, W., & Vrakking, B. (2008). *Homo zappiens: Growing up in a digital age*. London: Network Continuum Education.

Vermunt, J. K., & Magidson, J. (2002). Latent class cluster analysis. In J. A. Hagenaars & A. L. McCutcheon (Eds.), *Applied latent class analysis* (pp. 89–106). Cambridge: Cambridge University Press.

Fostering pupils' lifelong learning competencies in the classroom: evaluation of a training programme using a multivariate multilevel growth curve approach

Marko Lüftenegger ⓘ, Monika Finsterwald, Julia Klug ⓘ, Evelyn Bergsmann, Rens van de Schoot ⓘ, Barbara Schober and Petra Wagner

ABSTRACT
Evidence-based interventions to promote lifelong learning are needed not only in continuing education but also in schools, which lay important cornerstones for lifelong learning. The present article reports evaluation results about the effectiveness of one such training programme (TALK). TALK aims to systematically implement the enhancement of lifelong learning in secondary schools by optimizing teaching in terms of developing pupils' competencies for lifelong learning. TALK is conducted within the framework of a three-semester course of studies for secondary school teachers. In order to evaluate the effectiveness of TALK, a questionnaire study with 1144 pupils was conducted in the form of a pretest–posttest–posttest design for both training and control groups. Multivariate multilevel growth curve analyses showed the benefit of TALK in terms of both pupils' perceptions of classroom instructions and their individual motivation. Finally, TALK's contribution to promote lifelong learning in schools is discussed and implications are given.

Introduction

Lifelong learning has been seen as an important socio-political concern since the 1970s. Since then, there has been a shift in policy from lifelong learning as a means of personal development and social progress (Faure et al., 1972) to lifelong learning as an economic necessity (OECD, 1997). The process of personal development (known as "Bildung" in German or "formation" in French) consists of continuous learning and takes place across the lifespan. This development is an existential phenomenon because the knowledge, skills, attitudes and beliefs we have learned must be continually re-invented or renewed in novel situations. Besides personal development, the economic rationale for lifelong learning focuses on the necessity of being able to handle constant change and transition as a result of rapid technological and scientific changes, organizational innovation, and global competition (Field, 2012). This capacity to deal with the increasing insecurity of economic life requires the lifelong development of skills and knowledge. In our rapidly changing (Western) society, both rationales are crucial for the development of the individual.

As permanent learning is indispensable, the question arises as to what can be done to ensure successful lifelong learning. In our approach, lifelong learning is defined as the competence for learning throughout one's lifetime, a domain-specific competence that requires motivation and self-regulated learning (SRL) (Klug, Krause, Schober, Finsterwald, & Spiel, 2014).

Even though lifelong learning is often seen as primarily a topic for further education, school is considered by both researchers and politicians to lay the cornerstones for preparing pupils for lifelong learning (Gorard, 2009; OECD, 1997). However, "educational systems and practices in many countries are obviously poorly prepared, and often ineffective, concerning the development of lifelong learning competencies in schools" (Schober, Luftenegger, Wagner, Finsterwald, & Spiel, 2013, p. 116). This concerns both the motivational beliefs of pupils, which decrease the longer they stay in school (Wigfield, Eccles, Schiefele, Roeser, & Davis-Kean, 2006), as well as of teachers, who feel inadequately prepared to foster pupils' lifelong learning competencies (Hardré & Sullivan, 2008).

The Austrian Federal Ministry for Education, Arts and Culture tasked the Department of Applied Psychology of the University of Vienna (Austria) with developing, conducting and evaluating a teacher education programme for secondary teachers in the context of continuing education that enables them to promote core competencies for lifelong learning among their pupils within their regular teaching (this programme is called TALK[1]).

A sound literature review had shown that there are no evaluated programmes for teachers that explicitly deal with lifelong learning. Related programmes on motivation or self-regulated learning (=SRL; the two core determinants of lifelong learning) have rarely been implemented in regular classrooms, were usually restricted to an individual subject area (mostly math or reading/writing) and often focus only on single aspects of motivation (e.g., interest) or SRL (e.g., learning strategies; for an overview, see Schober et al., 2013). Hence, we developed

---

1. Training programme to foster teacher competencies to encourage lifelong learning—translation of the German title: Trainingsprogramm zum Aufbau von LehrerInnenkompetenzen zur Förderung von Lebenslangem Lernen.

and implemented a training programme to foster lifelong learning (Schober, Finsterwald, Wagner, Lüftenegger, Aysner, & Spiel, 2007) which follows standards for evidence and transfer to practice (e.g., Flay et al., 2005).

In this article, we evaluate whether the already proven gain in teacher competencies (Finsterwald, Wagner, Schober, Lüftenegger, & Spiel, 2013) through the TALK programme also led to corresponding, perceptual changes in teaching and pupils' competencies for lifelong learning.

Background of the teacher education programme TALK

Theoretical foundation of the content

Lifelong learning is, in its original form, a matter of social policy. Within educational and psychological science, two core determinants of lifelong learning independent of specific contextual features are discussed (Schober et al., 2007): (1) an enduring motivation and appreciation for learning and education and (2) those competencies that are needed to successfully realize this motivation through concrete learning activities. We assume an interactive effect of both determinants: To achieve a high lifelong learning competence, both motivation and self-regulated learning have to be high. If either motivation or SRL was low, high values on the other determinants are of little or no consequence for lifelong learning and behaviour. That is to say, individuals will successfully master the demands of lifelong learning when they see learning and the acquisition of knowledge as valuable and attractive (high *motivation*) and have the skills associated with SRL. Both are considered as modifiable by training, experience and reflection, for example.

Research on these two core determinants of lifelong learning is manifold and interconnected. Determinants can be identified that can be found in both research areas, especially when considering literature on how to foster them: Schunk and Zimmerman (2008), for example, presented how the complex construct of motivation is related to the complex construct of SRL and list different sources of motivation that can play a role in self-regulation (e.g., interest, goal orientation, self-efficacy, outcome expectations). Concerning motivation, TALK mainly focused on the expectancy–value theory (Wigfield & Eccles, 2000): According to this theory, pupils start to learn if they believe that they can be successful in performing a task (= expectancy), and if they consider the task to be important (= value). An example for an expectancy construct is self-efficacy (Bandura, 1997) and interest (Krapp, 2002) is considered a "value" construct.

Although reports of practical field applications and programmes in schools exist for fostering motivation and SRL (for an overview see Schober et al., 2013), not many have been tested in real classroom settings or focus, for example, on more than one aspect of motivation. However, empirical evidence from meta-analyses (Dignath & Büttner, 2008; Hattie, Biggs, & Purdie, 1996) showed medium to strong mean effect sizes of SRL intervention programmes on pupils outcomes (e.g., achievement, learning behaviour, motivation, emotions). Within the field of motivation enhancement (especially fostering interest), teaching according to the principles of self-determination theory (SDT; Ryan & Deci, 2000) is often recommended, particularly because of its practical utility (Niemiec & Ryan, 2009). This theory specifies three basic needs: autonomy, competence and relatedness. A multitude of empirical education studies exist about SDT, most emphasizing personal and contextual factors that facilitate optimal learning, engagement and well-being (see Guay, Ratelle, & Chanal, 2008). It has been shown that the degree of autonomy provided is associated with greater pupil engagement, enhanced intrinsic motivation/interest, higher self-esteem/perceived competence and a higher quality of learning (Guay et al., 2008). From a perspective of SDT (Deci & Ryan, 1985), autonomous behaviour constitutes self-regulation. Therefore, the relevance of providing autonomy is found very often in practical recommendations or teacher programmes within the context of motivation enhancement, like the TARGET framework[2] (Epstein, 1988; Lüftenegger, van de Schoot, Schober, Finsterwald, & Spiel, 2014).

But being supportive of autonomy does not imply that one should provide choices without any structure and supervision. Receiving information and adequate feedback about the learning progress as well as about successes and failures is important for both regulating one's own learning and motivation (Hattie & Timperley, 2007). Pupils should experience that it is normal to make errors; mistakes are allowed in the classroom and are important for the learning process and future learning since they help to establish accurate mental models (e.g., Hattie & Timperley, 2007; Steuer, Rosentritt-Brunn, & Dresel, 2013). Beyond this, feedback is relevant when considering pupils' basic need for perceived competence that is closely tied to the concept of self-efficacy. When studying the SRL literature about recommendations for classrooms, a large variety of different theoretical conceptions of SRL can be found. Our understanding of SRL is rooted in a social cognitive perspective in which some basic assumptions about the nature of SRL are common in most models (see e.g., Zimmerman & Moylan, 2009): (1) a set of skills or abilities are necessary for SRL as well as adaptive attitudes and beliefs that can be taught and learned by almost everyone. (2) The models stress the importance of setting goals or having performance standards/criteria. (3) Learners are active constructive participants in the learning process. (4) Self-regulated activities mediate between personal and contextual characteristics and the learning outcome. (5) SRL is seen as situation specific.

Although self-regulation in learning is inherent and ubiquitous (Winne, 2005), productive SRL does not take place automatically but SRL can be learned and improved in appropriate learning environments. Research about the conditions

---

2. The TARGET framework consists of six instructional strategies or dimensions (Task, Authority, Recognition, Grouping arrangements, Evaluation practices, Time allocation) with which a mastery goal orientation can be fostered in classrooms. These six instructional dimensions are assumed to overlap and interact.

that facilitate SRL showed, for example, that teachers can support pupils' SRL by providing differentiated help with generating goals and plans, self-monitoring and evaluating progress (Sierens, Vansteenkiste, Goossens, Soenens, & Dochy, 2009). A positive feedback culture is also needed to calibrate one's learning (Hattie & Timperley, 2007). Formulating clear expectations is another important issue (Sierens et al., 2009).

Structure of the teacher training programme

TALK was conceptualized for secondary school teachers who would participate in the training programme as school teams. It was delivered as a course of studies in a university setting and lasted three semesters. It embraces a total of 130 h (blocked into one or two-day workshops) and took place ten times in the first semester, six times during the second semester and four times in the third semester.

In the first two semesters ("intensive phase"), the focus was on encouraging teachers to reflect and optimize their classroom instruction in accordance with the session contents. The sessions explicitly covered the topic of lifelong learning as well as target variables from the fields of motivation and SRL (see Table 1 for an overview of the topics). The teachers learned about scientific results and how to transfer them into their daily classroom teaching and their schools.

Table 1. Overview of the topics addressed in the TALK sessions during the intensive phase.

Topics	Subtopics
Lifelong learning (LLL)	• Introduction to concept/reflection • Teachers plan LLL projects for their pupils and present the results of these projects
Motivation	• Motivation: introduction (action process model of motivation) • Learning motivation • Interest • Feedback (including self-worth, attribution theory, frame of references)
Self-regulated learning (SRL)	• SRL: introduction (process models; learning competences) & possibilities for promotion • Self-awareness: teachers plan their own SRL projects & work on them
Social competencies	• Cooperative learning • Conflict resolution (including violence prevention)
Cognitive competencies	• Critical thinking • Creative thinking (including problem solving)
School as an organization/project management	• School as a learning organization (incl. systemic view of organizations; importance of teacher cooperation) • Project management (how to implement projects in schools successfully)

BILDUNG-PSYCHOLOGY

In the third semester ("supervision phase"), the focus turned to ensuring sustainability: teachers planed and initiated projects within their classes directly tied to TALK. Correspondence between project plan and the principles of TALK was ensured, and teachers were supervised across all phases of the implementation of their projects (for more information about curriculum, structure and didactic principles of TALK see Schober et al., 2007).

Aims of the current evaluation

In this article, evaluation results of TALK, a pilot programme in the form of a three-semester teacher education programme for teachers in the context of lifelong learning, are presented. The effectiveness of TALK on teachers' competencies in fostering lifelong learning (= proximal goals) has already been shown (see Finsterwald et al., 2013). However, evidence of the transfer effect in daily classroom teaching is still lacking. More concretely, it was of interest to investigate whether this competence gain also led to (1) corresponding, perceptual changes in teaching and in (2) their pupils' competencies for lifelong learning.

The aim of this evaluation is to investigate whether these distal goals of TALK were reached.

Regarding the first goal, we assume that participating in TALK would lead to perceivable changes in teachers' classroom practice in comparison with classrooms of teachers who did not attend the programme. Concretely, we expect training effects concerning perceptions of the classroom that are considered useful in fostering motivation and SRL, namely reports of more autonomy, a good climate in handling failure and more opportunities for pupils to acquire competencies to manage all phases of SRL, in comparison with the control group.

Furthermore, we suppose that participating in TALK would have an impact on pupils' development of lifelong learning competencies. Concretely, the development of pupils' interest and self-efficacy and their competencies to manage all phases of SRL are expected to be affected. With respect to all goals formulated for the evaluation, it is assumed that the developments assessed for the classrooms and pupils in the training group would be more positive than those found in a corresponding control group. Figure 1 shows a graphical representation of the different goal levels.

Method

Design

In order to evaluate the summative effectiveness of TALK, surveys were conducted within the framework of a training and control group comparison (a pretest–posttest 1 [end of intensive phase]–posttest 2 [end of supervision phase] design). The control groups consisted of matched samples of teachers and pupils who did not participate in any intervention.

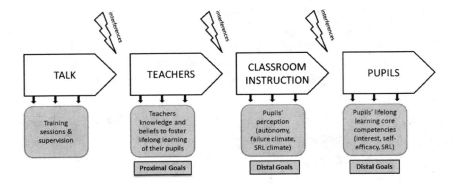

Figure 1. Goal levels, possible interferences during transfer and expected effects of the TALK programme.

Sample

In order to participate in the TALK programme, school principals of secondary schools in Vienna and Lower Austria were required to submit applications naming a team of teacher participants. In sum, 45 teachers from 14 Austrian secondary schools were admitted to TALK (two to five teachers per school); 40 teachers completed the training programme. At the start of the programme, each teacher chose one class where the content of the programme was tested and implemented.

The pupils completed questionnaires at the beginning of the school year (also the beginning of the TALK training programme; pretest), at the end of this school year (also the end the intensive phase; posttest 1), and nine months later, in the middle of the following school year (end of the supervision phase; posttest 2).

In recruiting the control group, an announcement calling for participation in a longitudinal study on lifelong learning was sent to secondary schools. A total of 13 principals expressed their interest in having their schools participate. In order to obtain an equivalent control group, a matching procedure was used as proposed by Spiel et al. (2008). Statistical matching is assumed to mimic the comparison of individuals in a randomized experiment (Rubin, 1977). Generally, in these cases, propensity score matching is applied, a method which has been shown to provide unbiased estimates of the average training effect (D'Agostino, 2005). Spiel et al. (2008) propose a procedure that allows one to perform matching based on multiple raw covariate scores. First, the variables which are to be matched were selected on a theoretical basis. *School grade, perceived autonomy in classroom, perceived promotion of self-regulation in classroom, self-efficacy* and *learning competencies* were chosen as matching variables. Then, using these variables, Euclidean distances were calculated for the pre-test data. Finally, matches were identified (for each training class a matched control class was established according to the defined matching variables). To clarify whether group equivalence was attained, a multivariate variance analysis with all dependent variables at the first measuring point was calculated which did not detect any significant differences between the training and control groups.

In sum, the sample for the evaluation of the training programme TALK consisted of 1144 pupils (514 in the control group) attending 58 classes in 27 secondary schools. 52.1% of the pupils were female. The pupils were enrolled in Grades 5 (37.6%), 6 (24%) and 7 (38.4%) and were between 10 and 13 years old at the first measurement point. The average number of children per classroom was 19.72 (SD = 7.51).

Measures

Data were collected with paper-and-pencil questionnaires at all three measuring points (pre-test, post-test 1, post-test 2). All of the items were developed in the context of the TALK project (Schober et al., 2007), and validity could already be shown for a subsample in an empirical study about lifelong learning (Lüftenegger et al., 2012) (for an overview see Table 2). Internal consistencies of scales (Cronbach's α) were found to range from satisfactory to good for all constructs and all three measurement points.

Analytical approach

Multivariate multilevel growth curve analysis was used to analyse the data. Growth curve modelling allows researchers to analyse the differences among individuals in their growth over time. Two growth parameters are used to characterize these individual paths: (1) an initial level growth parameter (= intercept) and (2) a linear growth rate parameter (= slope). Both these parameters are viewed as factors and vary between subjects.

In this study, the growth curve approach was applied for both the three classroom perception outcomes together (Models 1a, 2a, 3a; Research Question 1) and the three pupil outcomes together (Models 1b, 2b, 3b; Research Question 2). The advantage of this multivariate approach is that it also allows one to estimate the association between the growth trajectories of all three outcome variables for both research questions. Additionally, a multilevel approach was used to account for the nested structure of our data where individuals (pupils) are nested into groups (classes). This multilevel approach allowed us to model not only differences between pupils but also differences between classes in the growth trajectories of the investigated variables. For this study, a three-level analysis in terms of time (first level), individual (second level), and class (third level) was conducted.

The analyses were conducted in three steps, using Mplus 6.1 (Muthén & Muthén, 1998–2010). First, we analysed Model 1 with three latent growth curve models separately for each of the three outcome variables, considering

BILDUNG-PSYCHOLOGY

Table 2. Measures.

Variable	n^*	Reliability**	Sample item	Description
Interest in instruction	3	.72/.70/.74	In this class, I am learning something that I think is important	Value and emotional valence were considered (Krapp, 2002)
Self-efficacy	3	.70/.73/.80	When I make the effort, I can solve even the more difficult problems in class	The items focused on efficacy expectations among pupils (Bandura, 1997)
SRL competencies	6	.77/.80/.83	After studying in this class, I think about whether I have made proper use of the time I had	The items were based on existing instruments (Perels, Gürtler & Schmitz, 2005; Pintrich & de Groot, 1990)
Perceived autonomy	7	.63/.72/.77	In this class, we make important decisions with the teacher	The aspects autonomy while learning in school and joint social responsibility in the classroom were included
SRL climate	7	.75/.79/.81	In this class, we are asked to assess our own learning success	The extent to which pupils experience the encouragement of SRL in the classroom was assessed
Failure climate	1		In this class, it is not a big deal when someone makes a mistake	

Notes: All of the items were rated on a six-point scale ranging from "absolutely false" (1) to "absolutely true" (6). A higher score indicated a higher expression of the quality in question.*Number of items.**Cronbach´s α for three measurement points.

the multilevel structure (Model 1). Second, we analysed the outcome variables simultaneously (Model 2—unconditional model). In a final step, the time-invariant variable group (0 = control group; 1 = training group) was added at the class level as predictor of the growth parameters of the outcome variables to test whether there are training effects (Model 3—conditional model). For the sake of clarity, only estimates of the final model, Model 3, are provided. Goodness of fit of the models was evaluated using common fit indices.

The rate of individuals omitting items (nonresponse) in this study was below 5% (for all items) and, as such, very small. The imputation of the missing values was accomplished with the NORM programme (Schafer & Graham, 2002) using full information maximum likelihood estimation, whereby all variables were drawn on in the generation of estimations.

Results

Perception of changes in classroom

Table 3 provides descriptive statistics for all perceived class and pupil outcomes at the three measurement points.

In order to investigate the first research question, that is, whether pupils' perceptions of classroom instruction change in the TALK classes, three growth curve models were conducted. The results of the model selection procedure are presented in Table 4.

Table 3. Descriptive statistics for all perceived class and pupil outcomes at the three measurement points.

		Training group				Control group			
Item	Wave	M	SD	Min	Max	M	SD	Min	Max
Perceived class outcomes									
Autonomy	1	3.72	0.81	1.57	5.86	3.60	0.76	1.86	5.57
	2	3.59	0.84	1.00	5.86	3.42	0.84	1.00	5.71
	3	3.51	0.92	1.00	6.00	3.34	0.89	1.00	6.00
Failure climate	1	5.02	1.28	1.00	6.00	5.03	1.25	1.00	6.00
	2	4.92	1.29	1.00	6.00	4.76	1.30	1.00	6.00
	3	4.82	1.30	1.00	6.00	4.58	1.45	1.00	6.00
SRL climate	1	4.16	0.92	1.00	6.00	4.07	0.84	1.00	6.00
	2	4.01	0.93	1.00	6.00	3.73	0.95	1.00	6.00
	3	4.00	0.97	1.00	6.00	3.64	0.92	1.14	6.00
Pupils outcomes									
Interest	1	4.15	1.11	1.00	6.00	4.08	1.11	1.00	6.00
	2	3.77	1.14	1.00	6.00	3.60	1.23	1.00	6.00
	3	3.54	1.22	1.00	6.00	3.37	1.30	1.00	6.00
Self-efficacy	1	4.94	0.82	1.00	6.00	5.02	0.79	1.00	6.00
	2	4.93	0.89	1.00	6.00	4.83	0.93	1.00	6.00
	3	4.84	0.93	1.00	6.00	4.75	0.96	1.00	6.00
SRL competencies	1	4.09	1.00	1.00	6.00	4.09	1.02	1.00	6.00
	2	4.01	1.11	1.00	6.00	3.99	1.11	1.00	6.00
	3	3.90	1.15	1.00	6.00	3.81	1.07	1.00	6.00

Model 3a, the multivariate multilevel growth curve model with group as predictor, had the lowest AIC and BIC value, indicating that this model offers the best trade-off between model fit (likelihood of the data) and complexity (number of parameters). Furthermore, an evaluation of model fit indices indicated that Model 3a demonstrates a good fit.

Results, see Table 5, showed significant means of intercepts and slopes of failure climate, autonomy and SRL climate. Significant within-level variance and between-level variance of the intercept mean of failure climate, autonomy, and SRL climate indicated that pupils and classes differed in their baseline levels in terms of classroom perception. Significant within-level variance and between-level variance of slope means of failure climate autonomy, and SRL climate indicated that pupils and classes changed in their autonomy, failure climate and SRL climate over time.

The intercepts for failure climate, autonomy and SRL climate were not significantly predicted by group indicating that there were no differences in the initial status of these variables between the training group and the control group. Therefore, no pre-test differences can be assumed. There was a significant slope of failure climate and SRL climate indicating a training effect in classroom perception. Declines in the perception of a positive failure climate and climate

Table 4. Model fit indices and model comparison for perceived class and pupil outcome variables.

Models	χ^2 (N = 388)	df	CFI	TLI	RMSEA	SRMR-W	SRMR-B	AIC	BIC
Class outcome variables									
1a Outcomes separate & multilevel	1342.69*	78	.43	.47	.119	.183	.408	27940.22	27979.41
2a Outcomes simultaneously & multilevel	276.92*	66	.90	.90	.053	.031	.407	26909.54	26971.12
3a Conditional training effect	228.86*	66	.93	.91	.046	.032	.181	26866.00	26945.37
Pupil outcome variables									
1b Outcomes separate & multilevel	1440.22*	78	.57	.60	.124	.226	.477	27869.14	27908.02
2b Outcomes simultaneously & multilevel	162.28*	66	.97	.97	.036	.032	.474	26669.77	26731.35
3b Conditional training effect	131.91*	66	.98	.98	.032	.031	.131	26649.17	26727.54

Notes: CFI = comparative fit index; TLI = Tucker-Lewis index; RMSEA = root-mean-square error of approximation; SRMR-W = Standardized-Root-Mean-Square-Residual Within-Level; SRMR-B = Standardized-Root-Mean-Square-Residual Between-Level; Conventional guidelines were followed whereby fit is considered adequate if the CFI and TLI values are >.90, the RMSEA is <.08, and the SRMR is <.08; AIC = Akaike information criterion; BIC = Bayesian information criterion (sample size adjusted); Models with lower information criterion values indicate a better model fit.*p < .001.

fostering SRL were less strong in the training group. No associations between group and autonomy were found (Table 5).

Changes in pupils' development of lifelong learning competencies

In order to investigate the second research question, that is, whether pupils' interest, self-efficacy and SRL competencies changed in the TALK classes, three growth curve models were conducted. The results of the model selection procedure are presented in Table 4.

Model 3b, the multivariate multilevel growth curve model with group as predictor, had the lowest AIC and BIC value. Furthermore, an evaluation of model fit indices indicated that Model 3b demonstrates a good fit. Results, see Table 5, showed significant means of slope and intercept of interest self-efficacy, and SRL.

Significant within-level variance and between-level variance of intercept means of interest self-efficacy and SRL indicated that pupils and classes differed in their baseline levels of interest, self-efficacy and SRL. Significant within-level variance and between-level variance around the slope means of interest and self-efficacy indicated that pupils and classes changed in their interest and self-efficacy over time. SRL slope mean variance was only significant on the within-level.

The intercepts for interest, self-efficacy and SRL were not significantly predicted by group, indicating that there were no differences in the initial status of these variables between the training group and the control group. Therefore, no pre-test differences can be assumed. There was a significant slope for self-efficacy, indicating a training effect. The decline of self-efficacy was less strong in the training group. Non-significant, although positive, associations of both interest and SRL with group were found.

Discussion

Given the fact that schools and teachers are poorly prepared and often ineffective in preparing pupils for lifelong learning, there is a need for high quality intervention programmes to better equip teachers to face this. However, to our knowledge, no systematically evaluated teacher programme dealing with the promotion of lifelong learning competencies exists (Schober et al., 2013). Therefore, we developed, conducted and evaluated a theoretically grounded teacher training programme called TALK that aimed to foster lifelong learning competencies in schools and lasted 18 months. Having already been able to show the effectiveness of TALK on changing teachers` competencies in fostering lifelong (see Finsterwald et al., 2013), we aimed to examine also the more distal goals of changes in (1) pupils' perceptions of their classroom and (2) their

Table 5. Multivariate multilevel growth curve models with training as a time-invariant covariate (Model 3a & Model 3b).

| | Model 3a—Perceived Class outcomes | | | | | | Model 3b—Pupils outcomes | | | | | |
| | Autonomy | | Failure climate | | SRL climate | | Interest | | Self-efficacy | | SRL competencies | |
	b	p	b	p	b	p	b	p	b	p	b	p
Means												
Intercept	3.61	<.001	5.02	<.001	4.05	<.001	4.04	<.001	5.00	<.001	4.10	<.001
Slope	−0.13	.001	−0.23	<.001	−0.21	<.001	−0.34	<.001	−0.14	.021	−0.14	<.001
Training on intercept	0.12	.102	−0.01	.943	0.11	.169	0.13	.293	−0.03	.588	0.01	.901
Training on slope	0.03	.275	0.13	.034	0.13	.002	0.04	.255	0.08	.017	0.05	.099
Variances												
Individual level (Pupils)												
Intercept	0.18	<.001	0.19	<.001	0.26	<.001	0.47	<.001	0.23	<.001	0.49	<.001
Slope	0.02	<.001	0.06	.023	0.02	.001	0.06	<.001	0.05	<.001	0.04	<.001
Class level												
Intercept	0.05	<.001	0.05	.003	0.06	<.001	0.16	<.001	0.02	.005	0.04	.009
Slope	0.01	.011	0.02	.003	0.01	.011	0.02	.006	0.01	.036	0.00	.830

Note: b = unstandardized regression coefficient.

lifelong learning competencies. On the whole, the results indicate that TALK is effective in fostering lifelong learning competencies in schools on several levels.

Turning to the training results, we found effects for pupils' perceptions of their classroom instruction. The assumption was that teachers' competence gains should result in changes in their teaching—alterations that pupils could actually perceive. Compared to pupils in control classes, pupils perceived both a more positive failure climate (important especially for fostering motivation) and a classroom climate more supportive of SRL (important for pupils' SRL competencies).

Although pupils in the training group perceived that their classroom provided more opportunities to acquire competencies to manage SRL in comparison with the control group, pupils from both groups did not differ in their self-reported decrease in competencies to manage SRL. One possible explanation for this could be that although pupils in training classes experienced a more supportive SRL climate, it will take more time for them to (successfully) apply their SRL in the classroom ("sleeper effect"). However, also concerning lifelong learning competencies, we found that pupils' self-efficacy beliefs did not decrease in the training group. Self-efficacy beliefs are not only crucial for pupils' motivation, and they also matter in all phases of SRL. Pupils high in self-efficacy are more likely to apply self-regulatory strategies than pupils low in self-efficacy (Pintrich & De Groot, 1990). Thus, even if TALK pupils did not apply SRL more successfully in class in comparison with the control pupils, they at least kept their self-efficacy beliefs that empower them to act as self-regulated learners. These results concerning self-efficacy are in accordance with previous results (Steuer et al., 2013) on the positive association of failure climate and academic self-concept (an expectancy belief and a construct very similar to self-efficacy).

Against our expectations, we found no effects for the perception of more autonomy by pupils in training classes. Consequently, we could also not find higher levels of interest and SRL competencies among pupils in the training classes. These results are in accordance to previous results of SDT research (Deci, Eghrari, Patrick, & Leone, 1994), as the degree of autonomy provided in classroom is associated with pupils' interest and SRL competencies.

The transfer of knowledge, beliefs or competencies gained in a teacher training to actual changes in pupils' competencies is by far not a trivial issue. There are a couple of sources of interference imaginable that could have accounted for TALK's failure to reach all of its distal goals. One possible explanation could be the possible mediating effect of the heterogeneous classroom projects: TALK teachers themselves developed projects for their class with a special focus on addressing points relevant to the situation in their schools. Certainly, this flexibility in accounting for individual differences between schools is a strength, especially in terms of teacher commitment and in fostering teachers' competencies. On the other hand, it is more difficult to secure training effects with such heterogeneous class projects in comparison with intervention programmes with direct transfer of more standardized projects into the classroom. Of course, further studies are needed to fully understand the mechanisms and preconditions of the transfer of knowledge both from trainers to teachers and from teachers to pupils.

Limitations of the present evaluation

Two limitations of this evaluation study should be noted. First, the schools involved in the evaluation either as intervention or control schools volunteered to do so. Therefore, with regard to external validity, the programme effects can be generalized to schools and teachers that are willing to take part in the programme.

Second, the fit index SRMR-B for Model 3a und Model 3b is only mediocre. However, practices associated with model evaluation of complex multilevel modelling using SRMR are problematic due to the lack of empirical research (Hsu, 2009). Monte Carlo simulations show that SRMR-B is sensitive for complex models and shows only reasonable statistical power in models with high ICC (Hsu, 2009). Nevertheless, all the other descriptive measures of model fit (CFI, TLI, RMSEA, SRMR-W) indices clearly indicate a good model fit (Browne & Cudeck, 1993) for Model 3a and Model 3b. Additionally, the descriptive measures of model parsimony (BIC, AIC) for both models clearly show that we found the best trade-off between model fit and model complexity.

Implications

These findings are relevant both for educational policies and for evidence-based interventions in the field of (teacher) education. In the last 15 years, many calls have gone out for education and psychology to follow other fields (like medicine and agriculture) in placing more reliance on evidence as a basis for the adoption of programmes and practices (Spiel, 2009). Standards for evidence and transfer to practice have been extensively defined (e.g., Flay et al., 2005), but the broad-based implementation of an evidence base in education research and practice has not been achieved yet, and evidence-based reform has not yet been established in the federal policies of most European nations (Spiel, 2009). However, the work of teachers in the classroom should no longer be driven and perpetuated by subjective criteria but rather by scientific knowledge based on evidence on what works.

The evaluation of the theoretically grounded intervention programme TALK is a good example of considering standards of evidence (see Flay et al., 2005) while testing for effectiveness. TALK was evaluated in real-world conditions and considered methodically important features such as proper sample size, matched control design, multi-informant and multi-method outcome assessment

BILDUNG-PSYCHOLOGY

(see Schober et al., 2013), psychometrically sound measures, nested data structure and missing data imputation.

Acknowledgement

This research was supported by grants from the Austrian Federal Ministry for Education, Arts and Culture (bm:ukk). Rens van de Schoot served as an advisor on this project and assisted with the data analyses in Mplus.

Disclosure statement

No potential conflict of interest was reported by the authors.

ORCID

Lüftenegger Marko ⓘ http://orcid.org/0000-0001-8112-976X
Klug Julia ⓘ http://orcid.org/0000-0002-6595-4505
van de Schoot Rens ⓘ http://orcid.org/0000-0001-7736-2091

References

Bandura, A. (1997). *Self-efficacy: The exercise of control*. New York, NY: Freeman.
Browne, M. W., & Cudeck, R. (1993). Alternative ways of assessing model fit. In K. A. Bollen & J. S. Long (Eds.), *Testing structural equation models* (pp. 136–162). Newbury Park, CA: Sage.
D'Agostino, Jr., R. B. (2005). Propensity score. In B. S. Everitt & D. C. Howell (Eds.), *Encyclopedia of statistics in behavioural science* (pp. 1617–1619). Chichester: Wiley.
Deci, E. L., Eghrari, H., Patrick, B. C., & Leone, D. R. (1994). Facilitating internalization: The Self-determination theory perspective. *Journal of Personality, 62*, 119–142. doi:10.1111/j.1467-6494.1994.tb00797.x
Deci, E. L., & Ryan, R. M. (1985). *Intrinsic motivation and self-determination in human behavior*. New York, NY: Plenum.
Dignath, C., & Büttner, G. (2008). Components of fostering self-regulated learning among students. A meta-analysis on intervention studies at primary and secondary school level. *Metacognition and Learning, 3*, 231–264. doi:10.1007/s11409-008-9029-x
Epstein, J. L. (1988). Effective schools or effective students: Dealing with diversity. In R. Haskins & D. MacRae (Eds.), *Policies for America's public schools: Teacher, equity and indicators* (pp. 89–126). Norwood, NJ: Ablex.
Faure, E., Herrera, F., Kaddoura, A.-R., Lopes, H., Petrovsky, A., Rahnema, M., & Ward, F. C. (1972). *Learning to be. The world of education today and tomorrow*. Paris: UNESCO.
Field, J. (2012). Transitions in lifelong learning: Public issues, private troubles, liminal identities. *Studies for the Learning Society, 2*, 4–11. doi:10.2478/v10240-012-0001-6
Finsterwald, M., Wagner, P., Schober, B., Lüftenegger, M., & Spiel, C. (2013). Fostering lifelong learning – Evaluation of a teacher education program for professional teachers. *Teaching and Teacher Education, 29*, 144–155. doi:10.1016/j.tate.2012.08.009
Flay, B. R., Biglan, A., Boruch, R. F., Castro, F. G., Gottfredson, D., Kellam, S., … Ji, P. (2005). Standards of evidence: Criteria for efficacy, effectiveness and dissemination. *Prevention Science, 6*, 151–175. doi:10.1007/s11121-005-5553-y

Gorard, S. (2009). The potential lifelong impact of schooling. In P. Jarvis (Ed.), *The Routledge International Handbook of Lifelong Learning* (pp. 91–101). New York, NY: Routledge.

Guay, F., Ratelle, C. F., & Chanal, J. (2008). Optimal learning in optimal contexts: The role of self-determination in education. *Canadian Psychology/Psychologie canadienne, 49*, 233–240. doi:10.1037/a0012758

Hardré, P. L., & Sullivan, D. W. (2008). Teacher perceptions and individual differences: How they influence rural teachers' motivating strategies. *Teaching and Teacher Education, 24*, 2059–2075. doi:10.1016/j.tate.2008.04.007

Hattie, J., Biggs, J., & Purdie, N. (1996). Effects of learning skills interventions on student learning: A meta-analysis. *Review of Educational Research, 66*, 99–136. doi:10.2307/1170605

Hattie, J., & Timperley, H. (2007). The Power of Feedback. *Review of Educational Research, 77*, 81–112. doi:10.3102/003465430298487

Hsu, H.-Y. (2009). *Testing the effectiveness of various commonly used fit indices for detecting misspecifications in multilevel structural equation models* (doctoral dissertation). Texas A&M University. Retrieved from http://hdl.handle.net/1969.1/ETD-TAMU-2009-12-7411

Klug, J., Krause, N., Schober, B., Finsterwald, M., & Spiel, C. (2014). How do teachers promote their students' lifelong learning in class? Development and first application of the LLL Interview. *Teaching and Teacher Education, 37*, 119–129. doi:10.1016/j.tate.2013.09.004

Krapp, A. (2002). Structural and dynamic aspects of interest development: Theoretical considerations from an ontogenetic perspective. *Learning and Instruction, 12*, 383–409. doi:10.1016/S0959-4752(01)00011-1

Lüftenegger, M., Schober, B., van de Schoot, R., Wagner, P., Finsterwald, M., & Spiel, C. (2012). Lifelong learning as a goal – Do autonomy and self-regulation in school result in well prepared pupils? *Learning and Instruction, 22*, 27–36. doi:10.1016/j.learninstruc.2011.06.001

Lüftenegger, M., van de Schoot, R., Schober, B., Finsterwald, M., & Spiel, C. (2014). Promotion of students' mastery goal orientations: Does TARGET work? *Educational Psychology, 34*, 451–469. doi:10.1080/01443410.2013.814189

Muthén, B. O., & Muthén, L. K. (1998–2010). *Mplus* (Version 6). Los Angeles, CA: Muthén & Muthén.

Niemiec, C. P., & Ryan, R. M. (2009). Autonomy, competence, and relatedness in the classroom applying self-determination theory to educational practice. *Theory and Research in Education, 7*, 133–144. doi:10.1177/1477878509104318

OECD. (1997). *Lifelong learning for all*. Paris: Author.

Perels, F., Gürtler, T., & Schmitz, B. (2005). Training of self-regulatory and problem-solving competence. *Learning and Instruction, 15*, 123–139. doi:10.1016/j.learninstruc.2005.04.010

Pintrich, P. R., & de Groot, E. V. (1990). Motivational and self-regulated learning components of classroom academic performance. *Journal of Educational Psychology, 82*, 33–40. doi:10.1037/0022-0663.82.1.33

Rubin, D. (1977). Assignment to a treatment group on the basis of a covariate. *Journal of Educational Statistics, 2*(1), 1–26.

Ryan, R. M., & Deci, E. L. (2000). Self-determination theory and the facilitation of intrinsic motivation, social development, and well-being. *American Psychologist, 55*, 68–78. doi:10.1037/0003-066X.55.1.68

Schafer, J. L., & Graham, J. W. (2002). Missing data: Our view of the state of the art. *Psychological Methods, 7*, 147–177. doi:10.1037/1082-989X.7.2.147

Schober, B., Finsterwald, M., Wagner, P., Lüftenegger, M., Aysner, M., & Spiel, C. (2007). TALK – A training program to encourage lifelong learning in school. *Journal of Psychology, 215*, 183–193. doi:10.1027/0044-3409.215.3.183

Schober, B., Lüftenegger, M., Wagner, P., Finsterwald, M., & Spiel, C. (2013). Facilitating lifelong learning in school-age learners: Programs and recommendations. *European Psychologist 2013, 18*, 114–125. doi:10.1027/1016-9040/a000129

Schunk, D. H., & Zimmerman, B. J. (Eds.). (2008). *Motivation and self-regulated learning. Theory, research and applications*. New York, NY: Routledge.

Sierens, E., Vansteenkiste, M., Goossens, L., Soenens, B., & Dochy, F. (2009). The synergistic relationship of perceived autonomy support and structure in the prediction of self-regulated learning. *British Journal of Educational Psychology, 79*, 57–68. doi:10.1348/000709908X304398

Spiel, C. (2009). Evidence-based practice: A challenge for European developmental psychology. *European Journal of Developmental Psychology, 6*, 11–33. doi:10.1080/17405620802485888

Spiel, C., Lapka, D., Gradinger, P., Zodlhofer, E. M., Reimann, R., Schober, B., ... von Eye, A. (2008). A euclidean distance-based matching procedure for nonrandomized comparison studies. *European Psychologist, 13*, 180–187. doi:10.1027/1016-9040.13.3.180

Steuer, G., Rosentritt-Brunn, G., & Dresel, M. (2013). Dealing with errors in mathematics classrooms: Structure and relevance of perceived error climate. *Contemporary Educational Psychology, 38*, 196–210. doi:10.1016/j.cedpsych.2013.03.002

Wigfield, A., & Eccles, J. S. (2000). Expectancy-value theory of achievement motivation. *Contemporary Educational Psychology, 25*, 68–81. doi:10.1006/ceps.1999.1015

Wigfield, A., Eccles, J. S., Schiefele, U., Roeser, R. W., & Davis-Kean, P. (2006). Development of achievement motivation. In W. Damon & N. Eisenberg (Eds.), *Handbook of child psychology*. Chichester: John Wiley & Sons.

Winne, P. (2005). A perspective on state-of-the-art research on self-regulated learning. *Instructional Science, 33*, 559–565. doi:10.1007/s11251-005-1280-9

Zimmerman, B. J., & Moylan, A. R. (2009). Self-regulation: Where metacognition and motivation intersect. In D. J. Hacker, J. Dunlosky, & A. C. Graesser (Eds.), *Handbook of metacognition in education* (pp. 299–315). New York, NY: Routledge.

The implementation and evaluation of the ViSC program in Cyprus: challenges of cross-national dissemination and evaluation results

Olga Solomontos-Kountouri, Petra Gradinger, Takuya Yanagida and Dagmar Strohmeier

ABSTRACT

The ViSC program is a socio-ecological anti-bullying program that has been developed, implemented and rigorously evaluated in Austria. The main goals of the present study were (1) to implement the ViSC program with high fidelity in Cyprus and (2) to investigate the program effectiveness within a quasi-experimental longitudinal study. To tackle bullying on different levels in the educational system, a cascaded train-the-trainer model has been realized. Nine permanent staff members of the Cypriot Ministry of Education were trained as multipliers by researchers. These multipliers trained teachers in three Cypriot schools and teachers trained their students. To investigate the effectiveness of the program, data from students of three intervention and three control schools was collected via self-assessments at pre-test (October–November 2012), post-test (April–May 2013) and follow-up (March–April 2014). In total, 1752 grade 7 and 8 students (602 intervention, 1150 control group) with a mean age of 12.6 (SD = .60) at pre-test, nested in 82 classes and 6 schools participated. To investigate the program effectiveness regarding the reduction of victimization and aggressive behavior, multilevel growth models were applied (time points at level 1, individuals at level 2, and classes at level 3). The analyses revealed that the program effects differed depending on the grade level of the students. Overall, the program was more effective for grade 7 compared with grade 8 students. In grade 8, bullying and victimization increased more in the intervention group compared with the control group at time 2, but also steeper decreased at time 3 indicating a sensitizing effect of the program.

Evidence-based bullying prevention in schools is key area of Bildung-Psychology (Spiel, Reimann, Wagner, & Schober, 2008) and a research field of international interest (Ttofi & Farrington, 2011). Like in many other countries, bullying has also emerged as a serious problem in Cypriot schools indicating that 17% of students are involved as either bullies, victims or bully-victims (Stavrinides, Paradeisiotou, Tziogouros, & Lazarou, 2010). It was demonstrated that bullying is a serious threat for the mental health of Cypriot students and that there is an urgent need for evidence-based anti-bullying programs in Cypriot schools (Papacosta, Paradeisioti, & Lazarou, 2014). As some countries like Austria implemented evidence based programs nationwide (Spiel, Salmivalli, & Smith, 2011; Spiel & Strohmeier, 2011, 2012), a similar nationwide process has been initiated in Cyprus and the ViSC Social Competence Program (Strohmeier, Hoffmann, Schiller, Stefanek, & Spiel, 2012) has been implemented in Cyprus. Thus, taking advantage of the concept of Bildung-Psychology (Spiel et al., 2008) both a nationwide transformation process and an evidence-based bullying prevention program was cross nationally disseminated from Austria to Cyprus.

The goals of the present study are (1) to describe the steps necessary for implementing the ViSC program in Cyprus and (2) to investigate the program effectiveness regarding the reduction of victimization and aggressive behavior among Cypriote students.

ViSC social competence program

From a socio-ecological perspective, aggressive behaviour and bullying are understood as a complex systemic problem with mechanisms operating on several interacting levels (Bronfenbrenner, 1979; Swearer & Espelage, 2004). Therefore, a socio-ecological preventive intervention program not only targets individual students, but also aims to change the class and school environment. Because the main aim of the ViSC program is to enable a school transformation process, competencies on various systemic levels are fostered simultaneously by implementing measures for multipliers, teachers, students and parents with the goal to reduce various forms of bullying, aggressive behavior and victimization. While aggressive behavior comprises intentional harm doing; bullying also includes repetition and imbalance of power (Olweus, 1996; Roland & Idsøe, 2001). Both bullying and aggressive behaviour are expressed directly and indirectly and include a variety of negative forms, like physical attacks, verbal insults, relational harassments (Olweus, 1996) or offenses via electronic means (Smith et al., 2008). It is important to differentiate these different forms of bullying and aggressive behaviors as maladjustment differs for direct and indirect aggressive behaviour (Card, Stucky, Sawalani, & Little, 2008) for bullies and victims (Georgiou & Stavrinides, 2012); and for traditional bullying and cyber bullying (Gradinger, Strohmeier, & Spiel, 2009). Research also demonstrated that age is an important variable to consider in any study regarding bullying and aggressive behavior (Pellegrini & Bartini, 2000), especially also because nationwide anti-bullying programs might be more effective for younger children (Kärnä et al., 2011; Yeager, Fong, Lee, & Espelage, 2015).

The ViSC program creates a school development process to foster the shared responsibility between teachers to prevent aggressive behavior, bullying and victimization in their school. In line with social learning theory (Bandura, 1977), it is important that teachers have worked out a common understanding of the problem; agreed on procedures how to tackle acute cases and jointly implement preventive measures on the school and class level (Schultes, Stefanek, van de Schoot, Strohmeier, & Spiel, 2014). Furthermore, the program assumes that aggressive behavior and bullying have two underlying functions (Card & Little, 2006). Reactive aggression is theoretically grounded in the frustration–aggression model; instrumental aggression has its roots in social cognitive learning theory describing a planned behavior controlled by external rewards (Vitaro, Brendgen, & Barker, 2006). In addition, the program acknowledges that victimized students are heterogeneous (Yang & Salmivalli, 2013). While victims of bullying usually cannot easily defend themselves, reactive aggressive students are also often victims and thus labelled as bully-victims. Importantly, the program acknowledges that aggressive behavior, bullying and victimization co-occur and therefore aims to change these behaviors simultaneously. In many classes there is a rather big group of students who neither feel responsible for what happens around them nor intervene in critical situations (Craig, Pepler, & Atlas, 2000), moreover there is still a group of preadolescents who is not able to manage their negative emotions in a non-aggressive way (Salmivalli & Nieminen, 2002). Therefore, on the class level students are trained (a) to feel responsible when something negative is going on, (b) to react in a way which is likely to improve the situation, (c) to recognize their own emotions and the emotions of others, and (d) to cope with these emotions in a positive, non-aggressive way. Moreover, it is necessary to empower students who might get victimized easily as they often invite attacks with their non-assertive behavior (Veenstra et al., 2007). Thus, students are also trained how to best react when getting picked on by others.

To summarize, both on the school and the class level, the ViSC program aims to create an environment in which it is less likely that aggressive behavior, bullying and victimization occurs. The program also contains indicated measures. In line with the approach suggested by Roland and Vaaland (2006), teachers are trained how to respond when aggressive behavior or bullying has already been occurred in their school (for more details see Strohmeier, Hoffmann et al., 2012).

In Austria, the effectiveness of the ViSC program has been demonstrated in various studies (Gollwitzer, Banse, Eisenbach, & Naumann, 2007; Gollwitzer, Eisenbach, Atria, Strohmeier, & Banse, 2006; Gradinger, Yanagida, Strohmeier, & Spiel, 2015a, 2015b; Yanagida, Strohmeier, & Spiel, 2015). Using data of a large two wave cluster randomized control study the change of victimization was stronger in the intervention compared with the control group (Yanagida et al., 2015). However, the change of aggressive behaviour did not reach statistical significance, although the magnitude of the effect sizes was in favour of the program. Gradinger et al. (2015a, 2015b) demonstrated short and long term program effectiveness for cyberbullying and cyber victimization.

The present study

The present study investigated the effectiveness of the ViSC program in Cyprus regarding the reduction of perpetration and victimization of five different forms of aggression over two school years. Effectiveness of the program is indicated by a steeper decrease or lower increase in victimization and aggressive behavior in the intervention group compared to the control group. That is, we investigated the interaction of group (intervention, control) with the linear and quadratic effect of time over three time points for self-reported victimization and aggressive behavior. The quadratic effect of time was included in the analyses to examine whether the depended variables would change differently between pretest-posttest and posttest-follow-up-test.

We hypothesized that students in the ViSC intervention schools would show a better trend over time compared to students in the control schools regarding all five forms of perpetration and victimization. We hypothesized that grade would moderate the effectiveness of the program and we considered age as an additional covariate. Therefore, we examined grade 7 and grade 8 students separately controlling for age in each grade.

Method

Implementation process

The ViSC program has been implemented with the highest possible program fidelity, compared to Austria only few adaptations were necessary in order to respond to educational and cultural particularities in Cyprus (Solomontos-Kountouri & Strohmeier, 2013). Because the ViSC program targets multipliers, teachers, students and parents simultaneously, the implementation process is rather challenging.

Step 1: Partnerships with Stakeholders in Cyprus

The approval for piloting and implementing the ViSC program in secondary schools in Cyprus was achieved after several negotiations with relevant partner institutions related with the Ministry of Education.

Step 2: Training of the ViSC Multipliers in Cyprus

Like in Austria, the goal was to train permanent staff working at the institutions of the Ministry of Education to enable a sustainable knowledge transfer between research and practice. The ViSC multipliers consisted of nine highly experienced professionals (counselors, educational psychologists, teacher-researchers) from three partner institutions. To implement the ViSC program in Cyprus, all training materials were translated from German to Greek.

Step 3: Program Implementation in Cyprus Gymnasiums

In the 2012/13 school year the ViSC program has been implemented in three Cypriot schools located in three different provinces. To begin with, the ViSC multipliers received a 20 h training offered by the Austrian and Cypriote researchers over a period of one year. Second, the multipliers delivered five units of teacher training to all teachers during the available school time. Third, class teachers taught their students six 90 min lessons on social and cultural competences and to transfer the knowledge into real life, the students designed and exhibited a class activity with their classmates. Two new elements were (a) the chief educational officers were involved and an official inaugural meeting was launched to empower both the head teachers and the researchers in their mission; (b) two hours presentation of the ViSC program was offered to the parents in each school by the researcher, including discussion of how parents would help. Finally, a second year of implementation of the ViSC program was added in Cyprus. In the second year, three repetition trainings were offered to a small group of teachers who trained the rest of personnel, implemented the program to the new first year students and gave a presentation to parents. The parents were asked to discuss the program content with their children at home. In Cyprus, the students remain stable but several teachers in schools change every year, therefore the second year of implementation was very important to ensure the sustainability of the program.

Study design and procedure

Due to the small number of intervention schools, it was not feasible to undertake a randomized control trial. Instead, a quasi-experimental three wave longitudinal study was realized. Data was collected in six schools (82 classes) at pre-test (October–November 2012), post-test (April–May 2013) and follow-up (March–April 2014).

These six schools were located in three provinces (Nicosia, Larnaka and Pafos) and were chosen by the Secondary School Directory to participate as either intervention or control school. The schools were chosen based on convenience (which school collaborate better), demand (which school had a need for an intervention program) and equivalency (similar status schools were matched according to Directory criteria). This kind of school selection was used to make sure that the program would be implemented with high fidelity. Permission from the Centre of Educational Research and Evaluation in Cyprus was assured to conduct the longitudinal research. Active parental consent was granted by 88.6% of parents. Prior to data collection students were assured that their participation was voluntary and that their answers would be kept confidential. Data were collected with paper and pencil, during regular school hours by the first author and a group of research assistants with the help of the class teachers.

BILDUNG-PSYCHOLOGY

Table 1. Demographic characteristics of the sample (Grade 7, Grade 8) by intervention and control group at pretest.

	Grade 7 (N = 764)		Grade 8 (N = 822)	
	Intervention	Control	Intervention	Control
	(n = 286)	(n = 478)	(n = 280)	(n = 542)
Gender (% female)	48.9	44.6	52.3	50.9
Age, M (SD)	12.1 (.4)	12.1 (.3)	13.1 (.4)*	13.1 (.3)*
Country of birth (%)				
Cyprus	87.4	85.7	86.3	85.8
Other country	12.6	14.3	13.7	14.2
First language (%)				
Greek	88.8	89.1	93.2*	88.0*
Other language	11.2	10.9	6.8*	12.0*
Perceived financial situation (%)				
Very bad	4.6	6.0	6.1	4.5
Bad	8.5	7.2	6.9	3.9
Neither bad nor good	28.8	32.1	28.5	35.3
Good	39.9	35.1	40.4	39.8
Very good	18.1	19.6	18.1	16.5
Parent's working status (%)				
Working father	88.5	90.4	92.5	89.9
Working mother	73.9	70.9	75.5	74.2
Media usage at least once a day (%)				
Mobile phone	84.0	79.2	83.4	84.7
Internet	67.8	67.5	70.6	75.6

Note: Statistically significant differences between intervention- and control-group are indicated with asterisks.
$*p < .05**p < .01***p < .001$.

Participants

In total, 1652 grade 7 and 8 students (602 in intervention group, 1050 in control group) nested in 82 classes (30 in intervention, 52 in control group) and 6 schools participated in at least one measurement and were included. Gymnasium is the middle school between primary school and Lyceum and consists of 3 years of compulsory education. At wave 1 (pretest), the sample comprised 1586 students (48.9% girls) from 82 classrooms (40 seventh grade classes and 42 seventh grade classes) with a mean age of 12.6 years (SD = .6, Min = 12, Max = 15). Table 1 provides a description of the sample by intervention and control group, separately for grade 7 and grade 8. Intervention and control group were compared regarding pretest demographic characteristics using a series of Pearson's chi-square tests with Yates' continuity correction, and a two-sample t-test. In grade 7, the two groups were comparable. In grade 8, the students in the control group were slightly younger (t (806) = −2.188, $p < .05$, $d = .15$), and fewer students spoke Greek as a first language ($\chi^2(1) = 4.841, p < .05$) compared with the intervention group.

Missing data

In total, 677 records (47.9% in grade 7 and 52.1% in grade 8) were incomplete; 306 students showed wave non-response: 29 students were missing at wave 1,

81 students were missing at wave 2, 124 students were missing at wave 3, 37 students were missing at wave 1 and 3; and 35 students were missing at wave 2 and 3. According to the protocols of the data collection, these students missed one or more wave because of three reasons: They were (1) absent at the day of data collection, (2) choose to not participate or (3) completed the questionnaire in an invalid way. The remaining 371 students had a general missing data pattern with omitted items on single scales. The percentage of missing values across the 140 variables varied between 1.8 and 13.7% (1.5 and 13.7% in grade 7 and 2.0 and 13.7% in grade 8).

A series of two-sample t-tests was conducted to compare students with and without missing data on all study variables for grade 7 and 8 separately. Both grade 7 and 8 student with missing data had higher values in all scales with effect sizes ranging from $d = .06$ to $d = .31$ for grade 7 and effect sizes ranging from $d = .12$ to $d = .40$ for grade 8. These results indicate that missing data is systematically related to the study variables. Thus, all study variables are analyzed simultaneously based on a multivariate model accounting for the covariance among those variables making the missing at random assumption (MAR) more plausible. Full information maximum likelihood under the MAR assumption and Bayesian estimation were used to deal with missing data (Enders, 2010).

Measures

Aggressive behavior and victimization were measured with five self-report scales. The items cover specific aggressive behavior and victimization incidents during the last two months. Answers to all questions were given on a five-point response scale ranging from 0 (*never*), over 1 (*once or twice*), 2 (*two or three times a month*), 3 (*once a week*), to 4 (*nearly every day*).

Bullying perpetration and bullying victimization

The self-reported scales consist of one global item, and three specific items covering different forms (physical, relational and verbal) of bullying and victimization. The term "bullying" was not used in the items and no definition of bullying was provided. Instead very specific behavioral descriptions were used (Strohmeier, Gradinger, Schabmann, & Spiel, 2012). Cronbach's a coefficients were .74/.77/.76 (pretest/posttest/follow up) for the bullying perpetration scale and .75/.78/.78 (pretest/posttest/follow up) for the bullying victimization scale.

Cyberbullying and cyberbullying victimization

Cyberbullying and cyberbullying victimization were measured with two scales. Both scales contain one global and seven specific items related to different electronic means based on Smith et al. (2008). The different electronic means

BILDUNG-PSYCHOLOGY

Table 2. Model fit of the measurement models.

	χ^2	df	p	CFI	RMSEA	WRMR
Perpetration						
Bullying	393.49	182	<.001	.972	.038	1.892
Cyberbullying	7787.49	666	<.001	.994	.015	1.393
Physical aggression	183.27	106	<.001	.987	.030	1.349
Relational aggression	394.41	284	<.001	.989	.022	1.389
Verbal aggression	132.99	106	<.001	.996	.018	1.024
Victimization						
Bullying victimization	339.70	182	<.001	.986	.032	1.752
Cyberbullying victimization	782.18	666	<.01	.995	.015	1.351
Physical victimization	151.76	106	<.001	.990	.023	1.142
Relational victimization	413.22	284	<.001	.989	.023	1.446
Verbal victimization	174.05	106	<.001	.991	.028	1.209

Note: Models are based on measurement models with ordered-categorical indicators.

were calls, text messages, emails, chat contributions, discussion board, instant messages, and videos or photos. Cronbach's a coefficients for the cyberbullying scale were .84/.93/.92 (pretest/posttest/follow up) and .89/.93/.92 (pretest/posttest/follow up) for the cyberbullying victimization scale.

Physical aggression and physical victimization

The peer nomination measure developed by Crick and Grotpeter (1995) was modified into a self-report questionnaire and comprised three items. Cronbach's a coefficients were .79/.80/.84 (pretest/posttest/follow up) for the physical aggression scale and .80/.80/.78 (pretest/posttest/follow up) for the physical victimization scale.

Relational aggression and relational victimization

These five items were also adapted from the peer nomination measure originally developed by Crick and Grotpeter (1995). Cronbach's a coefficients were .84/.88/.89 (pretest/posttest/follow up) for the relational aggression scale and .85/.89/.86 (pretest/posttest/follow up) for the relational victimization scale.

Verbal aggression and verbal victimization

These three items were specifically constructed to cover active and passive verbal harassments (Strohmeier, Aoyama, Gradinger, & Toda, 2013). Cronbach's a coefficients were .77/.82/.79 (pretest/posttest/follow up) for the verbal aggression scale and .80/.84/.83 (pretest/posttest/follow up) for the verbal victimization scale.

Confirmatory factor analyses were conducted with Mplus Version 7.11 (Muthén & Muthén, 1998–2012) using robust weighted least squares estimator to establish measurement models with ordered-categorical indicators (see

Bovaird & Koziol, 2012) for the five different forms of aggression and victimization. Moreover, all scales were tested for strong longitudinal and between-group (control vs. intervention) measurement invariance (see Little, 2013). Results yield acceptable model fit (see Table 2) indicating sound measurement properties of all scales. In order to reduce model complexity (i.e., number of estimated parameters), factor scores for all scales were extracted and subsequently used in the main analysis.

Analytic strategy

Multivariate multilevel growth modelling (level 1: time, level 2: student, level 3: class) was conducted with Mplus Version 7.3 (Muthén & Muthén, 1998–2012) to test program effectiveness. Bayesian estimation with non-informative prior distributions based on the default settings of the program was used as estimation procedure. As recommended by Hox, van de Schoot, and Matthijsse (2012) convergence was assessed using Gelman–Rubin criterion using a stricter cutoff value (i.e., bconvergence = .01) than the default setting. We requested four chains for the Gibbs sampler and inspected all trace plots manually to check for convergence.

Program effectiveness was investigated based on the cross-level interaction *intervention × time* and *intervention × time*^{2} controlling for grand-mean centered age. That is, the difference in linear and quadratic change between control and intervention group for the five different forms of perpetration and victimization of aggression controlling for the mean age of the participants (see Tables 4 and 5). Age was included in the analyses to control for possible age variations within grades. We also computed standardized estimates for each effect. In order to compute these standardized estimates we re- run all analyses with standardized variables again. We added the standardized estimates in the tables only for the relevant effects (see Tables 4 and 5).

Results

Descriptive statistics for outcome variables

As a first step, the means and standard deviations of perpetration and victimization are reported by wave of data collection (pretest, posttest and follow up) in Table 3. Results are reported separately by grade level, intervention and control group, and wave.

Examining the means, aggressive behavior and victimization scores are higher in grade 8 than in grade 7, especially at pretest. Mostly, aggressive behavior and victimization increased between pretest and posttest, and then did not change or decreased again, especially in the intervention group. Changes

Table 3. Descriptive statistics for the criterion variables: means and standard deviations.

	Grade 7						Grade 8					
	Intervention			Control			Intervention			Control		
	Wave 1	Wave 2	Wave 3	Wave 1	Wave 2	Wave 3	Wave 1	Wave 2	Wave 3	Wave 1	Wave 2	Wave 3
Criterion	($n = 286$)	($n = 264$)	($n = 262$)	($n = 478$)	($n = 455$)	($n = 434$)	($n = 280$)	($n = 262$)	($n = 258$)	($n = 542$)	($n = 488$)	($n = 473$)
Perpetration												
Bullying	.42 (.58)	.54 (.62)	.55 (.62)	.40 (.56)	.53 (.68)	.52 (.64)	.61 (.69)	.81 (.87)	.66 (.68)	.63 (.70)	.62 (.68)	.61 (.72)
Cyberbullying	.06 (.19)	.10 (.31)	.09 (.25)	.08 (.22)	.12 (.46	.13 (.43	.16 (.37)	.31 (.66)	.16 (.42)	.12 (.36)	.13 (.42)	.14 (.42)
Physical aggression	.26 (.48)	.31 (.53)	.28 (.56)	.33 (.62)	.36 (.66)	.39 (.75)	.38 (.67)	.53 (.90)	.36 (.62)	.42 (.73)	.38 (.63)	.39 (.72)
Relational aggression	.09 (.26)	.17 (.49)	.12 (.37)	.13 (.36)	.20 (.56)	.21 (.57)	.19 (.45)	.38 (.75)	.20 (.53)	.17 (.48)	.18 (.46)	.20 (.49)
Verbal aggression	.39 (.54)	.52 (.79)	.54 (.72)	.40 (.66)	.48 (.76)	.57 (.84)	.62 (.77)	.76 (1.01)	.60 (.76)	.63 (.83)	.62 (.82)	.57 (.83)
Victimization												
Bullying victimization	.44 (.57)	.52 (.65)	.51 (.65)	.50 (.65)	.63 (.79)	.58 (.74)	.58 (.70)	.73 (.83)	.50 (.60)	.64 (.75)	.58 (.73)	.52 (.70)
Cyberbullying victimization	.12 (.33)	.14 (.37)	.12 (.34)	.12 (.34)	.16 (.46)	.15 (.44)	.18 (.44)	.36 (.71)	.18 (.45)	.18 (.47)	.16 (.49)	.15 (.45)
Physical victimization	.39 (.69)	.36 (.65)	.25 (.49)	.37 (.63)	.38 (.69)	.31 (.60	.40 (.68)	.45 (.75)	.28 (.59)	.46 (.84)	.36 (.70)	.34 (.64)
Relational victimization	.17 (.45)	.24 (.50)	.22 (.49	.20 (.49)	.29 (.64)	.26 (.58)	.28 (.60)	.43 (.69)	.25 (.53)	.26 (.58)	.27 (.63)	.23 (.59)
Verbal victimization	.45 (.80)	.60 (.88)	.49 (.73)	.54 (.77)	.66 (.95)	.57 (.85)	.61 (.84)	.67 (.97)	.53 (.78)	.66 (.93	.64 (.95)	.54 (.87)

Notes. Intervention $n = 602$; Control $n = 1150$. Sample size slightly differs by scale and wave due to missing values.

TABLE 4 Hierarchical linear modeling results: intervention effects for different forms of perpetration.

	Bullying		Cyberbullying		Physical Aggression		Relational Aggression		Verbal Aggression	
	Grade 7	Grade 8	Grade 7	Grade 8	Grade 7	Grade 8	Grade 7	Grade 8	Grade 7	Grade 8
	$N = 798$	$N = 851$	$N = 798$	$N = 854$	$N = 797$	$N = 853$	$N = 797$	$N = 852$	$N = 797$	$N = 853$
Level 1: Measurement										
Intercept	−.113	.245	.455***	.404***	.274**	.271*	.565***	.490***	.074	.264**
Time	.241**	.030	.087	−.017	.116	.009	.151	−.001	.065	.005
Time^2	−.073	−.028	−.022	.011	−.051	−.017	−.061	.008	.000	−.025
Level 2: Student										
Age	−.120	−.046	−.130	−.195*	−.145	−.124	−.099	−.168	−.152	−.008
Level 3: Class										
Intervention	−.101	−.064	.138	.335*	−.109	.003	−.082	.144	.003	.023
Intervention × time	.190	.537***	−.029	.423***	−.246*	.009	.299*	.720***	−.076	.080
Intervention × time^2	−.041	−.196***	.020	−.195***	.092	−.027	−.141***	−.363***	.044	−.014
Level 3: Class					*Standardized estimates*					
Intervention	−.084	−.049	.164	.338	−.100	.004	−.075	.124	.003	.028
Intervention × time	.160	.417	−.034	.424	−.228	.004	.281	.593	−.083	.069
Intervention × time^2	−.035	−.152	.023	−.195	.085	−.021	−.133	−.299	.048	−.008

Notes. Bayesian posterior median estimates of hierarchical linear modelling results. Statistically significant results based on two-tailed p-values are indicated with asterisks. Higher values of age represent older students. Intervention is coded as 0 = control group, and 1 = intervention group. *$p < .05$ **$p < .01$ ***$p < .001$.

BILDUNG-PSYCHOLOGY

between waves appeared to be bigger in the intervention than in the control group.

Baseline effects in perpetration and victimization

Regarding perpetration, the baseline effect *intervention* was significant for the perpetration of cyberbullying in grade 8 ($b = .335, p < .05$), indicating that the intervention group had higher scores than the control group at pretest. Regarding victimization, the baseline effect *intervention* was significant in grade 7 for verbal victimization ($b = -.321, p < .05$), indicating that the intervention group had lower scores than the control group at pretest.

Intervention effects on perpetration

As shown in Table 4, the overall pattern of results revealed that in grade 8 bullying, cyberbullying and relational aggression increased more in the intervention group compared with the control group over time (*intervention* × *time*). However, this effect was qualified by a quadratic intervention effect (*intervention* × *time*^{2}) indicating that the intervention group had a steeper decrease over time compared with the control group. For relational aggression, this pattern was also found for grade 7. Age was not significant in grade 7 and 8.

Bullying
In grade 7, bullying increased over time in both groups (*time*, $b = .241, p < .01$). In grade 8, there was a steeper increase over time in the intervention group compared with the control group (*intervention* × *time*, $b = .37, p < .001$) including a quadratic effect (*intervention* × *time*^{2}, $b = -.196, p < .001$), indicating that over time this increase became smaller in the intervention group compared with the control group.

Cyberbullying
In grade 7, there were no intervention effects. In grade 8, there was a steeper increase over time in the intervention group compared with the control group (*intervention* × *time*, $b = .423, p < .001$) including a quadratic effect (*intervention* × *time*^{2}, $b = -.195, p < .001$), indicating that over time this increase became smaller in the intervention group compared with the control group.

Physical aggression
In grade 7, there was a steeper decrease in the intervention group compared with the control group over time (*intervention* × *time*, $b = -.246, p < .05$). In grade 8, there were no intervention effects.

Table 5 Hierarchical linear modeling results: intervention effects for different forms of victimization.

	Bullying Victimization		Cyber Victimization		Physical Victimization		Relational Victimization		Verbal Victimization	
	Grade 7	Grade 8	Grade 7	Grade 8	Grade 7	Grade 8	Grade 7	Grade 8	Grade 7	Grade 8
	$N = 798$	$N = 849$	$N = 798$	$N = 854$	$N = 798$	$N = 854$	$N = 798$	$N = 854$	$N = 798$	$N = 854$
Level 1: Measurement										
Intercept	.159	.285*	.474***	.358***	.308***	.312**	.502***	.368***	.235*	.265*
Time	.285**	−.129	.115	−.005	.076	−.150*	.169*	−.004	.141	−.006
Time^2	−.115*	.001	−.046	−.008	−.058	.041	−.069*	−.022	−.068	−.033
Level 2: Student										
Age	−.194	−.071	−.178	−.196*	−.072	−.095	−.217*	−.247*	−.138	−.041
Level 3: Class										
Intervention	−.235	−.185	−.009	.150	.095	.025	−.230	−.079	−.321*	−.166
Intervention × time	.222	.799***	.207*	.620***	−.291*	.067	.931***	1.223***	.394**	.305*
Intervention × time^2	−.065	−.336**	−.054	−.251***	.102	−.066	−.387***	−.538***	−.127*	−.095
Level 3: Class					*Standardized estimates*					
Intervention	−.157	−.120	−.011	.164	.098	.024	−.218	−.068	−.288	−.142
Intervention × time	.146	.519	.258	.665	−.299	.060	.882	1.089	.354	.259
Intervention × time^2	−.042	−.218	−.69	−.270	.104	−.062	−.367	−.479	−.114	−.080

Notes. Bayesian posterior median estimates of hierarchical linear modelling results. Statistically significant results based on two-tailed p-values are indicated with asterisks. Higher values of age represent older students. Intervention is coded as 0 = control group, and 1 = intervention group. *$p < .05$ **$p < .01$ ***$p < .001$.

BILDUNG-PSYCHOLOGY

Relational aggression

In grade 7, there was an increase in the intervention group over time compared with the control group (*intervention × time, b* = .299, *p* < .01) which became smaller over time (*intervention × time², b* = −.141, *p* < .05). In grade 8, there was a steeper increase in the intervention group over time compared with the control group (*intervention × time, b* = .720, *p* < .001) including a quadratic effect (*intervention × time², b* = −.363, *p* < .001) indicating that over time this increase became smaller in the intervention group compared with the control group.

Verbal aggression

No intervention effects were found for both grade 7 and 8.

Intervention effects on victimization

As shown in Table 5, the overall pattern of results revealed that in grade 8 bullying victimization, cyber-victimization and relational victimization increased more in the intervention group compared with the control group over time (*intervention × time*). However, this effect was qualified by a quadratic intervention effect (*intervention × time²*) indicating that the intervention group had a steeper decrease over time compared with the control group. For relational victimization and verbal victimization, the same pattern was also found for grade 7. Age was significant regarding cyber victimization in grade 7 (*age, b* = −.178, *p* < .01) and grade 8 (*age, b* = −.196, *p* < .01), and relational victimization in grade 7 (*age, b* = .217, *p* < .05) and grade 8 (*age, b* = −.247, *p* < .01), indicating older students were less involved in victimization.

Bullying victimization

In grade 7, bullying victimization increased over time in both groups (*time, b* = .285, *p* < .01) and quadratic effect indicating that this increase became equally smaller in both groups (*time², b* = −.115, *p* < .05). In grade 8, there was a steeper increase over time in the intervention group compared with the control group (*intervention × time, b* = .799, *p* < .001) including a quadratic effect (*intervention × time², b* = −.336, *p* < .01), indicating that over time this increase became smaller in the intervention group compared with the control group.

Cyber victimization

In grade 7, there was an increase over time in the intervention group compared with the control group (*intervention × time, b* = .207, *p* < .05). In grade 8, there was a steeper increase over time in the intervention group compared with the control group (*intervention × time, b* = .620, *p* < .001) including a quadratic effect (*intervention × time², b* = −.251, *p* < .001), indicating that over time this increase became smaller in the intervention group compared with the control group.

Physical victimization

In grade 7, there was a steeper decrease over time in the intervention group compared with the control group (*intervention* × *time*, $b = -.291, p < .05$). In grade 8, physical victimization decreased in both groups (*time*, $b = -.150, p < .05$).

Relational victimization

In grade 7, relational victimization increased over time in both groups (*time*, $b = .169, p < .05$) and there was a quadratic effect of time indicating that this increase became equally smaller in both groups (*time²*, $b = -.069, p < .05$). There was a steeper increase over time in the intervention group compared with the control group (*intervention* × *time*, $b = .931, p < .001$) including a quadratic effect (*intervention* × *time²*, $b = -.387, p < .001$), indicating that over time this increase became smaller in the intervention group compared with the control group. In grade 8, there was a steeper increase over time in the intervention group compared with the control group (*intervention* × *time*, $b = 1.223, p < .001$) including a quadratic effect (*intervention* × *time²*, $b = -.538, p < .001$), indicating that over time this increase became smaller in the intervention group compared with the control group.

Verbal victimization

In grade 7, there was a steeper increase over time in the intervention group compared with the control group (*intervention* × *time*, $b = .394, p < .01$) including a quadratic effect (*intervention* × *time²*, $b = -.127, p < .05$), indicating that over time this increase became smaller in the intervention group compared with the control group. In grade 8, there was a steeper increase over time in the intervention group compared with the control group (*intervention* × *time*, $b = .305, p < .05$).

Discussion

Bullying prevention has emerged as a major need in Cypriot schools (Papacosta et al., 2014; Stavrinides et al., 2010) and the pilot implementation and evaluation of the ViSC program came as a successful respond. As suggested in the structural model of Bildung-Psychology (Spiel et al., 2008) the ViSC program covers the functional areas of intervention, prevention, counseling/teaching and research to tackle bullying on the micro-activity level of students, teachers, trainers, administrators and parents and on the meso-activity level of the involved schools and the Cyprus Ministry of Education. In that way, the implementation of the ViSC program enables sustainable knowledge transfer between research and practice for the benefit of the well-being of Cypriot students.

The ViSC program has been implemented with the highest possible program fidelity in Cyprus. Applying state of art statistical methods and ensuring reliability and validity of the measurements used, we obtained encouraging results. On the descriptive level, the aggressive behavior and victimization scores are higher in grade 8 than in grade 7. This result is in accordance with Pellegrini and Bartini's (2000) findings, who explained that the increase of bullying in middle school, especially among boys, was used to establish dominance in their peer group.

The decline in physical aggression and physical victimization among students in grade 7 with small to medium effect sizes based on standardized coefficients is a significant result. It indicates that the program was able to reduce physical aggression, which is the strongest violence form, already in the first year of implementation. This result confirms the program's efficiency, which has already presented in the evaluations of ViSC in Austria (Gollwitzer et al., 2007; Gradinger et al., 2015a).

Another important result is the quadratic intervention effect revealing that the phenomena increased more in the intervention group compared with the control group after one year of intervention and then the intervention group had a steeper decrease in the second year of implementation compared with the control group. Quadratic intervention effect found for relational aggression and relational victimization for both grade 7 and grade 8, for bullying perpetration, bullying victimization, cyberbullying and cybervictimization for grade 8 and for verbal victimization for grade 7. These results with small to medium effect sizes based on standardized coefficients can be interpreted as a promotion of sensitization for bullying amongst the students. The directors of the schools explained that the social and cultural competences program encouraged students to recognize all forms of bullying and victimization, to report them more, to uncover hidden victimization and even to report simple teasing. Directors added that the program enables school to handle appropriately all cases and by the second year, students kept sensitive but bullying episodes were much less.

The pilot implementation and evaluation of ViSC program in Cyprus provides significant results that can be used for further applications of the program, as well as for further research. Despite the limitations of implementing the program in a small number of schools and of using only self-reports, in a quasi-experimental design, ViSC evaluation results are very encouraging, especially when considering that the ViSC program is a primary preventive approach and not an anti-aggression training for highly aggressive youth. Therefore, the reduction of bullying, aggressive behavior and victimization is a tough evaluation criterion for ViSC and it also provides a very conservative test of its effectiveness (Gollwitzer et al., 2006). The program currently is implemented in four Cypriote schools, under the auspices of the Cypriot Minister of Education and Culture and it is scheduled to be offered to any school that will require it in the following years. In conclusion, the present study offers a strong example that a bullying prevention program can be disseminated with high implementation fidelity cross nationally.

Disclosure statement

No potential conflict of interest was reported by the authors.

References

Bandura, A. (1977). *Social learning theory*. Engleworth Cliffs, NJ: Prentice Hall.

Bovaird, J. A., & Koziol, N. A. (2012). Measurement models for ordered categorical indicators in structural equation modeling. In R. H. Hoyle, D. Kaplan, G. Marcoulides, & S. West (Eds.), *Handbook of structural equation modeling* (pp. 495–511). New York, NY: Guilford Press.

Bronfenbrenner, U. (1979). *The ecology of human development: Experiments by nature and design*. Cambridge, MA: Harvard University Press.

Card, N. A., & Little, T. D. (2006). Proactive and reactive aggression in childhood and adolescence: A meta-analysis of differential relations with psychosocial adjustment. *International Journal of Behavioral Development, 30*, 466–480. doi:10.1177/0165025406071904

Card, N. A., Stucky, B. D., Sawalani, G. M., & Little, T. D. (2008). Direct and indirect aggression during childhood and adolescence: A meta-analytic review of gender differences, intercorrelations, and relations to maladjustment. *Child Development, 79*, 1185–1229.

Craig, W., Pepler, D., & Atlas, R. (2000). Observations of bullying in the playground and in the classroom. *School Psychology International, 21*, 22–36.

Crick, N. R., & Grotpeter, J. K. (1995). Relational aggression, gender, and social-psychological adjustment. *Child Development, 66*, 710–722. doi:10.1111/j.1467-8624.1995.tb00900.x

Enders, C. (2010). *Applied missing data analysis*. New York, NY: Guilford.

Georgiou, S. N., & Stavrinides, P. (2012). Social-psychological profiles of early adolescents involved in bullying activities. *International Journal of Criminology and Sociology, 1*, 60–68. doi:10.6000/1929-4409.2012.01.5

Gollwitzer, M., Banse, R., Eisenbach, K., & Naumann, A. (2007). Effectiveness of the Vienna social competence training on explicit and implicit aggression. *European Journal of Psychological Assessment, 23*, 150–156.

Gollwitzer, M., Eisenbach, K., Atria, M., Strohmeier, D., & Banse, R. (2006). Evaluation of aggression-reducing effects of the "Viennese social competence training". *Swiss Journal of Psychology, 65*, 125–135.

Gradinger, P., Strohmeier, D., & Spiel, C. (2009). Traditional bullying and cyberbullying: Identification of risk groups for adjustment problems. *Journal of Psychology, 217*, 205–213. doi:10.1027/0044-3409.217.4.205

Gradinger, P., Yanagida, T., Strohmeier, D., & Spiel, C. (2015a). Prevention of cyberbullying and cyber victimization: Evaluation of the ViSC social competence program. *Journal of School Violence, 14*, 87–110. doi:10.1080/15388220.2014.963231

Gradinger, P., Yanagida, T., Strohmeier, D., & Spiel, C. (2015b). Effectiveness and sustainability of the ViSC social competence program to prevent cyberbullying and cyber-victimization: Class and individual level moderators. *Aggressive Behavior*. Accepted for publication.

Hox, J., van de Schoot, R., & Matthijsse, S. (2012). How few countries will do? Comparative survey analysis from a Bayesian perspective. *Survey Research Methods, 6*, 87–93.

Kärnä, A., Voeten, M., Little, T. D., Poskiparta, E., Alanen, E., & Salmivalli, C. (2011). Going to scale: A nonrandomized nationwide trial of the KiVa antibullying program for grades 1–9. *Journal of Consulting and Clinical Psychology, 79*, 796–805.

Little, T. D. (2013). *Longitudinal structural equation modeling*. New York, NY: Guilford Press.

BILDUNG-PSYCHOLOGY

Muthén, L. K., & Muthén, B. O. (1998–2012). *Mplus user's guide* (7th ed.). Los Angeles, CA: Muthén & Muthén.

Olweus, D. (1996). *The revised Olweus bully/victim questionnaire.* Bergen: Research Center for Health Promotion (Hemil Center).

Papacosta, E. S., Paradeisioti, A., & Lazarou, C. (2014). Bullying phenomenon and preventive programs in Cyprus's school system. *International Journal of Mental Health Promotion, 16*, 67–80. doi:10.1080/14623730.2014.888894

Pellegrini, A. D., & Bartini, M. (2000). A longitudinal study of bullying, victimization, and peer affiliation during the transition from primary school to middle school. *American Educational Research Journal, 37*, 699–725.

Roland, E., & Idsøe, T. (2001). Aggression and bullying. *Aggressive Behavior, 27*, 446–462.

Roland, E., & Vaaland, G. (2006). *ZERO teacher's guide to the zero anti-bullying programme.* Stavanger: Centre for Behavioural Research, University of Stavanger.

Salmivalli, C., & Nieminen, E. (2002). Proactive and reactive aggression among school bullies, victims, and bully-victims. *Aggressive Behavior, 28*, 30–44.

Schultes, M. T., Stefanek, E., van de Schoot, R., Strohmeier, D., & Spiel, C. (2014). Measuring implementation of a school-based violence prevention program. *Zeitschrift für Psychologie, 222*, 49–57. doi:10.1027/2151-2604/a000165

Smith, P., Mahdavi, J., Carvalho, M., Fisher, S., Russell, S., & Tippett, N. (2008). Cyberbullying: Its nature and impact in secondary school pupils. *Journal of Child Psychology and Psychiatry, 49*, 376–385. doi:10.1111/j.1469-7610.2007.01846.x

Solomontos-Kountouri, O., & Strohmeier, D. (2013, May). The implementation of the ViSC program in Cyprus. *EARA Newsletter*, p. 10.

Spiel, C., Reimann, R., Wagner, P., & Schober, B. (2008). Guest editorial: Bildung-psychology: The substance and structure of an emerging discipline. *Applied Developmental Science, 12*, 154–159. doi:10.1080/10888690802199426

Spiel, C., Salmivalli, C., & Smith, P. K. (2011). Translational research: National strategies for violence prevention in school. *International Journal of Behavioral Development, 35*, 381–382.

Spiel, C., & Strohmeier, D. (2011). National strategy for violence prevention in the Austrian public school system: Development and implementation. *International Journal of Behavioral Development, 35*, 412–418.

Spiel, C., & Strohmeier, D. (2012). Evidence-based practice and policy: When researchers, policy makers, and practitioners learn how to work together. *European Journal of Developmental Psychology, 9*, 150–162.

Stavrinides, P., Paradeisiotou, A., Tziogouros, C., & Lazarou, C. (2010). Prevalence of bullying among Cyprus elementary and high school students. *International Journal of Violence and School, 11*, 114–128.

Strohmeier, D., Aoyama, I., Gradinger, P., & Toda, Y. (2013). Cybervictimization and cyberaggression in eastern and western countries: Challenges of constructing a cross culturally appropriate scale. In S. Bauman, D. Cross, & J. Walker (Eds.), *Principles of cyberbullying research: Definitions, measures, and methodology* (pp. 202–221). New York, NY: Routledge.

Strohmeier, D., Gradinger, P., Schabmann, A., & Spiel, C. (2012). Gewalterfahrungen von Jugendlichen. Prävalenzen und Risikogruppen [Violence experiences among youth: Prevalence rates and risk groups]. In F. Eder (Ed.) *PISA 2009., Nationale Zusatzanalysen für Österreich* [Pisa 2009: National analyses for Austria] (pp. 165–208). Münster: Waxmann.

Strohmeier, D., Hoffmann, C., Schiller, E. M., Stefanek, E., & Spiel, C. (2012). ViSC social competence program. *New Directions for Youth Development, 2012*, 71–84.

Swearer, S. M., & Espelage, D. L. (2004). Introduction: A social-ecological framework of bullying among youth. In D. L. Espelage & S. M. Swearer (Eds.), *Bullying in American schools: A social-ecological perspective on prevention and intervention* (pp. 1–12). Mahwah, NJ: Lawrence Erlbaum Associates.

Ttofi, M. M., & Farrington, D. P. (2011). Effectiveness of school-based programs to reduce bullying: A systematic and meta-analytic review. *Journal of Experimental Criminology, 7,* 27–56. doi:10.1007/s11292-010-9109-1

Vitaro, F., Brendgen, M., & Barker, E. D. (2006). Subtypes of aggressive behaviors: A developmental perspective. *International Journal of Behavioral Development, 30,* 12–19. doi:10.1177/0165025406059968

Veenstra, R., Lindenberg, S., Zijlstra, B. J. H., De Winter, A. F., Verhulst, F. C., & Ormel, J. (2007). The dyadic nature of bullying and victimization: Testing a dual-perspective theory. *Child Development, 78,* 1843–1854. doi:10.1111/j.1467-8624.2007.01102.x

Yang, A., & Salmivalli, C. (2013). Different forms of bullying and victimization: Bully-victims versus bullies and victims. *European Journal of Developmental Psychology, 10,* 723–738. doi:10.1080/17405629.2013.793596

Yanagida, T., Strohmeier, D., & Spiel, C. (2015). Dynamic change of aggressive behavior and victimization among adolescents: Socio-ecological preventive intervention program ViSC. Manuscript submitted for publication.

Yeager, D. S., Fong, C. J., Lee, H. Y., & Espelage, D. L. (2015). Declines in efficacy of anti-bullying programs among older adolescents: Theory and a three-level meta-analysis. *Journal of Applied Developmental Psychology, 37,* 36–51. doi:10.1016/j.appdev.2014.11.005

∂ OPEN ACCESS

A Bildung-psychological investigation into student motives: McKinsey- or von Humboldt-oriented?

Willem Koops, Michael van den Kerkhof, Carlien Ostermeier and Rens van de Schoot

ABSTRACT

This study examined differential student motives among students from a social sciences bachelor's degree, and whether this difference related to participating in educational programmes for broader intellectual formation (Bildung). Survey research was conducted among 432 Dutch students (79.5% female), ranging in age from 17 to 32 years ($M_{age} = 21.12$, SD = 2.08). With five categories of questions, the survey assessed whether study motives corresponded to Bildung or vocational preparation. Results indicated an overall twocomponent structure, distinguishing Bildung motives (indicated as the von Humboldt component) from vocational preparation motives (indicated as the McKinsey component). In addition, respondents participating in a programme for broader intellectual formation or aspiring a research master's degree programme generally scored higher on Bildung and lower on vocational preparation compared to students who were not. Educational consequences of these findings are discussed. The main conclusion is that a von Humboldt perspective is feasible, since a substantial number of students share the von Humboldt perspective.

Bildung, a German word, refers to a concept that is difficult to translate into other languages. The philosopher and theologian Eckhart von Hochheim (according to historical inferences probably living from 1260–1328), in German usually indicated as *Meister Eckhart,* is considered as the scholar who introduced this concept (Spiel, Schober, Wagner, & Reimann, 2009, p. 5). For Eckhart, Bildung

---

ⓑ Supplementary material for this chapter can be found at:
http://www.tandfonline.com/doi/suppl/10.1080/17405629.2016.1230056
This is an Open Access article distributed under the terms of the Creative Commons Attribution-NonCommercial-NoDerivatives License (http://creativecommons.org/licenses/by-nc-nd/4.0/), which permits non-commercial re-use, distribution, and reproduction in any medium, provided the original work is properly cited, and is not altered, transformed, or built upon in any way.

was a divine process resulting in man becoming as close to the image of God as possible. God offers the image (in German: *Bild*), and to reach that image a process is needed called Bildung. So in that sense, Bildung leads to the desirable Bild. In later centuries the theologian context of the concept was lost, but Bildung still refers to a process leading to an ideal Bild. Mostly, this Bild has been defined in terms of what kind of personality is desirable for society. However, the ideas about what is desirable are changing over time.

Nowadays, the concept of Bildung is mostly connected with the work and the person of Friedrich Wilhelm Christian Karl Ferdinand Freiherr von Humboldt (1767–1835). von Humboldt became a very influential official in German education. The Prussian King asked him to lead the directorate of education. He installed a standardized system of public instruction, from basic schools until secondary education, and he founded Berlin University, that today bears the name Humboldt Universität. He created standardized state examinations and inspections and furthermore installed a sub department within the Ministry to oversee and design curricula, textbooks and learning aids.

The Humboldtian model of education goes beyond vocational training. In a letter to the Prussian king, Humboldt wrote:

> People obviously cannot be good craft workers, merchants, soldiers, or businessmen unless, regardless of their occupation, they are good, upstanding and – according to their condition – well-informed human beings and citizens. If this basis is laid through schooling, vocational skills are easily acquired later on, and a person is always free to move from one occupation to another, as so often happens in life. (Günther, 1988)

Today, many critics of the European universities are demanding Humboldtian Bildung instead of vocational preparation.

One of these critics, the philosopher *Julian Nida-Rümelin*, criticised discrepancies between Humboldt's ideals and the contemporary European education policy. He argued that our modern Bachelor-Master Bologna University system is too much oriented towards the labour market and to a lesser extent towards Bildung (Nida-Rümelin, 2009). He urges policymakers to make a choice between von Humboldt and McKinsey, or at least to find an optimal compromise between both positions.

James Oscar McKinsey (1889–1937) was a famous professor of accounting in the University of Chicago School of Business (Flesher & Tonya, 1996), who wrote the first book in history on *management accounting* (McKinsey, 1922), and founded the well-known and still worldwide operating *McKinsey and Company*. He was a university professor and a member of an accountancy practice when he founded McKinsey in 1926 to give financial and management advice to corporations. His firm concentrated on production or pricing, in the context of the political, social, and economic climate. McKinsey was a great example of applying knowledge to business, accounting and management. In that sense he is totally the opposite of von Humboldt, who in the first place valued personal development or Bildung, while McKinsey is in the first place oriented on vocational training, on what is called today knowlegde economy. We think that this dilemma is a very important issue for the so-called Bildungpsychology (Spiel et al., 2009). Bildungpsychology is a specific psychological discipline, founded by Spiel and Reimann (2005). Spiel and colleagues developed a model for the study of Bildung as a lifelong learning process. This model is three dimensional, existing of *activity levels* (micro, meso, and macro level), *functional areas* (research, counselling, prevention, intervention and controlling), and the *Bildung-career*, running from infancy and early childhood to advanced adulthood. If Bildungpsychology studies Bildung, then it should go beyond studying the way that individuals are prepared for the labour market, or for the knowledge economy. Looking at the universities, there is indeed a call for more Bildung.

However, this call predominantly comes from policymakers, senior scholars and intellectuals. Very little is known about the motivation and the attitudes of the students themselves. We think that the design of study programmes should be informed by knowledge about students' motivations. It is therefore that we study the opinions and attitudes of university students with respect to the dilemma McKinsey vs. von Humboldt. In other words: Bildung vs. job market and knowledge economy. This research is in the segment of the model of Spiel et al. (2009), that is found by choosing at the level of activity: the micro level (it is about individual attitudes and motivations), the functional area of research (we hope to gather data that can be used in devising university curricula) and looking at the Bildung career it is on the level of the tertiary school.

Bildung at Utrecht University

The Faculty of Social Sciences (FSS) at Utrecht University (UU) offers 7 bachelor programs: general social sciences, cultural anthropology, pedagogical sciences, psychology, sociology and a specicific bachelor for the education of future teachers of elementary schools. In addition to these regular bachelor programs students can apply for additional extra-curricular programs that offer general academic formation (Bildung). There are three such programs: the Descartes program, the von Humboldt program and participation in Liberal Arts and Science program.

The Descartes program is for students, who want to participate in a program (in addition to their regular bachelor program) that offers broader multidisciplinary insights (from humanities to physics) and historical and societal contexts. Students are selected from all the disciplines of the University. Within the FSS there is a possibility for so-called honor students to follow in their second and third bachelor years the von Humboldt program offering in total half a year of study in ethical, philosophical and methodological aspects of the social sciences.

The UU also offers a full three year bachelor in Liberal Arts and Science, which offers a multidisciplinary education. There is a differentiation in three groups of core disciplines: (1) history, language, culture, religion and philosophy; (2) physics, geology and artificial intelligence; and (3) social sciences, geography and economy. Only this last choice is exceptionally combined with a study in one of the social science bachelor programs.

The present study

In the current study, we answer four research questions; the first being whether the questionnaire we developed can be used to assess Bildung or the von Humboldt motive, as well as the contrasting McKinsey motive. In the study reported in this paper we asked Bachelor students in the social and behavioural sciences of Utrecht University to indicate why they studied their particular Bachelor programme. Moreover, we asked them the same questions about their opinion on the relevance of science, the aims of universities, the student's own general academic attitudes. Lastly, we asked them whether they are planning to make the choice for a research master or a professional, in the UU always indicated as 'academic master'. Those who chose the option 'research master' were asked why they made this choice. We hypothesized to find a two-component factor structure across the Likert scales that we used: a component referring to Bildung, which we will call the *von Humboldt component*, and one referring to preparation for the Job Market, to be indicated as the *McKinsey component*. All questions with our hypothesized two-component structure are presented in Table 1.

The second question is about motives and attitudes of the students who are participating in the programmes, which explicitly are offered for students who are longing for a broad intellectual academic formation. We expect, and that is our second hypothesis, that students who already made the choice at our university for special programmes that offer broader intellectual formation will have higher scores on the von Humboldt component than on the McKinsey component, while in contrast their counterparts show the opposite pattern.

Thirdly, we want to compare students who make the choice for applied and practical work and therefore choose a professional oriented master ('academic master') with students who choose a 'research master'. Our third hypothesis states that those students who aspire after a research master will score higher on the von Humboldt component than on the *McKinsey* component, while those aspiring after an academic master will score higher on the McKinsey component than on the von Humboldt component.

To exclude the potential confounding effect of study achievement here, we also expected, and that is the fourth hypothesis, that students who aspire after a research master will score higher on the von Humboldt component than on the *McKinsey* component, and vice versa, even after controlling for differences in study achievement.

BILDUNG-PSYCHOLOGY

Table 1. Questionnaire items including hypothesized component classification (McKinsey vs. von Humboldt).

Questionnaire item	Component classification
Main objective of a bachelor's degree programme	
1. Intellectual education	Hum
2. To develop research skills	Hum
3. Career orientation	McK
4. To prepare for the job market	McK
5. To learn to think critically	Hum
6. To prepare for a specific master's degree programme	McK
7. To learn to see the interconnection between disciplines	Hum
8. To lay a foundation for further specialisation	McK
9. To learn to be sociocritical	Hum
10. To acquire the necessary basic knowledge	McK
Importance of science	
1. To be able to base your assessments on knowledge files	Hum
2. To contribute to democratic political objectives	McK
3. To train critical and outspoken citizens	Hum
4. To allow for technological applications	McK
5. To be able to base decisions on validated knowledge	Hum
6. To encourage critical thinking	Hum
7. To train useful specialists	McK
8. To build a strong knowledge economy	McK
9. To further economic prosperity	McK
10. To create independent, autonomous personalities	Hum
Aim of the university	
1. To train students to practice intellectual professions	McK
2. To strengthen the knowledge economy	McK
3. To create independent 'headstrong thinkers'	Hum
4. To connect and harmonise with the societal requirements	McK
5. To further democracy	McK
6. To be able to practise science independently (free from church and state)	Hum
7. To educate free and universal citizens	Hum
8. To solve societal issues	McK
9. To further freedom of speech	Hum
10. To practice teaching and research comprehensively	Hum
General opinions	
1. An academic degree prepares you for a career of 'lifelong learning'	Hum
2. Academic training is the main objective; being trained for a specific profession is a secondary aim	Hum
3. When I read a scientific article, I find it more important to critically reflect on it than to learn from it	Hum
4. When I study, I find it more important to understand the content than to be able to apply it to other areas	Hum
5. The main objective of an academic degree programme is to learn to theorise creatively	Hum
6. Scientific knowledge is empirically validated knowledge	McK
7. What I learn should be immediately useful; I need to be able to apply it	McK
8. Theories must have a practical use	McK
9. Practical skills are important elements of a scientific education	McK
10. To really understand always means: to be able to apply it in practice	McK
Motivation to pursue a research master's degree programme	
1. To increase my chances on the job market	McK
2. To practice a profession at a higher level	Hum
3. To be able to find a better salaried job	McK

(Continued)

Table 1. (Continued)

Questionnaire item	Component classification
4. To acquire scientific knowledge	McK
5. To be able to critically contribute to the societal debate	Hum
6. To become an independent thinker	Hum
7. To be able to obtain an intellectually superior position	McK
8. To write a research thesis	McK
9. To learn to conduct research independently	Hum
10. To prepare for an academic career	Hum

Note: McK = McKinsey component; Hum = von Humboldt component.

Method

Procedure

An invitational link to an online survey (using the software LimeSurvey) was send via email to all students attending a bachelor's degree programme at the Faculty of Social and Behavioural Sciences at Utrecht University (total $N = 3359$), the Netherlands. The online survey remained active for 11 weeks between April and July 2015.

Before completing the questionnaire, students were informed on the aim of the study: to investigate student motives and how this correlates to opinions on science and the university. Despite participants' having answered several demographic variables, it was made clear all data would be collected and processed anonymously. Participation was voluntary, could be ended at any point without further notice, and no (monetary) incentive was provided. Respondents who indicated they were interested in the results of this study were requested to send a separate email to one of the authors.

Sample

Out of all the students who received the invitation, 699 students clicked on the survey link (79.2% non-response). Of the students that responded, only students who reported on the key study variables were included for further analyses ($n = 472$). Subsequent screening of the data revealed that 40 respondents did not participate in a bachelor's degree programme. We excluded these respondents from further analyses, yielding a final sample of 432 students, ranging from 17 to 32 years of age ($M_{age} = 21.12$, SD $= 2.08$, 79.5% female). Respondents were predominantly of Dutch origin (96%) and were distributed among the six bachelor's degree programmes at the Faculty of Social and Behavioural Sciences as follows: General Social Sciences (16.9%); Cultural Anthropology and Developmental Sociology (7.9%); Educational Sciences (5.1%); Pedagogical Sciences (16.2%); Psychology (48%); Sociology (6%). The distribution among the first, second, and third year of the study was 25.5, 26.4, and 48.2%, respectively. Out of the 432 students who replied to the von Humboldt questions, 361

BILDUNG-PSYCHOLOGY

students provided information about whether they are planning to proceed with either an academic master ($n = 298$) or a research master ($n = 63$). The rest of the respondents indicated they don't know yet what to do after finishing their bachelor, or they have other plans like traveling. GPA scores are missing for another six students. We report the exact sample sizes used for each analysis in the tables.

In Table 2, we compared our respondents with the student population on several background characteristics, showing our sample to be representative for the entire population (i.e., bachelor students at the Faculty of Social and Behavioural Sciences in Utrecht). That is, for our final sample ($n = 432$), chi-square goodness of fit tests revealed no significant distributional differences in terms of gender, year of study, and bachelor's degree programme between our sample and the total population of bachelor's degree students ($N = 3359$). We also tested for age differences and our sample was 0.25 years significantly (but not substantially) younger, $t(431) = -2.497$, $p = .013$. More details are provided in the online supplementary materials: questionnaire, data-set and logbook with syntax files and detailed results.

Measures

Student motives were assessed with a custom-made questionnaire using five categories of questions, each consisting of 10 items of which five were intended to measure the von Humboldt component and five to measure the McKinsey

Table 2. Comparison of sample characteristics with population data using χ^2 goodness of fit tests.

	Population ($N = 3359$) N (%)	Sample		χ^2 (df)
		Observed n (%)	Expected n	
Gender[a]		$n = 431$		.42 (1)
Male	689 (20.51)	83 (19.26)	88.41	
Female	2670 (79.49)	348 (80.74)	342.59	
Year of study[b]		$n = 432$		5.14 (2)
1st	1019 (30.34)	110 (25.46)	131.05	
2nd	861 (25.63)	114 (26.39)	110.73	
3rd	1479 (44.03)	208 (48.15)	190.21	
Degree[c]		$n = 431$		5.02 (5)
CUL	265 (7.89)	36 (8.35)	34.00	
EDU	170 (5.06)	31 (7.19)	21.81	
GSS	566 (16.85)	73 (16.94)	72.62	
PED	544 (16.20)	63 (14.62)	69.80	
PSY	1611 (47.96)	200 (46.40)	206.71	
SOC	203 (6.04)	28 (6.50)	26.05	

[a]In our sample, 1 respondent indicated having an 'other' gender than male/female. For analytical purposes, this respondent was excluded from the χ^2 test (but not from main analyses).
[b]Since respondents were forced to select bachelor year 1–3 in our survey, the 600 students from our population at bachelor year ≥ 4 were merged with the 3rd year students.
[c]CUL = Cultural anthropology and developmental sociology; EDU = Educational sciences; GSS = General social sciences; PED = Pedagogical sciences; PSY = Psychology; SOC = Sociology.

component, see Table 1. Two of the authors of this paper (W. K. and C. O.) gathered recent Dutch and German literature on von Humboldt and McKinsey, as far as Bildung and vocational formation and economic thinking about knowledge and science are considered. The two authors independently derived from the chosen set of texts the most frequently used adjectives referring to both orientations. For von Humboldt adjectives like democratic, socio-critical, and autonomous were found. For the McKinsey orientation adjectives like useful, practical and technological were found. The common set of adjectives was then used to formulate the items of Table 1. All items were rated on a 5-point magnitude scale (1 = *not important at all* to 5 = *very important*). The first category referred to the opinion on the *main objective of a bachelor's degree programme* (e.g., 'to learn to be socio-critical' for the von Humboldt and 'to prepare for a specific master's degree programme' for the McKinsey component, Cronbach's α = .66). For the second category, respondents were asked for their opinion on the *importance of science* (e.g., 'to be able to base decisions on validated knowledge' for the von Humboldt and 'to train useful specialists' for the McKinsey component, Cronbach's α = .74). The third category referred to the opinion on the *aim of the university* (e.g., 'to create independent "headstrong" thinkers' for the von Humboldt and 'to strengthen the knowledge economy' for the McKinsey component, Cronbach's α = .71). For the fourth category, respondents were asked to what extent they *subscribed to a number of opinions* (e.g., 'when I read a scientific article, I find it more important to critically reflect on it than to learn it's contents' for the von Humboldt and 'practical skills are important elements of a scientific education' for the McKinsey component, Cronbach's α = .41). For the fifth, and last, category, respondents who indicated wanting to pursue a research master's degree programme were asked for their motive as to *why they would start a research master's degree programme* (e.g., 'to learn to conduct research independently' for the von Humboldt and 'to increase my chances on the job market' for the McKinsey component, Cronbach's α = .64).

In addition, the following demographic variables were assessed: gender (male/female/other; age; native language (Dutch/non-Dutch); year of study (year 1, 2 or 3); year of enrolment (2010–2015); bachelor's degree programme (General Social Sciences/Cultural Anthropology and Developmental Sociology/Educational Sciences/Pedagogical Sciences/Psychology/Sociology); enrolment in a special programme for broader intellectual formation (von Humboldt programme/Descartes programme/Liberal Arts and Sciences); previously completed higher education degree programme (yes/no); involvement in extracurricular activities (e.g., 'membership of a board' or 'committee work'); and finally Grade Point Average (GPA).

Analytic strategy

To assess our first hypothesis whether a two-component structure (von Humboldt vs. McKinsey component) would emerge in our data, separate exploratory factor analyses (EFA) with direct oblimin rotation and maximum likelihood extraction were conducted for all five categories of questions using IBM SPSS Statistics Version 22. In case the initial factor structure is not readily interpretable in two components but the scree plot, Eigenvalues and factor loadings do indicate two components to be viable, subsequent two-factor EFAs were conducted. In case the initial factor structure was readily interpretable in more than two components, we adhered to this structure. In the main text, we summarized findings of the EFAs and more detailed information can be found in the supplementary materials which includes not only all analytic steps, but also all the results from SPSS.

For our second hypothesis, we expected that students, who already made the choice at our university for special programmes that offer broader intellectual education, would have higher scores on the von Humboldt component than on the McKinsey component. Based on the most viable factor solution, composite factor scores were created for each of the factors. Note that factor scores take cross loading into account. Higher factor scores indicated scoring higher on the von Humboldt component, with zero indicating an average score. Multivariate analyses of variance, corrected for multiple testing (Bonferroni), were used to examine differences between students in special programmes and those who were not.

As third hypothesis, we expected that those students who made the choice for a research master would score higher on the von Humboldt component than on the *McKinsey* component. To test this hypothesis, separate multivariate analyses of variance were used on the factor scores of each of the categories of questions (with, of course, the exception of the pursuit of a research master's degree programme), corrected for multiple testing (Bonferroni).

While multivariate analyses of variance could show strong evidence for an effect of master's degree programme choice on student motives, there is reason to believe this effect might as well be caused by differences in study achievement, as reflected by respondents' GPA. Therefore, for our fourth hypothesis, we conducted the previous analyses of variance for the effect of master's degree programme choice on student motives again, but this time with a posthoc subgroup analysis. Since admission to a research master's degree programme is primarily based on a having a GPA of 3.43 and higher, this criterion was used to distinguish between categories of students that were admissible and/or aspired such a programme. We proceeded with the following variables: academic master and low GPA (Acad/low); academic master and high GPA (Acad/high); research master and low GPA (ReMA/low); research master and high GPA (ReMa/high). More detailed information about these steps can be found in the supplementary materials. Primary interest goes to the comparison of students having a low GPA but also aspired a research master's degree programme vs. students having a high GPA but did not aspire a research master's to exclude the potential confounding effect of study achievement.

Results

EFA results

Main objective of a bachelor's degree programme

For the first category of questions, referring to the opinion on the main objective of a bachelor's degree programme, the factorability of the 10 items was explored. Initial Eigenvalues and the scree plot were examined, showing two factors with an Eigenvalue larger than 1 that explained 25.5 and 20.9% of the variance respectively. This two-factor solution seemed to be readily interpretable as all items on the von Humboldt component showed high loadings on one factor and low on the other one, while the reverse was found for the items hypothesized belong to the McKinsey component.

Importance of science

With regard to the second category of questions, the opinion on the importance of science, factorability examination revealed no clear component structure in the inter-item correlation matrix. To assess the number of factors to be retained, initial Eigenvalues and the scree plot were examined, showing three factors with an Eigenvalue larger than 1 that explained 30.3, 13.8, and 12.3% of the variance respectively. However, based on the scree plot, a two-factor solution may have also been viable. Therefore, a subsequent EFA with two fixed factors was conducted. This two-factor solution showed two factors with an Eigenvalue larger than 1 to be retained, explaining 30.3 and 13.8% of the variance respectively. However, based on the structure matrix, this two-factor solution did not seem to be easily interpretable, giving preference to the initial three-factor solution. In this solution, the first factor was interpreted to represent economic importance, the second freedom and autonomy, and the third the importance of science and its applications.

Aim of the University

With regard to the opinion on the aim of the university, results showed three factors with an Eigenvalue larger than 1, with the first two factors explaining 29.1 and 13.5% of the variance respectively. In addition, the scree plot supported this two-factor solution. Upon assessing the zero-order correlations, four out of five questions regarding the von Humboldt component had high loadings on one factor and low loadings on the other one. For three out of five questions assessing the McKinsey component, a reverse result was found, leaving three ambiguous loadings on both factors.

General opinion

For the category of questions in which respondents were asked to what extent they subscribed to a number of opinions, results indicated three factors with an Eigenvalue larger than 1, with the first two factors explaining 28.2 and 15.7% of the variance respectively. In addition, the scree plot supported this two-factor solution. Upon assessing the zero-order correlations, four out of five questions regarding the McKinsey component had high loadings on one factor and low loadings on the second one. For all five questions assessing the von Humboldt component, the reverse was found.

Master's degree choice

With regard to the category of questions on which respondents, who indicated wanting to pursue a research master's degree programme, were asked for their motive as to why they would start a research master's degree programme, inter correlations showed signs of a three-factor structure (all p's < .05). Eigenvalues and the scree plot were examined, showing three factors with an Eigenvalue larger than 1 that explained 25.8, 22.6, and 14.8% of the variance respectively. In addition, the scree plot supported an initial three-factor solution. Based on the structure matrix, the three factors seemed to represent more personal motives for choosing a research master's degree programme, instead of Bildung or vocational motives, with the first factor representing job and economical security, the second factor furthering academic competence, and the third factor representing becoming an autonomous and sociocritical citizen.

Differential study motives by study programme

In this paragraph, the multivariate effects for Special Program on each of the five categories of questions are presented, as summarized in Table 3.

Main objective of a bachelor's degree programme

For the category of questions on the main objective of a bachelor's degree programme, based on the factor scores of the initial two-factor solution, a statistically significant difference in factor scores was found based on enrolment in a special educational programme, $F(2, 429) = 10.09$, $p < .001$; Wilk's $\Lambda = 0.955$, partial $\eta^2 = .045$. This result indicated that students who participated in one of the programmes at the Faculty of Social and Behavioural Sciences for a broader intellectual formation, compared to those who do not, had stronger motives that correspond to the von Humboldt component when it comes to their opinion on the objective of a bachelor's degree programme. Exactly the opposite holds for the McKinsey component, see Table 3).

BILDUNG-PSYCHOLOGY

Table 3. Multivariate effects for special programme on each of the five categories of questions.

| | Special programme | | | | | |
| | Yes | | | No | | |
	N	M	SD	N	M	SD
Main objective of bachelor's degree programme	380			52		
1. McKinsey		−.41[a]	1.09		.06[a]	0.98
2. von Humboldt		.40[b]	0.76		−.05[b]	1.02
Importance of science	380			52		
1. Economy		−.36[c]	1.14		.05[c]	0.97
2. Freedom/autonomy		.33[d]	0.95		−.05[d]	1.00
3. Science		.39[e]	0.95		−.05[e]	1.00
Aim of the university	380			52		
1. McKinsey		<−.01	1.02		<.01	1.00
2. von Humboldt		.14	0.92		−.02	1.01
General opinion	380			52		
1. McKinsey		−.40[f]	1.00		.05[f]	0.99
2. von Humboldt		.36[g]	1.03		−.05[g]	0.99
Motives to pursue research master's degree programme	25			38		
1. Job security		−.14	0.98		.09	1.02
2. Academic competence		.07	1.13		−.04	0.92
3. Autonomous/critical		.32[h]	0.88		−.21[h]	1.03

Note: Means with the same upper script differ significantly ($p < .05$), corrected for multiple testing (Bonferroni).

Importance of science

For the opinion on the importance of science, analyses were based on the initial three-factor solution that was found. Results showed a statistically significant difference in factor scores based on enrolment in a special educational programme, $F(3, 428) = 8.03$, $p < .001$; Wilk's $\Lambda = 0.947$, partial $\eta^2 = .053$. On closer inspection, it seemed that students from a special educational programme, compared to those who were not, valued the importance of science more in terms of fostering freedom and autonomy, in addition to valuing knowledge-based decisions, that is the importance of science and its applications (in Table 3 simply indicated as 'Science'). On the other hand, students who were not enrolled in a special educational programme had more economical motives for the importance of science.

Aim of the University

With regard to the opinion on the aim of the university, multivariate analyses of variance on the two-fixed factor solution showed no statistically significant difference in factor scores based on enrolment in a special educational programme, $F(2, 429) = .545$, $p = .580$; Wilk's $\Lambda = 0.997$, partial $\eta^2 = .003$. Accordingly, students from a special educational programme did not seem to differ from students not in a special educational programme on the opinion whether the university should provide vocational preparation or broader intellectual formation.

BILDUNG-PSYCHOLOGY

General opinion

For the category 'which opinions do you subscribe to', analysis on the two-fixed factor solution showed a statistically significant difference in factor score based on enrolment in a special educational programme, $F(2, 429) = 8.68$, $p < .001$; Wilk's $\Lambda = 0.961$, partial $\eta^2 = .039$. This result seemed to indicate that, in general, students from a special educational programme tended to subscribe more to Bildung-related opinions, referring to the von Humboldt component, whereas students not in a special educational programme subscribed more to practical opinions, referring to the McKinsey component.

Master's degree choice

From the analysis of variance on the three initial factor scores of the pursuit of a research master's degree programme, there was no overall statistically significant difference in factor scores based on enrolment in a special educational programme, $F(359) = 1.78$, $p = .161$; Wilk's $\Lambda = 0.917$, partial $\eta^2 = .083$. However, upon assessing the pairwise comparisons, it appeared that one effect was significant. Nevertheless, due to our correction for multiple testing we have refrained from interpreting this result.

Differential study motives by master's degree choice

Main objective of a bachelor's degree programme

With regard to the opinion on the main objective of a bachelor's degree programme, results indicated a significant difference between respondents who indicated wanting to pursue a research master's degree programme and those who did not, $F(2, 358) = 18.51$, $p < .001$; Wilk's $\Lambda = 0.906$, partial $\eta^2 = .094$. This result suggested that students who aspired a research master, scored significantly higher on the von Humboldt component and lower on the McKinsey component compared to students who aspired an academic master (Table 4).

Table 4. Multivariate effects for master's degree choice on opinion on main objective of a bachelor's degree programme (with posthoc analysis).

	N	1. McKinsey		2. von Humboldt	
		M	SD	M	SD
Master's choice					
Academic	298	.20[a]	0.90	−.03[b]	0.97
Research	63	−.51[a]	1.08	.35[b]	1.00
By subgroup					
Acad/low GPA	227	.16[c]	0.94	.01[f]	1.01
Acad/high GPA	58	.34[de]	0.76	−.14[g]	0.83
ReMA/low GPA	27	−.32[d]	0.90	.19	1.15
ReMA/high GPA	33	−.64[ce]	0.98	.62[fg]	0.76

Note: Means with the same upper script differ significantly ($p < .05$), corrected for multiple testing (Bonferroni).

Importance of science

For the opinion on the importance of science, the analysis showed a significant overall effect of aspiration for a research master's degree programme, $F(3, 357) = 8.31, p < .001$, Wilk's $\Lambda = 0.935$, partial $\eta^2 = .065$. More specifically, pairwise comparisons indicated that respondents who wanted to pursue a research master had significantly higher scientific motives and lower economical motives that respondents who aspired an academic master's degree. For the third factor, that seemed to reflect motives of freedom and autonomy, no significant differences were found (Table 5).

Aim of the University

On the category of questions regarding the opinion on the aim of the university, an overall significant effect was found by master's degree programme choice, $F(2, 358) = 5.50, p < .01$, Wilk's $\Lambda = .970$, partial $\eta^2 = .030$. However, as indicated by the pairwise comparisons, this effect seemed only to apply to the McKinsey component, where the respondents who indicated wanting to pursue a research's master's degree programme scored significantly lower than students who aspired an academic master (Table 6).

General opinion

Analysis on the factor scores of the last category of questions, those on general opinions on broader intellectual education vs. vocational education, showed a significant effect of the aspiration for a certain type of master's degree programme, $F(2, 358) = 20.33, p < .001$, Wilk's $\Lambda = .898$, partial $\eta^2 = .102$. Here, students who aspired a research master had a significant higher score on the von Humboldt component and a lower one on the McKinsey component, whereas the opposite was found for respondents who wanted to pursue an academic master's degree programme (Table 7).

Table 5. Multivariate effects for master's degree choice on opinion on the importance of science (with posthoc analysis).

	N	1. Economy		2. Freedom/autonomy		3. Science	
		M	SD	M	SD	M	SD
Master's choice							
Academic	298	.12[a]	0.93	−.03	1.02	−.06[b]	0.99
Research	63	−.30[a]	1.21	.11	0.96	.46[b]	0.96
By subgroup							
Acad/low GPA	227	.12[c]	0.94	−.04	1.05	−.10[d]	1.00
Acad/high GPA	58	.08	0.93	.10	0.93	.09	0.93
ReMA/low GPA	27	−.11	1.28	.01	0.83	.36	0.97
ReMA/high GPA	33	−49[c]	1.11	.26	1.03	.53[d]	0.95

Note: Means with the same upper script differ significantly ($p < .05$), corrected for multiple testing (Bonferroni).

BILDUNG-PSYCHOLOGY

Table 6. Multivariate effects for master's degree choice on opinion on the aim of the University (with posthoc analysis).

	N	1. von Humboldt		2. McKinsey	
		M	SD	M	SD
Master's choice					
Academic	298	−.01	0.98	.14[a]	0.96
Research	63	−.03	1.11	−.31[a]	1.07
By subgroup					
Acad/low GPA	227	<.01	0.98	.15	0.96
Acad/high GPA	58	−.05	1.00	.01	0.99
ReMA/low GPA	27	< −.01	1.18	−.36	0.83
ReMA/high GPA	33	.13	0.92	−.32	1.18

Note: Means with the same upper script differ significantly ($p < .05$), corrected for multiple testing (Bonferroni).

Subgroup analysis – GPA

Main objective of a bachelor's degree programme

With regard to the opinion on the main objective of a bachelor's degree programme, results indicated a significant difference between respondents within each of the four subgroups (combining type of master's degree with high/low GPA), $F(6, 680) = 6.97$, $p < .001$; Wilk's $\Lambda = .888$, partial $\eta^2 = .058$. Posthoc comparisons showed that the group of respondents from the ReMa/high group scored significantly lower on the McKinsey component and higher on the von Humboldt component than pursuers of an academic master (Table 4). Results also indicated that respondents from the ReMa/low group scored lower on the McKinsey component than respondents from the Acad/high group. For the von Humboldt component, however, no significant difference between these two groups was found.

Importance of science

For the opinion on the importance of science, the analysis showed a significant overall effect of group membership, $F(9, 825.19) = 3.35$, $p < .001$, Wilk's $\Lambda = .916$, partial $\eta^2 = .029$. However, this difference was only significant for the ReMa/high

Table 7. Multivariate effects for master's degree choice on general opinions (with posthoc analysis).

	N	1. McKinsey		2. von Humboldt	
		M	SD	M	SD
Master's choice					
Academic	298	.13[a]	0.96	−.06[b]	1.01
Research	63	−.56[a]	0.95	.40[b]	0.96
By subgroup					
Acad/low GPA	227	.12[c]	0.98	<.01[f]	1.03
Acad/high GPA	58	.10[de]	0.93	−.25[g]	0.90
ReMA/low GPA	27	−.50[cd]	0.93	.15	0.98
ReMA/high GPA	33	−.53[ce]	0.95	.64[fg]	0.94

Note: Means with the same upper script differ significantly ($p < .05$), corrected for multiple testing (Bonferroni).

vs. the Acad/low group, where the former scored lower on economical motives and higher on scientific motives (Table 5).

Aim of the University
On the category of questions regarding the opinion on the aim of the university, an overall significant effect was found for group membership, $F(6, 680) = 2.14$, $p < .05$, Wilk's $\Lambda = .963$, partial $\eta^2 = .019$. However, as indicated by the posthoc analysis, no significant differences were found between the subgroups (Table 6).

General opinion
Finally, analysis on the factor scores of the last category of questions, those on general opinions on broader intellectual formation vs. vocational preparation, showed a general significant effect of subgroup, $F(6, 680) = 6.76$, $p < .001$, Wilk's $\Lambda = .891$, partial $\eta^2 = .056$. More specifically, students who aspired a ReMa scored lower on the McKinsey component than students who wanted to pursue an academic master, regardless of GPA, where the ReMA/low group also scores significantly lower than the Acad/high group. For the von Humboldt component, only a general significant difference was found for the ReMa groups vs. the Acad groups (Table 7).

Discussion

Our data overall confirms our first hypothesis: there is evidence that students are thinking in terms of von Humboldtian Bildung vs. McKinsey like job preparation. Looking at the student motives to study the bachelor programme of their choice, there is a clear two factor structure with a von Humboldt and a McKinsey component. Further support is offered by the two factor structures for the opinions on the aim of the University and by the two factor structure for the general set of opinions asked. With respect to the motives to pursuit a research master programme, a first factor represents job and economic security, but the other two factors together represent a typical von Humboldt stance: academic competence and becoming an autonomous and sociocritical citizen. It should be realized that the first factor is not necessarily contrasting with the Bildung idea, it is quite probable that students are hoping for a secure job within typical academic (Bildung-) environments instead of hoping for applied practical jobs. Finally, in the structure of the students' opinions on the importance of science a first factor was found that stresses economic value, while the two other factors still stress a Bildung idea: freedom and autonomy, the importance of science and its applications. Opinions on the importance of science may be different from the motives for students' own choices: in their general opinions, economical importance may be accepted by students who are personally striving for Bildung instead of a position on the job market.

Our second hypothesis stated that students who already chose to follow programmes for broader intellectual formation (here further indicated as 'Bildung-students') would have higher scores on the von Humboldt- motives and lower scores on the Mc Kinsey motives compared to students who did not participate in these programmes. Based on factor scores, it is clear that Bildung-students indeed have stronger Bildung motives for their bachelor study than students who do not follow the special programmes. Analysis on the opinions on the importance of science shows that Bildung-students value the importance of science in terms of fostering autonomy and sociocriticism more than their counterparts, who prefer economic motives. With respect to the aim of the university, the Bildung-students and their counterparts do not differ in opinion. Of course, these opinions do not reflect students' personal university aims, but general ones instead. Apparently, both groups accept von Humboldt-as well as McKinsey-values as general aims of the university. With respect to their general opinions, Bildung-students subscribe more Bildung-related opinions, while their counterparts prefer practical opinions. Finally, there is no general difference by Bildung-students who want to pursue a research master's degree vs. counterparts who pursue a research master's degree, but do not participate in special programmes. This suggests that the preference for following a research master programme as such relates to Bildung-motives. The only difference is suggested (but not statistically proven) by the data in Table 7: Bildung students may be more interested in independence and critical thinking.

Our third hypothesis stated that students who aspire to pursue a research master's degree would score higher on the von Humboldt component than on the McKinsey component, and more so than their counterparts who prefer to purse a professional master (at Utrecht University called 'academic master'). The data on the opinions on the main objectives of a bachelor's degree programme confirms this hypothesis. Data on the opinions of the importance of science confirm the hypothesis too: students who aspire to pursue a research master's degree score higher on scientific and lower on economical motives than their counterparts do. Opinions on the aim of the university differ in the expected direction too: students aspiring after a research master score lower on the factor of vocational education than their counterparts. Finally, for the questions on general opinions, those same students score higher on the von Humboldt component and lower on the McKinsey component than the students who pursue a professional 'academic master'.

Since student motives may be related to their GPA we analysed the differences between four groups of students: (1) students choosing an academic masters with low GPA; (2) idem, but with high GPA; (3) research master with low GPA; (4) idem, but with high GPA. The overall results show that students from groups three and four systematically score higher on the von Humboldt component and lower on the McKinsey component than those of groups one and two. This is independent of the GPA: even students of group three score lower on the McKinsey component than those of group two. These data quite convincingly show the principal difference in students' perspectives: von Humboldt vs. McKinsey.

Despite these conclusive results, this study has a few limitations. In the first place, the instruments used were devised for this particular research (tailor made), and their psychometric qualities have not been investigated independently from this study. This of course may have consequences for the reproducibility of our findings. Relatedly, we decided to keep all items even if there were high cross loadings. This strategy negatively affects the psychometric properties. More research is needed to find out whether the questionnaire could be improved without the items with such cross loadings. Secondly, our research suffered from a high non-response percentage, although at the same time our final sample turned out to be statistically representative. Furthermore we only investigated the Faculty of Social and behavioural sciences and although that faculty is in between the humanities and the sciences, we cannot be sure that it is representative for the other faculties. Finally, we cannot be sure that the situation at Utrecht University is representative of other European universities. Therefore, substantial research still has to be conducted to permit generalization to other European universities.

Such research would be important for educational purposes. For the education of university students, it is essential to know their motives and attitudes. If we know, as this research indicates, that students differ fundamentally in their appreciation of a von Humboldt perspective and/or a McKinsey perspective, this has consequences for the universities' curricula. If, as nowadays is strengthened in the discussions, we opt for a von Humboldt university conception we should offer the programs that part of the students are longing for.

Following the view of von Humboldt, we conclude with our conviction that Bildungpsychology (Spiel & Reimann, 2005) should investigate student motives, in an attempt to realise a mentality of academically studying for Bildung, which is lifelong learning with professionality as a respected, but secondary goal. Happily enough, quite a substantial number of students share this perspective and will be intrinsically motivated to develop themselves as intellectuals.

Acknowledgement

The last author was supported by a grant from the Netherlands organization for scientific research: NWO-VIDI-452-14-006.

Disclosure statement

No potential conflict of interest was reported by the authors.

Funding

This work was supported by the Netherlands organization for scientific research [grant number NWO-VIDI-452–14-006].

ORCID

Rens van de Schoot ⓘ http://orcid.org/0000-0001-7736-2091

References

Flesher, D. L., & Tonya, K. F. (1996) McKinsey, James O. (1889–1937). In M. Chatfield & R. Vangermeersch (Eds.), *History of accounting: An international encyclopedia* (pp. 410–411). New York, NY: Garland Publishing.

Günther, K.-H. (1988). Profiles of educators: Wilhelm von Humboldt (1767–1835). *Prospects, 18*, 127–136. doi:10.1007/bf02192965

McKinsey, J. (1922). *Budgetary control*. New York, NY: Ronald.

Nida-Rümelin, J. (2009, October 29). Die Chance zum Kompromiss ist da [A compromise is possible]. *Die Zeit*. Retrieved from http://www.zeit.de/2009/45/Bachelor-Kritik

Spiel, C., & Reimann, R. (2005). Bildungpsychologie [Bildungspsychology]. *Psychologische Rundschau, 56*, 291–294. doi:10.1026/0033-3042.56.4.291

Spiel, C., Schober, B., Wagner, P., & Reimann, R. (2009). Vorwort [Preface]. In C. Spiel, B. Schober, P. Wagner, & R. Reimann (Eds.), *Bildungspsychologie* (pp. 5–6). Göttingen: Hogrefe.

Index

Note: Numbers in **bold** refer to tables
Numbers in *italics* refer to figures

ability perception 57–8, 61, 63
absorption 80, 83
academic achievements 65, 68
academic competence 146–8
academic self-concept and gender role 6, 56–78
accomplishment 81
achievements in mathematics and reading 56–78
action orientation 35–6
active engagement 43
active implementation frameworks 47–8
activity areas of Bildung-Psychology 3, 13–14
addiction 82
ADHD *see* attention deficit/hyperactivity disorder
adjusted Lo-Mendell-Rubin likelihood ratio test 84–5
adolescence 91–2
advanced socio-digital competency 83
affective components of gender role self-concept 64–5
affective-motivational reaction 57–8, 61, 63
affective–motivational reactions 61–3
affirmative components of academic self-concept 67–8
aggression 35–6, 113–15
aggressive behaviour disorders 31, 113
aim of Utrecht University 140, 142–4, 146
aims of TALK evaluation 99
alienation 90
alpha error 65
analytic strategy 120
ANOVA 84

anti-bullying program 112–30
anxiety 31
approach to taking responsibility 19–21
Arens, A. K. 74
Arrow, Kenneth 49–50
aspects of Bildung-Psychology *see* crucial aspects of Bildung-Psychology
assertion 32
attention deficit/hyperactivity disorder 35–6
attention problems 31
Austria 112–30
autonomy 14, 19, 28, 33, 97, 100, 103, 107, 146–8

Banaji, M. R. 62
Bartini, M. 127
Bartley, L. 47
baseline effects in perpetration 123
basic approach to taking responsibility 19–21
Bayesian Information Criterion 84–5, 103, 105, 118
behavior-based femininity 64, 66–8, 71–2
behavior-based masculinity 64, 66–7, 69, 71–2
Bell Labs 50
belonging 32, 35
Bem Sex Role Inventory 59–60, 64
BIC *see* Bayesian Information Criterion
Biernat, M. 59
Bildung-career 2–3, 7, 72, 133
Bildung-psychological investigation into student motivation 131–49
biological gender 68–70
Blase, K. A. 44

INDEX

bodily functions 28–9
Boldizar, J. P. 60, 64
Bonferroni variance 139
bootstrap sampling 65
Bronfenbrenner, U. 3, 13
BSRI *see* Bem Sex Role Inventory
bullying 8, 35–6, 112–30; perpetuation 118; victimization 118, 125

calibration of learning 98
cascading logic model 47–51, **48**
causality of self-ascription 74–5
caution in analysis 90–91
central role of universities 16–18
challenges of cross-national dissemination 112–30
changes in pupil development 105
Chi square analysis 59
children and SED 27–40; importance of understanding 30–31
Children's Sex Role Inventory 64–6
classroom competencies 94–111
Clover model 31–6, *33*; and dimensions of SED *33*
cognitive components of academic self-concept 67–8
cognitive skills 32–3
collaborative learning 17–18, 89
competency in lifelong learning 3, 94–111
concrete interventions 6
confirmative factor analysis 66–7
connectivity 49–50
consistent self-ascription 59
core dimensions of SED 28–30
correlations, means, SDs **88**
Cowan, G. 59
Craven, R. G. 62
Crick, N. R. 119
Cronbach's α 65, 83, 102, 118–19, 138
cross-national dissemination 112–30
crosstabulation 84
crucial aspects of Bildung-Psychology 11–26; approaches to ensure transfer 16–18; conclusion 21–2; relevance of progress 11–12; taking responsibility 19–21; transfer as emerging challenge 14–16; transfer as immanent characteristic 13–14
custom-made questionnaires 137–8
Cvencek, D. 58
cyberbullying 118–19; victimization 118–19, 125
cynicism 7, 79–83, 85, 87–90
Cyprus 8, 112–30

dedication 80, 83
delinquency 6
demographic characteristics **117**
depression 31
Descartes program 133–4
descriptive statistics 102–5, **103**, 120–23, **121**; development of lifelong learning competencies 105; perception of classroom change 102–5
design of TALK program 99–100
design of ViSC 116–17
DESSA *see* Devereux Student Strengths Assessment
development of gender stereotypes 57–8
development of high quality interventions 105–9; implications of study 108–9; limitations of study 108
development of lifelong learning competences 105
development psychology 2–3
developmental approach to SED 31–4
developmental psychology ideas 9–10
Devereux Student Strengths Assessment 34
Deweyan Model 16–17
diagnostic accuracy 37
differential study motives by master's degree 143–5; aim of Utrecht University 144; general opinion 144–5; importance of science 144; objective of BA program 143
differential study motives by program 141–3; aim of Utrecht University 142; general opinion 143; importance of science 142; master's degree choice 143; objective of BA program 141–2
digital natives (Finland) 79–93
dimensions of SED *33*
direct effects of self-ascription 69–71
disengagement 79–81, 89–92
dissemination of knowledge 42
distal attitude 81
diverse patterns of burnout 87–92
Dwyer, C. 58

e-competence 17–18
Early Development Instrument/Middle Years Development Instrument 34
early indicators of gender role self-concept 74–5
Eccles, J. S. 90
EDA *see* Schoolwork Engagement Inventory

INDEX

EDI/MDI *see* Early Development Instrument/Middle Years Development Instrument
education 'experiments' 11–12
educational phases 13–14
educational psychology 16, 47
educational science 3
EFA *see* exploratory factor analysis
effect of gender role on performance of school reading 56–78
effective use of educational innovations 46–9, 51
effectiveness surveys 99–102; analytical approach 101–2; measures 101; participants 100–101; survey design 99–100
EFPA *see* European Federation of Psychologists Association
Egan, S. 60
Eigenvalues 140–41
Ellis, L. A. 62
emergence of implementation science 43–6
emergence of Third Mission 21–2
emerging challenges 14–16
emerging cynicism 79, 85, 87–90
emotion control 32–3, 35
emotional engagement 79–93
empathy 32–3
encapsulating Bildung-Psychology 91
engagement with Bildung 87–90
engagement profiles 79–93
enhancing SED 27–40; *see also* social-emotional development
ensuring transfer 16–18
Euclidean distances 100–101
European Federation of Psychologists Association 22
evaluation of TALK 99
evaluation of ViSC program 112–30
evolution of gender role concept 58
exhaustion 79–83, 87–9
expectancy belief 107
expectancy–value theory 96
explaining educational trajectories 57–8
explaining gendered cognitive self-concept 71–5; limitations of study 74–5
exploratory factor analysis 138–41; results of survey 140–41
expressing emotions 5, 28–30, 114

factorability of surveys 140–46; differential study motives by degree choice 143–5; differential study motives by study program 141–3; EFA results 140–41; subgroup analysis – GPA 145–6
factors of gender role self-concept *66*, **66**
failure climate 103, 107
feminine orientation 62
fidelity criteria 44–5, 50, 115–16
field of education: progress of transfer 11–12
Finland 79–93
fit index SRMR-B 108
Fixsen, D. L. 44, 49
fostering lifelong learning competencies 94–111; aims of evaluation 99; conclusion 105–9; introduction 94–6; research method 99–102; results 102–5; teacher training programme TALK 96–9
functional areas of Bildung-Psychology 3, 13–14
future burnout research 90–91

Gelman–Rubin criterion 120
Gender Competence through Reflective Coeducation *see* REFLECT
gender constancy 58, 62, 64
gender equality 19
gender identity 58
gender self-concept 6, 56–78; conclusion 71–5; incorporation of gender stereotypes 57–63; introduction 56–7; research method 63–6; results 66–71
gendered ability perceptions 61–3
gendered pathways 81
general student opinion 141, 143–6
generation of digital natives 79–93; *see also* school burnout
Gibbs sampler 120
Goodwin, H. 60
Gradinger, P. 115
Great Society programs 43
Greenwald, A. G. 58, 62
Grotpeter, J. K. 119
growth curve modelling 101–2

Halverson, C. F. 59, 72
Heidelberger Rechentest 65
Henderson, N. 60
hidden victimization 126–7
hierarchical linear modelling **122, 124**
Higgins, M. 49
high cynicism 79, 85, 87–9
Hoffman, C. D. 59
Holistic Student Assessment 5
Hox, J. 120

153

INDEX

HSA psychometric properties 35–7
HSA/3–18 caregiver report *36*
Hubner, J. J. 61
Humboldtian Model 16–17
hypothesized component classification **135–6**

identity development 29
immanence of transfer 13–14
impact of gender role on academic self-concept 56–78
Implementation 43
implementation capacity building 47
implementation science 5, 41–55; and Bildung-Psychology 46–9; conclusion 51; emergence of 43–6; introduction 41–3; theoretical base for future 49–50
implementation of ViSC program 112–30; conclusion 126–7; introduction 112–13; measures used 118–20; present study 115; research method 115–18; results 120–26; social competence program 113–15
implementing interventions 35–7
Implicit Association Test 58, 62
importance of science 140, 142, 144–6
importance of understanding SED 30–31
in vivo modeling 44
inadequacy 79, 81–3, 87–9
incorporation of gender stereotypes 56–63; development of gender stereotypes 57–8; individual difference variable 58–61; into self 58; predictor of gendered ability perceptions 61–3
indirect effects of self-ascription 69–71
individual difference variable 58–61
individual motivation 7–8
individualization 19
inferences from TALK *100*
information economics 49–50
information maximum likelihood estimation 65
innovation 46–7
innovative approaches 16–18
Inoff, G. E. 59
institutional autonomy 14
integration of gender role 59–61
integrative perspective 4–5
intensity of socio-digital participation 83
inter-individual differences 31–2
intercepts for failure climate 103
interconnectedness 33
International Panel on Social Progress 15
intervention effects on perpetration 123–5; bullying 123; cyberbullying 123; physical aggression 123–4; relational aggression 125; verbal aggression 125
intervention effects on victimization 125–6; bullying victimization 125; cyber victimization 125; physical victimization 126; relational victimization 126; verbal victimization 126
intra-individual differences 31–2
investigation into student motivation 131–49; *see also* student motivation from Bildung-psychological approach
I³ approach 14
ivory towers 11–26

Jelenec, P. 58
job satisfaction 11–12

kinds of school engagement 85–7
knowledge economy 133, 135, 138

latent profile analysis 84–5
Lewin, Kurt 12
lifelong learning 2–3, 9–10, 37–8, 41–2, 50–51, 94–111
Likert scale 64, 134
LimeSurvey online 136–40; analytic strategy 138–40; measures 137–8; procedure 136; sample 136–7
LLL *see* lifelong learning
LMR *see* adjusted Lo-Mendell-Rubin likelihood ratio test
localization of REFLECT *21*
localization of VEL *17*
longitudinal study research 63–6; research instruments 64–6; research participants 63–4
LPA *see* latent profile analysis

McGeown, S. 60, 662
McKinsey and Company 132
McKinsey, James Oscar 132–3
McKinsey orientation to motivation 8–9, 131–49
macro level of Bronfenbrenner model 3, 5, 21–2, 42, 133
maladjustment 113
management accounting 132–3
MAR *see* missing at random assumption
Marsh, H. W. 62–3, 74
Martin, C. L. 72
master's degree choice 141, 143
mathematics performance 61–3
Matthijsse, S. 120

INDEX

maturity 37–8
mean difference variables **86**
measuring gender role self-concept 64
measuring SED 34–5
mediation effects 71
Meltzoff, A. N. 58
mental health 27–8, 30–31
meso level of Bronfenbrenner model 3, 5–6, 21–2, 42, 133
methods used in ViSC program 115–18; implementation process 115–16; missing data 117–18; participants 117; study design/procedure 116–17
Metz, A. 47
micro level of Bronfenbrenner model 3, 5–6, 21–2, 42, 133
Mind-the-Gap Survey 2013 83–4; data analyses 84; measures 83–4
missing at random assumption 63, 65, 118
missing data 65–6, 117–18
model fit indices **104, 119**
moderate cynicism 79, 85, 87–9
Monte Carlo simulations 108
Morris, P. A. 3
motivation enhancement 19–20
motive and opinion correlation 136
Mplus 65, 84, 101–2, 119–20
multivariate effects **142–3, 145**
multivariate multilevel growth curve analysis 7, 94–111, **106**

Napoleonic Model 16–17
need for bullying prevention 126–7
networking 18
Newmanian Model 16–17
Nida-Rümelin, Julian 132
Noack, P. 58
Nobel Prize 49
non-assertive behavior 114
NORM program 102
NOsek, B. A. 62
novel information technologies 91
nurturance 59

objective of BA program 140–43, 145
obsession 82
other-oriented sympathy 30
outcome expectation 96
outcome variables 120–23
overcoming ivory tower 11–26

Pajares, F. 62
paper-and-pencil questionnaires 101
PAQ see Personal Attribute Questionnaire

parameters for approach to responsibility 19–21
participants in longitudinal study 63–4
participants in TALK program 100–101
participants in ViSC program 117
path models of analysis 65–6, *68, 70*
PDSA see Plan-Do-Study-Act cycles
Pellegrini, A. D. 127
perception of change 102–5
performance in mathematics due to gender role 56–78
perpetration of bullying 118, 123–5; baseline effects 123; intervention effects 123–5
Perry, D. 60
person-centred data analysis 84; comparison of groups 84; latent profile analysis 84
person-oriented approach to burnout 79–93
Personal Attribute Questionnaire 59–60
personal development 94–6
personality traits 72
Phelps-Zientarski, D. 58
physical aggression 119; victimization 119, 126
PISA see Program for International Assessment
Pizzigati, K. A. L. 59
Plan-Do-Study-Act cycles 43–4, 46, 49–51
planning interventions 35–7
polynomial school systems 12
positive failure climate 7–8
potential of Bildung-Psychology 9–10
Pottorff, D. D. 58
predicting academic achievement through gender self-concept 56–78
prediction of mathematic achievements 70–71; direct effects 70–71; indirect effects 71
prediction of reading achievements 68–70; direct effects 69; indirect effects 69–70
predictor of gendered ability perceptions 61–3
preparation for job market 134–6
Pressman, J. L. 43
preventive measures 114
processes of learning 41–3
profiles of school burnout in Finland 79–93
program fidelity 44–5, 115–16
Program for International Assessment 80, 89
progress in transfer 11–12

INDEX

propensity score matching 100
proximal goals 99
psychological distress 90–92
psychological risk buffering 37
Psychologische Rundschau 1
psychopathology 31

quality assurance 19
quality chasm 47

re-negotiating social contract 14–15
reactive aggression 114
reading performance 61–3
reduction of violence program 115
redundant knowledge 49
REFLECT 5, 19–22
reflective coeducation 19–22
regional knowledge transfer 15–16; *see also* transfer
Reiman, R. 1–4, 41–2, 72–3, 133
relational aggression 119; victimization 119, 123, 126
relationship between SED and Bildung-Psychology 37–8
relevance of progress 11–12
Renkl, A. 3
research 19–21
resilience 30, 32, 37–8
results of EFA survey 140–41; aim of Utrecht University 140; general opinion 141; importance of science 140; master's degree choice 141; objective of BA program 140
results from Mind-the-Gap Survey 2013 85–7
results of longitudinal study 66–71; academic achievements 68; cognitive/affective components of academic self-concepts 67–8; gender self-concept 66–7; predicting mathematic achievements 70–71; predicting reading achievements 68–70
results of ViSC study 120–26; baseline effects 123; descriptive statistics 120–23; intervention effects on perpetuation 123–5; intervention effects on victimization 125–6
risk-and-resilience perspective 37
Roeser, R. W. 90
Roland, E. 114
role self-concept *see* gender self-concept

Salmela-Aro, K. 81
Sameroff, A. J. 90
SBI *see* School Burnout Inventory

scaled redundancy 49
Schober, B. 3–4, 41–2, 72–3
school burnout 7, 79–93; conclusion 91–2; discussion 87–90; implications 91; introduction 80–82; limitations 90–91; research method 83–4; results 85–7
School Burnout Inventory 83
school start and gender role 56–78
Schoolwork Engagement Inventory 83–4
Schunk, D. H. 96
SDT *see* self-determination theory
SEARS *see* Social-Emotional Assets and Resilience Scales
SED *see* social-emotional development
SEL *see* social-emotional learning; *see also* social-emotional development
self-ascription 6, 56–78
self-awareness 29
self-concept 58–61
self-description 60–63
Self-Description Questionnaire for Preschoolers 64
self-determination theory 97, 107
self-directed activity 89
self-efficacy 20, 81, 96, 99–100, 102, 105, 107
self-esteem 97
self-government 43–4
self-incorporation of gender stereotype 58
self-monitoring 98
self-reflection 32
self-regulated learning 7–8, 19, 95–107
self-reporting scales 118–20; analytic strategy 120; cyberbullying 118–19; perpetuation/victimization 118; physical aggression/victimization 118; relational aggression/victimization 119; verbal aggression/victimization 119–20
sense of achievement 81
Shavelson, R. J. 61–3
silent reading 65
Skovera, M. E. 58
sleeper effect 107
Smith, P. 118
social competence program 113–1534
social learning theory 114
social policy 96
Social-Emotional Assets and Resilience Scales 34
social-emotional development 5, 27–40; and Bildung-Psychology 37–8; core dimensions of 28–30; developmental

156

INDEX

approach to SED 31–3; introduction 27–8; measuring SED 34–5; understanding of SED in children 30–31; using SED tools 35–7

social-emotional development theory 34–5

social-emotional learning 27–8, 35–7

socially shared beliefs 57–8

societal responsibility 11–26

socio-digital participation 7

socio-digital technologies 90–91

socio-political concerns 94–6

sociocriticism 147

Spiel, C. 1–4, 9–10, 41–2, 72–3, 80, 100, 133

SRL see self-regulated learning

standardized means 87

Stanton, G. C. 61

statistical matching 100

Steffens, M. C. 58

stereotyping 6, 56–63; see also gender self-concept

Stokes, D. E. 2

stress 79–80, 85, 87–90

structural model of Bildung-Psychology 2

structure of TALK 98–9

student motivation from Bildung-psychological approach 131–49; Bildung at Utrecht University 133–4; conclusion 146–8; introduction 131–3; present study 134–6; research method 136–40; results 140–46

subgroup analysis 145–6; aim of Utrecht University 146; general opinion 146; importance of science 145–6; objective of BA program 145

successful use of educational innovations 46–9, 51

sustainability 19, 21–2

systematic structure 3–4, 13, 15–16

T-values 65

taking responsibility 19–21

TALK program 7–8, 96–9; structure of program 98–9; theoretical foundation of content 96–8

TALK session topics **98**

TARGET program 97

taxonomical description of SED dimensions 28–30

taxonomy of SED *30*

teacher education programs 96–9; see also TALK program

teaching 16–18

Teaching-Family Association 45–6

Teaching-Family Model 6, 42–7, 50–51

tertiary school 5

TFA see Teaching-Family Association

theoretical base for future 49–50

theoretical foundation of TALK 96–8

theoretical ideas of developmental psychology 9–10

theory of basic research 1–10; conclusion 9–10; introduction 1–4; potential of structural model 4–9

theory into practice 27–40; measuring SED 34–5; see also social-emotional development

Third Mission 3–5, 9–10, 15–18, 21–2; emergence of 21–2

tools of SED 28, 34–7

traditional schooling 2–3

training programme evaluation 94–111

trait-based femininity 64, 66–7, 71–2

trait-based masculinity 64, 66–7, 71–2

transfer 11–26; approaches to ensure transfer 16–18; emerging challenge for universities 14–16; as immanent characteristic 13–14; progress in transfer 11–12; and societal responsibility 11–26

Tukey HSD comparison 84

Tuominen-Soini, H. 81

understanding SED 27–40; see also social-emotional development

University of Chicago School of Business 132

University of Mannheim 4

use inspired basic research: introduction to 1–10

using SED tools 35–7

Utrecht University 131–49; Bildung at 133–4

Vaaland, G. 114

Valiante, G. 62

value construct 96–7

van de Schoot, R. 120

VEL see Vienna E-Lecturing

verbal aggression 119–20; victimization 119–20, 123, 126

victimization 112–30; baseline effects 123; bullying 118; cyberbullying 118–19; physical 119; relational 119; verbal 119–20

Vienna E-Lecturing 5, 16–18

ViSC program 8, 112–30

VLMR see Vuong–Lo–Mendell–Rubin likelihood ratio test

INDEX

vocational aspirations 19
von Hochheim, Eckhart 131–2
von Humboldt, Friedrich Wilhelm 2, 131–2
von Humboldt orientation to motivation 8–9, 131–49
Vuong–Lo–Mendell–Rubin likelihood ratio test 84–5

Wagner, P. 3–4, 41–2, 72–3
Weiner, J. 49
'whole child' focus 28
Wildavsky, A. 43
Wilk's 141–6

WLLP *see* Würzburger LeiseLeseprobe
Wolf, M. M. 44
Wright, P. 60
Würzburger LeiseLeseprobe 65

X^2 goodness of fit tests 66–7, 70, 85, 117, 137, **137**

Yates' continuity correction 117
Young, L. 49

Zgaga, P. 16
Zimmermann, B. J. 96